Charles Curtice McCain

Compendium of Transportation Theories

A Compilation of Essays upon Transportation Subjects by eminent Experts

Charles Curtice McCain

Compendium of Transportation Theories
A Compilation of Essays upon Transportation Subjects by eminent Experts

ISBN/EAN: 9783337187422

Printed in Europe, USA, Canada, Australia, Japan

Cover: Foto ©ninafisch / pixelio.de

More available books at **www.hansebooks.com**

TRANSPORTATION THEORIES.

KENSINGTON SERIES.—FIRST BOOK.

A COMPILATION OF ESSAYS UPON TRANSPORTATION SUBJECTS
BY EMINENT EXPERTS.

PUBLICATION OF SERIES UNDER DIRECTION OF
C. C. McCAIN.

WASHINGTON, D. C.:
KENSINGTON PUBLISHING COMPANY
1893.

"The best that we can do for one another is to exchange our thoughts freely, and that after all is but little."

—*Froude.*

CONTENTS.

1. The Railway Problem Defined. Hon. Thomas M. Cooley.
2. The Railroad Malady and its Treatment. Hon. Augustus Schoonmaker.
3. The Railroad Problem. Hon. Joseph D. Potts.
4. The Public and the Railways. Hon. Shelby M. Cullom.
5. The Railroads and the Public. Mr. Frank J. Firth.
6. The Future of the Railroad Problem. Mr. A. B. Stickney.
7. Unity of Railways and Railway Interests. Hon. Augustus Schoonmaker.
8. The American Railroad System. Hon. Joseph Nimmo, Jr.
9. Federal Regulation of Commerce. Hon. Shelby M. Cullom.
10. Federal Regulation of Commerce. A Reply. Mr. George R. Blanchard.
11. Limitations upon Railway Powers. Hon. Augustus Schoonmaker.
12. Railway Legislation. Hon. Walter D. Dabney.
13. Amendment of the Interstate Commerce Law. Hon. Aldace F. Walker.
14. Legal Aspects of Railroad Strikes. General Wager Swayne.
15. Services of a Bureau of Railway Statistics. Professor Henry C. Adams.
16. English and American Railways. Mr. W. M. Acworth.
17. High Speed Railroad Travel. Mr. Theodore Voorhees.
18. Relations between Canadian and American Railways. Mr. A. C. Raymond.
19. Some Characteristics of the American Railway System. Hon. Joseph Nimmo, Jr.
20. Development of Railway Freight Classifications. Mr. C. C. McCain.
21. The Interstate Commerce Law. Hon. Charles Francis Adams.
22. Discrimination by Railways. Hon. Martin A. Knapp.
23. Discriminations from the use of Private Cars of Shippers. Hon. Augustus Schoonmaker.
24. Long *versus* Short Haul. General E. P. Alexander.
25. Treatment of Railway Employees. Mr. B. B. Adams.
26. Brotherhood of Engineers. Mr. Nat. Sawyer.
27. The Necessity of Railway Compacts under Governmental Regulation. Mr. James Peabody.
28. Apportionment of Traffic. Hon. Joseph Nimmo, Jr.
29. Popular and Legal View of Traffic Pooling. Hon. Thomas M. Cooley.
30. Pooling and Combinations. Hon. Thomas M. Cooley.
31. A Plea for Railway Consolidation. Mr. Collis P. Huntington.
32. Railroad Consolidation. General E. P. Alexander.
33. Government Interference in English Railway Management. Mr. W. M. Acworth.
34. Railway Associations. Hon. Aldace F. Walker.

THE RAILWAY PROBLEM DEFINED.

Address of Hon. Thos. M. Cooley.

Our purpose in coming together on this occasion is for consultation upon subjects of mutual interest, and for the discussion of questions which either pertain directly to the official duties we have severally taken upon ourselves, or which have at least some bearing upon the proper performance of those duties. We are not all clothed with the same powers; there has not been prescribed for all of us the like obligations; but in our official action we all have the same general purpose in contemplation, and it may justly be assumed that the views we may severally hold will be of common interest, and that in so far as there has been experience in dealing with practical questions, this experience will be not interesting merely but of high value.

It has been assumed by the people in creating the offices which are represented in this meeting, that there are mischiefs, of some considerable magnitude in the railroad service of the country; and the existence of these mischiefs is the justification for creating such offices. No class of persons in the country will admit more freely the existence of serious evils than those who are managers of the railroads or who are interested as stockholders or bondholders in the results of the management; but as this class look upon the existing evils from the standpoint of corporate interests, they are likely to see them as they exist mostly in the relations between the roads themselves, while the public, regarding them from a different standpoint, naturally see most distinctly the mischiefs which spring from the relations of the railroads to their customers or which affect the political society.

When the legislation which was intended to bring the transportation business of the country under public control was first entered upon, there were persons interested as managers or otherwise in railroad property, and possibly some others, who denied that any such legislation was fairly warranted by just principles of constitutional law. This denial is not often heard now, but it is very generally conceded that inasmuch as the railway is a public agency, its management is a public trust; and that as such it is as

---

Reprinted from Proceedings of National Convention of Railroad Commissioners held at Washington, March, 1891.

legitimately to be regulated by law as is the management of any other trust in which the public are directly concerned. There are doubtless still some persons, however, who believe that in point of policy, public regulation was uncalled for at the time it was entered upon, and that the results will not justify the expectations upon which the legislation hitherto adopted has been based. This last proposition, I do not see that this convention need care to controvert. It is likely to be the case with all attempts at important reforms in public affairs, that the results will not equal the antecedent expectations; and one of the consequences must be, that those who are officially connected with the effort will be compelled to share among them, to some extent, the blame that inevitably follows the impossibility of giving complete satisfaction to extravagant hopes.

Whether the views of those who have not favored public regulation of railways are or are not justified by the situation, or by the prospects for the future, it seems to be taken for granted now that statutes for the purpose not likely to have a place among the laws for an indefinite period; though to what extent they shall go in regulation, and how far they may justly and properly subordinate the interests of stockholders and bondholders to the rights and convenience of the general public, are questions upon which the differences of opinion are not likely to be reconciled, and may be expected to be hereafter, as they are now, somewhat radical. There are many who believe that the Government should not regulate merely, but should manage the roads; that its hand should be felt continuously and everywhere; while others look upon the existing legislation as having gone quite as far as can be justified by the expectation of useful results. Others, holding views differing from both these classes, might be mentioned, but it is not important: the future alone, after much more practical experience than the country has had as yet, will determine which of them, if indeed any, are right in their anticipations and prophecies. For our present purpose it is sufficient for us to say, that it is agreed on all hands by those who undertake to deal with the subject of railway regulation, that there are many evils here which ought to be remedied; and whoever speaks of these evils is likely in general terms to talk of a "railroad problem" to be solved: those interested in the roads for the reason already mentioned appearing to look for it mainly in the relations between the roads themselves, while others regard it as existing somewhere in the defective performance by the roads of their public duties, and therefore, perhaps to be solved through the exercise of such governmental power as shall compel proper performance.

It is a noticeable fact that when this railroad problem is spoken of, the mention is likely to be vague and indefinite, whether it is receiving attention at the hands of those representing the roads or from those who speak in the interests of political economy, or as representing the public authorities. If a legal discussion is being had, however narrow may be the point involved, the parties are not unlikely to make use of this phrase "railroad problem," as if a decision upon the matter then in controversy was to solve the problem, or at least was to dispose of some portion or lead up to some final solution. This same phrase may be used in the very next controversy, though equally narrow, but quite different, and the same expectation of the result may seem to be in the minds of those who represent the contestants. When, however, public authorities are making use of a phrase which pertains to their official duties, and which to the mind of the hearer may seem to indicate their understanding of what their jurisdiction is, in part or in whole, it is important that they employ the phrase with some degree of exactitude; and perhaps no better use can be made of the opening hour of our meeting than to devote it to an endeavor to ascertain precisely what it is that is meant by the "railroad problem," not merely when it is used by ourselves, but also when it is used by those who are connected directly with railroad management. In doing this, however, we shall be under the necessity of going beyond the terms employed in the several acts of legislation under which we are acting, for in none of them is this phrase defined: the laws point out the scope of our duties, and it is easy to see that many of these are of minor importance and stand by themselves, so that they cannot be considered with reason as constituting a part of any great problem; while the evils at which others are aimed may possibly be traced to a common source, and the correction of one through the proper treatment of that common source, may be a correction of the others also. Certainly nothing can fairly be dignified with the appellation of "railroad problem" which does not concern the foundation cause or causes of the principal evils which in the railroad service beget injury or annoyance and excite complaint.

In an attempt to ascertain what the railroad problem (treating the designation in the sense indicated) must be held to be, it may be well at first to point out what it is not; and this I shall now proceed to do.

It is certainly not to be found in the legislation authorizing the building of railroads, or in that which prescribes the terms and conditions under which the building shall be carried on and completed. It is unfortunate no doubt that the laws for this purpose are so wanting in homogeneity, and in provisions for the protection against the mischiefs with which the exercise of such important powers, when they may be assumed by any one at discretion, are likely to be attended. The authority comes in the main from the legislation of the states and territories; and if we examine these we shall find that apparently the most important object in the minds of the law-makers in granting charters of incorporation for railroads, or in passing general laws which shall stand in the place of such charters, has been to invite and secure the construction;—to invite capitalists, or others who can secure capital by whatever means for the purpose, to expend it to that end; and that with this object in view they have been far more anxious to make their legislation satisfactory to the promoters of roads than they have been to take care to satisfy themselves that the building of a particular road is important on public grounds, or that the road when constructed will, in the service it will perform, meet a public demand. In every section of the country, instances may be pointed out of roads which have been built without any legitimate demand for them whatever, so that the money invested in them has for the most part been as completely wasted as if it had been sunk in the sea. Either there has been no sufficient traffic that at fair rates would support them when built and keep them in suitable condition, or the traffic of the region which must support them was already so far provided for that a new road could only come in as a disturbing factor, to render those already in existence unprofitable, or to force itself upon them as a marketable commodity under circumstances which could be considered as little less than the levying of black-mail. There is reason for saying that when the interest of the whole country is considered, it would be better if the necessity or propriety of every proposed new road were required to be passed upon by competent public authority before the state should delegate to anyone the eminent domain to be employed for its construction; but this is not now required, and under existing laws, a new railway project is in very many cases little more than a mere demand by mercenary speculators upon the credulity of the public, who, understanding very little about the elements that must constitute railroad prosperity, are ready enough to believe that riches are to be found in any plausible scheme that projectors put before them. In some instances, we feel warranted in saying that the building of a road is entered upon with a full understanding, by those who plan and manage the construction, that the road itself, when complete, can have no value to stockholders except as a means of forcing the owners of roads already in existence and performing valuable service to the country, to pay for that which has no intrinsic value, a price measured by its power to do mischief.

There is an evil here which is of no small magnitude; it may be measured in part by the millions which credulous people, often people of very small means, have invested in worthless roads, but in part also by other millions which have been paid for roads which even those who built them knew were not called for. Nevertheless, the great mass of the people of the country are only indirectly injured by the construction of such roads. The roads do not go out of existence even though it be fully demonstrated they ought never to have been built: everyone of them has local communities more or less numerous for which it performs convenient service: they come into business relations with the other roads of the country; their operations are likely to be conducted in the same methods as those of other roads; and the great railway questions which concern and disturb the public, as well as those which trouble the railroad world, are likely to remain the same and to require the same discussion and demand the same final settlement as would have been essential if these needless roads had never been constructed.

The "railroad problem" is also not to be found in the condition in which the roads may be put by the projectors or managers, or the manner in which they are equipped for the purposes of operation. A road in bad condition is likely, for that reason, to cause great annoyance to the general public and to its customers. It may result in great delays and possibly in the loss of life as well as of property: a road badly equipped may also, for that cause, be of little or no service to the community; it may possibly be even detrimental, as standing in the way of something better. But commonly the difficulties which are found to arise from these deficiencies in construction or equipment are of a minor character and do not to any great extent affect the general public. They certainly do not rise to the dignity of being considered the "railroad problem" of the age. Neither are they likely to any very great extent to affect the relations of the roads with each other; and we must therefore assume that the problem which we are endeavoring to indicate and define ,would exist in nearly the same force as now, were these deficiencies entirely cured: if, in other words, every road was in perfect condition and was fully equipped for any business likely to be offered to it. In point of fact, if we examine the roads of the country, we are not unlikely to be led to the conclusion that the equipment of roads may also go beyond any just demand that business makes upon it, as well as fall short of the proper business necessity. This is especially the case with the preparation made for passenger service, since the earnest and somewhat bitter competition that has existed between the leading lines of the country has begotten an extravagance in equipment which presents us the spectacle of palaces moving on wheels across the continent and inviting the traveling public, when upon journeys which but a few years ago could only be made under circumstances of great hardship and privation, to a participation now in comforts and even luxuries which in the case of most of them are quite beyond their ordinary life at home. But this causes no complaint: the railroad company voluntarily supplies the luxuries and the traveling public voluntarily pay for and enjoy them.

If the freight traffic is not provided for bountifully and extravagantly, it is but just to say for the roads that deficiences are not often serious, and when they are met with are usually found to exist in the case of roads which have come into existence under circumstances of doubtful expediency, and which since their construction have been unable to command the business that would secure and keep up their adequate equipment. But any amount of imperfection in these particulars will at most only touch upon outlying questions affecting slightly the railroad problem and not the main problem itself.

The relations between the railroad corporations and their employes do not present the "railroad problem" that is troubling the country. We may say this with great confidence because neither the corporations themselves nor their employes seem to take a different view, and because also most of the laws which undertake to provide for the regulation of railways do not confer upon the authorities which they create for the purpose any jurisdiction over these relations. It is no doubt true that the public authorities might with entire propriety take them somewhat under consideration, since it not infrequently happens that the just performance of their own duties is impeded, or to some extent at least disturbed by the disputes which arise in railroad service, and by the controversies which sometimes injuriously affect public transportation in considerable sections of the country. It might not only be admissible but important, and even a matter of duty, that in some cases railroad commissions should recommend legislation bearing upon these relations; legislation, for example, in regard to the use of machinery better calculated to protect employes against injury or loss of life; and legislation that would tend to lessen the injurious consequences of disturbances that arise over the question of wages, or of the unjust discharge of faithful servants. Possibly also it might be, if not strictly within their province, certainly not foreign to their duties, to recommend to the railroads of the country and to the employes the adoption of some system of insurance, under which either the railroad companies or the employes themselves, by some general rule of voluntary adoption, should provide a fund for the protection of families against the evils of poverty and destitution, especially in cases of accident resulting in death or in inability to perform labor. But whatever may be done on this subject, the fact would remain that after all that was possible had been considered and provided for by the parties to this service in regard thereto, the great railroad problem would still remain unsolved, and still demanding the best attention of railroad managers and of the public authorities. The relation of employer and employe touches it but lightly; and even on occasions when strikes affect the business of large sections of the country, so as to seem for the time being to make the relation between the strikers and their employers more important than anything else in those sections, yet they are seldom of such magnitude that the business of the country at large is seriously disturbed, and they are seldom of long continuance; so that if they constituted the only difficulties in railway service, the mischiefs which are felt on all hands would be far less serious than now; and it it can scarcely be doubted that they would find speedy and satisfactory solution.

The "railroad problem" is not to be found, exclusively at least, in the diversities which exist between the legislation of the several states when compared with each other, or between the same legislation when compared with that of the Federal Government. These diversities necessarily aggravate the existing difficulties and constitute obstacles in the way of the speedy and effectual removal of some of the worst in which the general public is concerned; but the difficulties existing in the relations between the roads themselves are affected but slightly by differences in legislation. Remove these, and the clashing of interests between the roads will be the same as now: the temptation to unfriendly action for the very purpose of inflicting injury upon rivals or of embarrassing their operations with a view to forcing what cannot be accomplished by negotiation, will be as strong as ever. I need not enlarge upon this for it is obvious; and so long as the fact is as stated the railroad problem must remain, whatever may be the laws that state or territory or nation may have passed and enforced in mitigation of the evils.

The "railroad problem" is not to be found altogether in the fact that railroad rates are supposed by the public to be in a great many cases much too high; or that there is unlawful discrimination in the transportation of freights and of passengers, and that many persons are carried free who are not entitled to it by law; or that in the cases in which exceptions are made by law to the general rules which are prescribed, the railroad corporations contrive to increase these exceptions in inadmissible or unwise ways to the detriment of their own revenues, or to the increase of the charges that are made against the community in general. The problem without question is present here, but not in its entirety. There is no reasonable doubt that railroad charges are often made higher than they should be. This is sometimes made clear on an investigation into the facts, where those who make them are given the amplest opportunity to justify their rates if they can do so. And it may not unjustly be said that they themselves in many cases furnish evidence of more or less conclusive nature that the public complaints are not without foundation: they do so when they cut rates in the warfare with each other to an extent that greatly reduces their annual income and still leaves them in a condition to make respectable dividends to stockholders. They also furnish evidence tending in the same direction when they carry great numbers of persons free of charge; a number which we hope is diminishing from year to year, but which nevertheless, when the whole country is considered, is still enormous; embracing as it does among the private citizens who are thus favored, not the men of small means to whom the charge of transportation would be a serious burden and must therefore very much restrict their means of indulgence, but the men of large means who, because they are such, have no claim whatever to the favor; embracing also officials of all grades, and especially such as are empowered to make state and municipal laws or regulations bearing upon the subject of railway management. The discredit into which the use of the ordinary evidence of a right to free transportation has fallen is so great, that both the corporations and the persons who receive it deem it politic to resort to other devices, the most frequent perhaps being the giving of mileage books; so that a state legislator or city mayor or other officer, when he uses it, may appear to be paying his passage though in fact he is receiving it free. I need hardly say that the giving the transaction this form does not in any degree relieve it of the discredit which fairly attaches to it, or lessen in the least its moral turpitude: on the contrary, it adds to the main offence of obtaining transportation at the cost of the public, the cowardice of going through the forms of payment, that by this false pretence the offender may cheat his fellow-passengers into the belief that he is doing what a proper regard for the rights of others would require him to do. In some sections of the country the practice here referred to has continued for such a length of time that it seems to be expected by the general public that, as a matter of course, it will be continued indefinitely, and it is therefore believed to be practiced by every successive incumbent of certain offices. Whoever would investigate the sources of political corruption in such sections would do well to inquire to what extent they had their origin in public opinion being debauched by these corrupt practices until at length the grosser forms of political misconduct came to be looked upon as matters of course, and tolerated or excused for that reason.

The manner in which advantage is taken of the exceptions of the statute in order to avoid charging the regular rates also has a tendency in the direction of showing that the regular rates are higher than they should be. Thus the statute in forbidding discriminations in passenger carriage makes exceptions for the case of excursions; and how diligent some roads are in finding excuses for excursions in which they are to carry the passengers for a mere fraction of the customary rates is well known to us all. The excuse advanced may be that thereby they create business which would not otherwise come to them; that they gain favor by giving special accommodation to communities or societies at particular times and on special occasions, and so on; but we have a right to assume that they nevertheless expect to make and do, as a general fact, make some profit on every such occasion, except when calamities befall them through the accidents which are much more likely to attend special trains, running on unusual time, than the regular trains. A person investigating the subject with a view to reaching the underlying reasons for their action would be very likely to inquire why, instead of manifesting great anxiety to increase the number of occasions for exceptional trains carrying passengers below the regular rates, the company does not make the regular rates as low as can reasonably be afforded, and thereby invite the public to make excursions, not on special occasions merely, but continuously; thus increasing the aggregate passenger traffic though taking it by the ordinary and safe trains, as the railroads of some foreign countries have done without loss by a similar reduction of rates. The reason for making this inquiry would seem to be specially forcible when it is borne in mind that the exceptional trains that are run at reduced rates furnish to a very considerable extent the opportunities which the class of people known as scalpers embrace to make great profits out of the railroad companies, and, through them, out of the general public who, in their regular travels, must pay rates which are maintained above what would otherwise be necessary, that those who charge them may not be the losers through the operations of this class of persons.

But if the railroad companies were chargeable with no breach of law or of sound morality, or with want of good policy in the carriage of passengers free, or of either passengers or freight at unjustly discriminating rates, and if they made use of their privileges under the exceptional provisions of the statutes wisely and justly, there would still be the same railroad problem that exists now—not, it is true, accompanied by as many evils as now, but nevertheless demanding solution as it now demands it, only somewhat less importunately.

Many other things in railroad service are causes of annoyance to the public, or tend to break up friendly and useful relations as between the roads themselves, but they may be passed over lightly at this time because they touch but lightly upon the great problem that confronts the public and makes such serious demand upon the best thought of the country. Thus the refusal of one road to unite with another in making convenient arrangements for the transfer of freight or passengers from one line to the other without unneccessary delay; or the making of arrangements with one company which are unjustly discriminating as against another, are seen in some cases to be evils of no slight magnitude; but such cases are not numerous; they are believed to be diminishing in number from year to year; and for the most part they can be dealt with by the public authorities on a consideration of all the facts with no great difficulty.

The troubles that are always present, always annoying, and always difficult of adjustment, are those which relate to the making of rate sheets, and to the manner in which these are observed or treated after they are made. It is here that we discover a problem that is not narrow or temporary, and that does not touch lightly upon the relations between the railroads themselves, but is seen in nearly all their controversies and misunderstandings, and that is the prolific parent of nearly all the difficulties between the railroads and those who have occasion for their services. It is the unjust nature of the rate sheets when the rights of the public or of other roads are considered; it is the refusal to join with other roads in making them, or the demand of an unreasonable share of a joint rate when one is made; it is the sudden reduction in rates when injury can be done to a rival by resorting to that measure, or when it is hoped that the rival can be compelled thereby to give assent to some measure to which assent cannot be obtained by negotiation; it is the refusal to unite in through bills of lading at agreed rates, or to receive for the transportation of persons the tickets that have been given by other roads; it is the failure to abide by understandings concerning rates when a disregard of them seems to promise a temporary advantage; in short, it is the manner in which this whole subject of making rates is dealt with and treated by the railroad companies, and the effect thereby upon their own interests respectively, the interests of stock and bondholders, and the interests of those who, willingly or unwillingly, are their customers, that present the fundamental and still unsolved problem which must necessarily address itself, first of all to the railroad managers of the country, and after that to the public authorities. The evils in railroad service nearly all find there origin here; and especially is this true of those that are most difficult and inveterate. The railroad problem will be dealt with effectually when the power to fix the rates for railroad transportation is placed upon such a basis that the evils now so prominent and troublesome and persistent, which spring from its exercise, shall be cured and the power itself brought under effectual regulation.

When the number of railroads which are now merely subsidiary to other and stronger lines, either through being brought into the same interest or from being leased or otherwise effectually controlled, are left out of account, there are something like five hundred in this country still remaining, whose boards have the power to make rates for the carriage of passengers and property. These boards are by the law left to exercise in the first instance what is practically a free and unlimited authority in the making of rate sheets. They may make them low or high, just or unreasonably discriminating as between persons and property, or different classes of property, or between different centers of trade, at pleasure: the few instances in which the laws have undertaken to prescribe a precise limit being in the main confined to passenger transportation. The several boards are not obliged to agree with each other as to what the rates shall be: it may be their policy to come to agreement, and it may be assumed that they will recognize this fact and endeavor to come to some understanding in advance; but this is not compulsory; and it not unfrequently happens that a single road will proceed to make rates wholly irrespective of what has been done or proposed by other roads with which it must come into competition or relations of some sort in respect to business. It was at first thought by those who made the laws for the building and management of roads, that to leave the authority thus unrestricted was the best possible condition of things: that it would lead to active competition in rates, of which the general public would have the benefit: that the competition would as a matter of course force the rates down to a reasonable point: in short, that the competition would act precisely as it does in other lines of business. Experience has shown that this idea of railroad competition is a mistaken one: that it cannot be compared with competition in the channels of commerce in general: that there are no such tests of the value of railroad service as can fix the limit down to which a road may go without inevitable loss upon its business as an aggregate: that it may carry some classes of its business at impolitic if not in fact at losing rates and yet make profits upon its whole operations by charging to other classes of its business rates which may perhaps seem to be excessive and yet cannot clearly be shown to be so because of the absolute impossibility of making distinct apportionment between the cost of the service rendered to one class and that rendered to the other. Indeed, it is now very well known that in many cases where roads are carrying freights at what seem to be no more than reasonable rates, on lines leading directly from one great business center to another, other roads whose lines are of twice the distance in length, may be carrying the like freights at the same or at even less rates, though the expense to them is presumably twice as great. This they do because they are forced to do so by a situation which they find absolutely controlling. The general fact is that in severe competition between business centers, the very long route carries, not at the same rate merely, but at a lower rate because otherwise it would not get the business to carry. How distinctly it is seen here that it is utterly impossible to judge of railroad competition and its effects, its usefulness and its mischiefs, by comparing it with competition as we encounter it in other lines of business.

We have said that every one of these five hundred operating roads, through its managing officers, may make rate sheets at pleasure. The rates are subject to be changed to some extent afterwards when they are found to be violative of public rights or interests, but the public authorities are not consulted and their consent is not asked as a prerequisite to putting the rate sheets in force. If a rate sheet affected only the road itself and its customers, the fact stated would in a great many cases be of local importance only, and other roads not directly competing with the road making it need not concern themselves specially with its being put in force. But so inextricably are the railroads of the country intermingled in interest; in so many ways do they form routes from business center to business center; from the lakes to the gulf and from ocean to ocean; so easy is it for almost any seemingly unimportant road to be made a part of some direct or indirect route which shall constitute a great channel of commerce, that any considerable change in the rate sheets by any one of these five hundred boards is not only likely to affect the business and the rate sheets of the roads which are its immediate rivals, but to reach out also in its influence from road to road in all directions; not over small neighborhoods, but from state to state, until what seemed to be the action, and was perhaps the hasty and reckless action, of a mere local board may become almost of continental importance. An ill-advised act possibly resulting from passion or from a belief that a power to do mischief when thus exercised will compel others to do what they would not otherwise consent to, by way of purchasing peace, may thus carry disorder into the railroad system of a large section of the country if not into the whole of it, and may compel a change in the rate sheets of all the roads which form the lines competing with those of which the road whose rate sheet causes the disorder is or can be made to become a constituent part.

Now it need hardly be said in this convention that one of the most important things to be accomplished in the regulation of railroads is to secure steadiness of rates: I do not mean that sort of steadiness that would prevent the gradual reduction of railroad charges as it should be seen to be practicable and just for the railroads to make it; but I mean the sort of steadiness that makes changes only in the proper direction, and when it does make them, does so deliberately, carefully, after consideration of all the interests involved, and after such reasonable notice to the public as well as to the railroad interests, as will enable due provision to be made by others to prevent heedless loss and injury therefrom. All sudden changes are necessarily to some extent injurious: they are injurious even though they are made in the direction of lower rates and when as a matter of right they ought to be made in that direction: for they force sudden changes also in the values of property; they affect in unexpected ways contracts made in the commercial world; and they give abundant opportunities for fraudulent understanding as between railroad officials and large dealers: opportunities which the public are certain to suspect are not unfrequently availed of. The law does well when it requires that a notice reasonable in point of time shall be given not merely of advances in rates but of reductions also. This is right and proper even when the reductions result from competition properly so called in railroad service; but the sudden cutting of rates is usually an act which can by no proper use of terms be called a result of legitimate competition. Almost invariably it is an act of open and avowed warfare, entered upon not to benefit the public, but to injure a rival line. It differs from the warfare between nations in this, that in the case of international war the effects can commonly be limited for the most part to those who engage in it, while the rate war on the other hand injures not merely the parties engaged but possibly to an equal extent other railroads whose operations reach the same sections, while injuring also far more than it benefits, the business community that seeks to take advantage of it.

This, then, is the "railroad problem:" there are mischiefs in railroad service that are outside of it, but we distinctly indicate the main source of difficulty when we place our finger upon the power as it exists now, to make and unmake the rates for passenger and freight transportation. So long as five hundred bodies of men in the country are at liberty to make rate sheets at pleasure, and to unmake or cut and recut them in every direction at their own unlimited discretion or want of discretion, and with little restraint on the part of the law except as it imposes a few days' delay in putting changes in force, the problem will remain to trouble us; the mere existence of the power making losses, disorder, and confusion constantly imminent. The authority to reduce rates when they are found to be excessive is but a slight corrective, and reaches the evils only on the public side; and I need hardly remind you who understand it so well, that in this matter of rates, the power on the part of the public authorities to compel the railroads to do what is just to each other in respect to observing rates which they have once made, and to adhering to rate sheets until there is reasonable ground for changing them, is so very slight that it may really be regarded as too insignificant to be spoken of as possessing substantial value.

A problem so momentous as that described, the members of this convention may very well decline to discuss in its totality, or even at all, except as by law they may have been given authority to deal with minor questions embraced within it; but this need not hinder a recognition of its difficulties nor of the infinite powers of mischief which are involved. The first effective step towards the removal of any great public evil is to have distinctly pointed out its scope and its proportions, that those who undertake a reform may not be misled into accepting some single feature as constituting the whole, or some minor consequence as embracing the aggregate of all the mischiefs which do or may result from it.

In the preparation of this paper, the purpose to limit it strictly to indicating what the railroad problem is, has been closely adhered to, and no attempt whatever has been made to indicate what should be the solution.

THE RAILROAD MALADY AND ITS TREATMENT.

By Hon. Augustus Schoonmaker.

So much has been said and written about the misconduct and the troubles of railroads that the general public is familiar with the oft repeated tale. Railroads complain that their revenues are insufficient, that the properties are unprofitable, that rates are constantly demoralized and declining, and that government regulation is a hindrance to their prosperity. The public complains that railroad management is dishonest, that unjust discriminations and stealthy trickery are practiced, that equality and justice are disregarded, and business rendered precarious by the instability of transportation charges and its effect on commercial values. The public often ascribes these conditions to the depravity of railroad officials and agents, and their consequent disregard of business morality and fair dealing. Railroad managers protest that their methods and practices are forced upon them by conditions surrounding them beyond their control, compelling a struggle for existence; that it is their duty to protect and sustain the properties they manage, and that the multitude of railways and the competition between them lead to the troubles and evils whose recitals weary the public ear.

There is enough truth in what is charged by the public and what is said by the roads in exculpation of themselves, to give reasonable foundation for the accusations and extenuating pleas. But half truths are of little value, and the whole truth is essential to furnish the real explanations of the conditions admitted to exist.

One has not far to go to find the active and potent cause of the contentions and practices that hurt the railways, and the unjust discriminations and irregularities that prejudice the public. Multiplication of roads and competition are not the primary causes. They are secondary or resulting causes, and aggravate the disordered condition; but the efficient cause lies back of them. It is none other than the independent power of every railroad or consolidated system of roads to establish and change rates at will, with no control or restriction except the trifling provision of law requiring ten days' notice of advance and three days' notice of reduction. This power is the Pandora's box out of which proceeds

---

Reprinted by permission from the Railway Review of August 15, 1891.

the whole scandalous horde of evils—premature and speculative construction of roads, reckless competition in prices for business, evasions of the law, shrinking revenues, the various forms of unjust discrimination, rebates and devices for getting business from competitors. And this pernicious power is the creation of law, and is protected by law, upon the antiquated and once respectable theory, but now fully demonstrated fallacy, that unrestricted competition among railroads is a public benefit, that the public interest is subserved in getting its transportation service for the lowest prices at which it may be publicly or privately offered for sale, and that any restraints on competition would tend to raise or keep prices high, and therefore prejudice the public. The law protects this power by its omission to control or regulate it, and by prohibiting under high penalties any efficient efforts to regulate it on the part of the roads. The power, therefore, is the favorite of the law, as the instrument by which competition is to be preserved and low rates secured. The competition so sedulously guarded by law is solely in rates. Competition in other respects, such as facilities, quality of service, accommodations for the public, have been left to shift for themselves.

What is this power? In the shortest phrase, it is a power to do infinite mischief—a power by every road to do as it pleases; to separate from the general railroad system of the country, which to the eye of the government, as an agent of government, and in its relations to the public, is essentially a unit; to unsettle rates; to bring on railroad wars; to diminish revenues; to disturb values and demoralize trade and commerce: to induce unjust discriminations, with their train of attendant evils.

Is evidence needed in support of these facts? One has only, for confirmation, to turn his ear to the complaints that come up from all parts of the country, voiced by railway associations, and daily rehearsed in the public press, that rates can not be maintained, that agreed schedules have been wantonly changed or violated, that some competitor, like a Canadian line, or a circuitous water and rail rival of the trunk lines, or a superfluous line between Chicago and St. Paul, or between Chicago and the Missouri river, is cutting rates, that business is being diverted and revenues falling off; or, for additional evidence, to open his eyes to the scores of traffic associations supported at great expense for the sole purpose of regulating competition by agreements for fixing and maintaining competitive rates. The roads endeavor to do by voluntary action what the government has failed to do for them, and 90 per cent. of their efforts is wasted, because the government withholds its sanction.

Mr. Stickney, whose experience and knowledge as a practical railroad man qualify him to speak with authority, in his recent vigorous and very frank book on the railway problem, furnishes, under cover of a discussion of various topics, an instructive commentary on the dangerous power of independent rate making. At pages 6 and 7 he says: "This unrestricted power to discriminate in the matter of rates, lodged in the hands of one man, the manager, say, of five thousand miles of railway; the power, through malice, ignorance or stupidity, to decree which out of a thousand cities and villages located on his lines should prosper, and which should not, which individuals out of, say, ten thousand merchants doing business in those cities and villages should make a profit or a loss, * * * such enormous power over the fortunes of so many should never be lodged in the hands of any human being."

At page 31, after illustrating the effect of slight concessions in rates, he says; "With these facts fresh in mind, who is willing to say that the power to discriminate in freight rates ought to be lodged in the control of one man or a few men? Under such conditions what business is safe?"

And in commenting on the report of the senate committee, he says, at page 146: "The whole discussion by the committee tended towards one conclusion—that the traffic on railways should be regulated by law, in the interest of the carrier as well as of the people, since every evil which was pointed out by the committee grew out of the schedule of rates. With a properly arranged and enforced schedule, none of these evils would be possible." And once more (page 153): "The railway companies and the public both suffer from the confusion in rates; since when the rates in the various schedules conflict, the lowest prevails, which results in loss of revenue to the companies and in unjust discrimination to the public."

Judge Cooley, whose competence to speak will not be questioned, in his able address at the convention of railroad commissioners at Washington in March last, says: "The troubles that are always present, always annoying, and always difficult of adjustment, are those which relate to the making of rate sheets, and to the manner in which these are observed or treated after they are made. It is here that we discover a problem that is not narrow or temporary, and that does not touch lightly upon the relations between the railroads themselves, but is seen in nearly all their controversies and misunderstandings, and that is the prolific parent of nearly all the difficulties between the railroads and those who have occasion for their services."

Then, after discussing the independent power of the different roads to make and change rates, and the manner in which the power is exercised, he continues "This, then, is the railroad problem; there are mischiefs in railroad circles that are outside of it, but we distinctly indicate the main source of difficulty when we place our finger upon the power as it exists now to make and unmake rates for passenger and freight transportation. So long as 500 bodies of men in the country are at liberty to make rate sheets at pleasure, and to unmake and cut and recut them in every direction at their own unlimited discretion, or want of discretion, and with little restraint on the part of the law except as it imposes a few days delay in putting changes in force, the problem will remain to trouble us; the mere existence of the power making losses, disorder and confusion constantly imminent."

It may seem superfluous to refer to evidence or to quote authorities in support of a proposition that should be evident in the nature of things, and be matter of general knowledge. But there are many who do not understand it, and least of all, unfortunately, the majority of those who are charged with the responsibility of making laws. This is proven conclusively by the character of the laws framed. Unjust discrimination was found to be the crowning sin of railroads, and the evil intended to be cured. This was done by enacting into a statute a few sound ethical principles, long recognized as legal rules, and declaring that their violation should be unjust discrimination, to be punished with fire and sword, while the cause of all the wrongs intended to be corrected was left untouched and active. It was like enacting that "honesty is the best policy," or like a father giving excellent advice to his son and then filling his pockets with money and sending him forth to spend it in dissipation. Stickney says of the law: "It attempted to destroy discrimination, while preserving the cause of discrimination—competition, so called." Page 140.

As long ago as 1885 Judge Cooley, in a letter to the Cullom committee, with a prescience evincing his thorough comprehension of the subject, wrote: "There is a demand for legislation that will secure at the same time steadiness of rates and unrestrained and even active competition, things which necessarily kill each other; and those who make the demand, if compelled to choose between the two, would be almost certain, in the present state of public opinion, to choose that which was least beneficial." * * * "But it is thought by many that a complete remedy could be found in legislation that should require rates to be made public, and adhered to for a definite time without change, under penalty, and that should at the same time prohibit the common understandings that the railroads have endeavored to harmonize upon. The prohibition would necessarily destroy the remedy; that is to say, the attempt at such a remedy would be more mischievous than beneficial, unless it had for its basis a general predetermination of rates. Such most certainly would be the case as to all the business in respect to which rates are now so unsteady as to make legislation important; that, namely, in respect to which there is competition, which of course is the major part of all."

How completely these predictions have been verified it is unnecessary to spend time in pointing out. It is enough to say that the mischiefs intended to be cured by the law was framed on the theory indicated, have increased and multiplied, and the law itself has fallen largely into disrespect.

THE RAILROAD MALADY.

The preservation of free and active competition has been the favorite theory upon which all laws for the regulation of railways have hitherto been framed. No doubt the idea had its origin in the natural dread of combination and extortion. Competition has therefore been the *ignis fatuus* that has allured theoretical writers and led astray lawmakers. But experience, which is the test of all human plans, has demonstrated the fallacy of the theory. It is a fact now as well known as any fact of human experience that free and active competition is inconsistent with regulation, that, in the language of Judge Cooley, it kills the remedy. So long as the power to compete in prices for service exists and is authorized by law, and the demand for business is greater than the supply, it will be exercised to the extent and in the manner deemed necessary. The scramble of a flock of chickens for a few grains of corn scattered on the ground is only an illustration of the competition of railroads for business.

Is there any plan that affords promise as a practicable and efficient remedy? Any untried theory must rest largely in opinion until tested by experience. Obviously, regulation, to be of value, must regulate the whole subject to which it is applied. The cause that produces mischievous results must be reached or there can be no effective regulation. Regulation is as essential to the railways as to the public. This is abundantly shown by their own well meant but ineffectual attempts at voluntary regulation. From the side of the public, stability and uniformity of reasonable rates, with exclusion of undue preferences and unjust discriminations, are the things of importance, and they are no less important to the railroads. In these respects the interests of the public and the roads are mutual. In depriving the roads of the power to hurt each other, they will be divested of the power to injure the public. On the part of the railroads, what is most needed is that a single road, and one perhaps of least importance and usefulness, shall not have the power to demoralize the business of competitors and drive them to bad practices and financial disaster.

Where the whole subject of the remedy to be applied that shall be potential and free from vital objections is theoretical, there must be various theories and honest differences of opinion. The accepted governmental theory is regulation of the conduct of railways in transportation only, without interfering with active competition between roads and their independent power of rate making, which is the motor of competition. The conviction has become general that this mode is inadequate and that something else is necessary.

A theory that has apparently a large body of adherents is government ownership and operation of the railways This is the most objectionable of all. It involves the purchase of eight to ten billions, nominal value, of railway property; the maintenance and operation of some 170,000 miles of railway with its equipment, and with the control, management and payment of some 800,000 employes necessary to its operation; and the making, printing and publishing of all the classifications and tariffs for the enormous amount of traffic carried—upwards of half a billion tons of freight annually—and nearly half a billion passengers.

In the single matter of the relations to employes with the ever impending and embarrassing questions they involve, new and serious problems would certainly arise. And what additional elements of public peril and demagogic disturbance these relations would afford.

It also involves the wielding of a tremendous political power, with the complications and abuses inevitable to its exercise. The management of the post-office department is insignificant in comparison. These objections are insuperable. Whatever a despotic government like Russia may find practicable in this regard, in a republic like ours it cannot be done. The attempt to assume this gigantic undertaking would speedily shatter the government to fragments.

Another theory proposed is that the roads should remain in private hands for purposes of ownership and operation, as at present, but that the government should establish and change whenever necessary the schedules of rates, and exercise summary powers for their enforcement. This is the argument of Mr. Stickney's book, and the conclusion to which the whole discussion apparently is directed. This plan, which has its germ in the English system in the powers of the board of trade, and is possible under the conditions and with the limited scale of railways of that country is, to those who believe in the infallibility and omnipotence of government, plausible theoretically, but, under the railway and governmental conditions of this country, is open to grave objections.

Those are, briefly, the nature and magnitude of the work, with its endless complications and intricacies, and the impossibility of its being done directly by Congress or by any commission method at all likely to be created; the political *animus* inseparable from nearly everything done through government agencies which are liable to frequent changes for partisan reasons; the repugnancy of the plan to the spirit of our institutions, and the American idea that a citizen should have at least a part in the management of his own business affairs, and non-interference by government beyond certain necessary safeguards required by the general public interests.

A unique theory emanates from an exalted source while this paper is in preparation. A member of the supreme court of the United States in a grave judicial opinion suggests that the "powers of a court of equity may yet be found adequate to the situation—that such courts may yet lay strong hands upon these railroad corporations, and by compelling performance of contracts secure stability, uniformity and justice to all, and thus quiet the clamor and avoid any necessity of governmental possession and management." He declares that "the powers and processes of a court of equity are equal to any and every emergency. They are potent to protect the humblest individual from the oppression of the mightiest corporation, to protect every corporation from the destroying greed of the public; to stop state or nation from spoliation or destroying private rights; to grasp with strong hand every corporation and compel it to perform its contracts of every nature and do justice to every individual."

As an illustration he says that a judge "on the bench" of a certain court "not only took possession of and managed great railroad corporations by receivers; but built hundreds of miles of railroads and created millions of dollars of obligations against those roads."

This language is strong and significant and implies more perhaps than is expressed.

If the court be the *imperium in imperio* it is declared to be, most of our governmental machinery is surperfluous.

Within judicial limits the enforcement of lawful contracts is sound doctrine. But contracts of *every nature* are not and ought not to be always enforced. "Circumstances alter cases." When statute law shall have declared what contracts railroad companies may enter into "to secure stability, uniformity and justice," such contracts should very properly be enforced. The phrase "powers of a court of equity" is misty and undefinable. Practically, it is whatever a court in a particular case may see fit to do. "Grasping," "building" and managing railroads, if they are functions of a court, imply the absorption by the judiciary of the powers of the legislative and executive departments of the government, and the exercise of all the powers lodged in its different departments, by one man sitting as a court of equity and determining the extent of his own jurisdiction.

Applied in this manner the theory means independence of all law and of all interference by any public authority. The judge who sways the limitless powers of a court of eqnity is monarch of all he surveys. His receivers come to him with *ex parte* applications for "instructions" and for authority to do various things, and the judge, without the benefit of discussion. and drawing from his own wells of wisdom only, issues his edicts. Within their ordinary jurisdiction of deciding controversies between parties, and enforcing judgments rendered, these courts are indispensable and invaluable, but for purposes of regulating and operating railroads they have not in all cases been a shining success. The experience of numerous roads managed by courts through receivers has not been such as to commend that plan to public approval.

The late Justice Miller, in a dissenting opinion (104 U. S. 137), in speaking of receivers of railroads, said: "The appointment of receivers, as well as the power conferred on them, and the duration of their office, has made a progress which, since it is wholly the work of courts of chancery and not of legislatures, may well suggest a pause for consideration. He (the receiver) generally takes the property out of the hands of its owner, operates the road in his own way, with an occasional suggestion from the court, which he recognizes as a sort of partner in the business; sometimes, though very rarely, pays some money on the debts of the corporation, but quite as often adds to them, and injures prior creditors by creating a new and superior lien on the property pledged to them."

Another, and so far as can be judged without previous trial, a preferable theory, is to combine the authority of the government with the exercise of responsible power by the roads themselves acting by some joint or federated method instead of every road acting independently. Federation for common purposes and to promote the common good, is a plan approved by the experience of mankind for centuries. It is especially the mode among races endowed like the Anglo-Saxon with a genius for government by lawful and peaceful means, and is illustrated in its grandest form in the structure of our national government. Federation among railroads, which are creatures and agents of governments, should be compulsory. This theory requires the withdrawal or surrender of the separate power of every road to make and change rates at its own pleasure, and substitutes for it a sort of parliament of roads to fix schedules of common rates by agreement, which shall be binding on all and be enforceable in a summary manner by authority of the government. The fact that nearly all rates are interdependent or related as between competing lines, as well as regards localities and individuals served by a particular line, is a controlling reason for authoritative federated action, as well to preserve peace as to promote common prosperity. It is implied that in instances in which agreements can not be arrived at, the government, by some office or tribunal, shall act as arbiter to decide the points of difference. Of course it is also implied that the reasonableness of all rates and their freedom from unjust discrimination and undue preference shall be subject to review and correction by the government, through some appropriate tribunal possessing judicial powers and capable of prompt action—constituted perhaps on the general pattern of the present commission, with suitable modifications, but with a sufficient number of auxiliary commissioners, to be territorially distributed, who should act as arbiters in the rate-making federations, conduct *ex parte* investigations, and have charge of prosecutions for violations of the law in their respective districts. And the decisions of the tribunal of commerce should be final in all cases, unless appealed from within a limited time, upon the record in the case, to the appellate courts of the United States.

As a subsidary matter arrangements for the distribution or equalizing of transportation among roads legitimately entitled to participate could be anthorized as part of the general scheme ahd become an important factor in controlling the forces of discord and preserving harmony.

This theory assigns to government its true function in the business pursuits of its citizens, as the great reserve force to secure justice and impartiality, leaving to those interested in the business scope for judgment, and to enterprise and capacity, freedom of action, within limitations that shall guard the public against imposition and wrong-doing.

With the independent power of rate making extinguished the means of reckless competition ceases, and it would seem that stability and uniformity of reasonable rates might be maintained.

It is not to be expected that any plan can be free from objection, or prove an absolutely perfect remedy. In the affairs of the world, and with the constant friction of the separate and often opposing interests, only an approximation to ideal results is possible.

The power of congress to require interstate rates to be established by federations of railways—which would be little more than an enlargement of existing associations, and legalization of their acts in establishing schedules—would seem to be as clear as the powers already exercised. The power to regulate commerce, as defined and amplified by the courts, is co-extensive with the subject to which it relates, and embraces not only the traffic carried, but the means and instrumentalities of carriage, and the terms and conditions of carriage, together with the business conduct of the carriers in their relations to the public. And it is not to be assumed that the limit of the power has yet been reached.

The powers of railway corporations are delegated powers, and may be revoked, or be limited and governed in their exercise in such a way as the sovereign authority may prescribe. "Shall the thing formed say to him that formed it, Why hast thou made me thus?"

The relinquishment of the independent power of rate making is only the surrender of a power that may be exercised, and in its untrammelled state is constantly exercised, to do irreparable mischief, and which, while it remains, renders government efforts at regulation mostly abortive. The general result of its surrender would inevitably be a maximum of good and minimum of evil.

Judge Cooley's letter in 1885 to the Cullom committee contained this significant paragraph:

"The question then presents itself whether the final solution for the 'railroad problem' is not likely to be found in treating the railroad interest as constituting in a certain sense a section by itself of the political community, and then combining in its management the state, representing the popular will and general interests, with some definite, recognized authority on the part of those immediately concerned, much as state and local authority are now combined for the government of municipalities. Something of the sort would neither be unphilosophical nor out of accord with the general spirit of our institutions, and it is therefore likely at some time to be taken into serious consideration by law makers. If the state reserves to itself the necessary authority to protect the public against unfair practices, she may well leave the roads to quarrel over the infinite variety of detail in the adjustment of rates, taking care, however, that their adjustment shall not be, as it often is now, purely nominal, but one to be adhered to."

Would it not be wise for railroad managers and the public to direct their efforts to some such solution of the railway puzzle ?

Kingston, N. Y., Aug. 6, 1891.

COMMENT OF HON. ALDACE F. WALKER, CHAIRMAN WESTERN TRAFFIC ASSOCIATION.

To the Editor of The Railway Review :

I am obliged for the opportunity you have given me to examine the proofs of Judge Schoonmaker's interesting article entitled "The Railroad Malady and its Treatment," and for your request that I also write you upon the subject. My time permits no more than a hasty illusion to a single point. I think that Judge Schoonmaker's severe arraignment of Justice Brewer's recent utterance on the subject of the enforcement of contracts must have been written without having read the opinion as a whole and without understanding the precise point of the remarks which are criticised. Judge Schoonmaker apparently thinks that Justice Brewer's suggestion implies that railways may be operated through receiverships established by the court of equity, and that it is proposed to substitute that power for government ownership and control. Having this thought he enlarges upon the danger of the absorption of authority by courts.

I am satisfied, however, that nothing was further from Mr. Justice Brewer's mind. On the contrary his suggestion varies in one respect only from that made by Judge Schoonmaker himself. The proposition of Judge Schoonmaker is that congress should require the establishment of railway federations for the preparation of interstate tariffs, which he says would be little more than the enlargement of existing associations and the legalization of their acts. Justice Brewer's proposition implies that the existing federations are legal and require no act of congress to compel their formation or to recognize their legality; and that being legal contracts they are enforceable as are other contracts in the courts.

For a court of equity to compel the specific performance of contracts duly made between competent parties is no new jurisdiction; the application of established principles to new cases at times seems doubtful until it has become an accomplished fact, when its propriety is so evident that one is surprised that the doubt could have existed. The agreements under which railway associations are formed constitute a class of contracts which as yet have not been submitted to the courts. It may possibly be found that in some of these agreements single clauses may exist of which some courts would decline to take cognizance, but the contracts as a whole, and especially the features of such contracts which relate to the establishment of interstate rates by federated action subject to arbitration of differences, are unquestionably legitimate at the present time, and, more than this, are absolutely required by existing legislation, which would not be workable in their absence.

Justice Brewer's suggestion then is: that the courts of equity may compel the performance of contracts of this character as well as of other contracts of a continuing nature. This thought being admitted, the railway situation is at once clarified. The "railroad malady" is seen to be susceptible of treatment in the precise line suggested by Judge Schoonmaker, namely, by federation in the establishment of rates, subject to restraint in case rates so made become excessive. No further legislation is required. As in thousands of other instances, there has been too much legislation already. All that is necessary to treat existing difficulties in the line desired by Judge Schoonmaker is simply to proceed under existing laws in the making and execution of contracts according to existing association methods, and in case parties to such contracts should refuse to be bound by the terms of their obligations thereunder, submit to the courts the question of the right of their associates in the agreement to compel a specific performance thereof.

Chicago, Aug. 14, 1891.   ALDACE F. WALKER.

THE RAILROAD PROBLEM.

Hon. Joseph D. Potts.

The question of transportation is one of the weightiest of living topics. It has grown more rapidly than it has been comprehended; and the commercial health of the nation requires that this condition be changed; that its essential principles be broadly understood, and the proper regulation of its great power be intelligently, justly, and completely established.

I hope you will not consider it unfitting if I refer, by way of a short prelude, to what may be deemed the genesis of transportation; to the imperative character of the instincts it has been created to gratify—instincts which have grown, and which will continue to grow in volume and force, as means for their gratification increase in extent, in excellence, and in cheapness.

The impulse to movement, to motion, to change of locality, seems inherent in all matter. The great spheres which occupy space are forever moving; the infinitesimal atoms of which matter consists are never quiet, excepting under restraint. Animal life has its recurring periods of restlessness, and the human animal, man, is dominated by the same irresistible law. Only the restraints of inconvenience, lack of physical power, and lack of time, keep mankind within reasonable bounds of quietude. The possession of money in modern times somewhat lessens the force of these restraints, and the palpable results of such possession have led an acute observer to say that "when a rich American has built himself a house in the city, another in the country, and a cottage by the sea or in the mountains—then—he travels." The motives to movements are multitudinous; to movements of persons, of property, of ideas; motives of pleasure, of sorrow, and of gain; the supply and reception of news, and the demand and supply for and of materials for use and gratification. These motives are endless in quantity and variety, but they are all in constant activity; and they all impel and compel movement.

The palliation and the partial removal of the forms of restraint just named, which so hamper these ever-present impulses to movement, has become in modern days one of the greatest of human industries. It is the science and the art of transportation.

Address delivered before the Contemporary Club, Philadelphia. Reprinted by permission from the Railway Review of June 4, 1892.

Let us glance briefly at some of the achievements of this immense industry. Instead of the rugged and broken natural surface of the earth, to be wearily and slowly plodded over on foot, in danger, with exhausting toil, with great loss of useful time, and with the most barbaric discomfort, we have the smooth railway and vestibule train, and we eat and sleep in luxury, comfort, and safety, while gliding easily along at 50 miles an hour. The great water surfaces of the globe, upon which in his early history man could not safely venture, are now traversed in huge vessels, safely, comfortably, and swiftly, and with such certain punctuality that spaces of thousands of miles are covered with variations of but a few hours in the times of the voyages; and, indeed, under favoring conditions of sea and weather, these differences are measured by minutes.

Our ideas are passed from point to point with still greater perfection of method. The telegraph, the telephone, and the extraordinary postal systems of civilized countries, especially that of the United States, make the interchange of ideas rapid and cheap to a degree which but a short time since would have appeared impossible, unless it had been wrought miraculously.

If we turn from what has been done in the way of removing restraints on the movement of man and his belongings to the effect which such partial removals have worked, we will find the most abundant confirmation of the declaration already made, that the tendency to movement is constant and all-pervading, and that nothing but natural hindrances prevent its increasing conversion from tendency to deed.

Bear in mind that transporters have not wholly removed difficulties; they have only modified some of them, and this, in part, by converting them into a new form of difficulty, the new form being a charge of money. Instead of spending time and strength in tramping from place to place, the traveler buys a ticket, for which he disburses money; instead of carrying his goods on his back through the wilderness, he pays a freight rate, and for the sending of his letters 3,000 miles, he uses a stamp which costs him two cents.

He can earn the requisite cash for the ticket, for the freight rate, and for the stamp, with much less outlay of time and of labor than was required, when, by his own efforts, his person or his property was moved; so that, while this movement is still under restraint, still subject to whatever difficulties may be represented by the rates of charge and the conditions made by transporters, his restraint has been greatly lessened, and the extent of movement has, therefore, been greatly enlarged.

I don't wish to worry you with statistics, but I will venture to give you a few figures, because in no other way can you be so briefly shown how increases in movement have followed the physical improvements and the lessened cost already established by transporters.

Take an example from the movement of property:
On the railroads of the United States the average charge for moving one ton of property one mile was—

In 1880 . . . . 1, 29-100 cents
In 1890 . . . . 93-100 cents

The tons moved one mile per each person of the entire population of the United States were—

In 1880 645
In 1890 1,265

That is, the reduction in rates was a little more than one-fourth per ton, while the increase in movement, per person, was nearly doubled.

Take an example from the movement of letters:
The rate of letter postage charged by the United States was—

In 1880, for half ounce or less . . . . . . 3 cents
In 1890, for an ounce or less . . . . 2 cents

The movement of letters through the mails during the same years, for each person of the entire population, was—

In 1880, approximately, ... 21
In 1890, approximately, ... 30

Disregarding the effect of the change in maximum weight, as an effect, the extent of which cannot now be ascertained, we find the result in the reduction of charges of one-third per letter, and an increase in movement of nearly one-half per person.

All hindrances to movement, however, are not yet represented by a charge. Some loss of time is yet involved, and in the cases of long journeys, very much time which often can be illy spared. Our practical speed, however, is yet slow—not over 50 miles an hour—and betterments in this respect can be reasonably hoped for. It is much slower than certain varieties of birds are said to have attained, and what birds have done, man can probably do. Some bodily wear and tear is yet a necessity, and this may never be wholly removed, but it is certainly lessened yearly.

The chief hindrances of to-day are represented in part by the tariff conditions of transporters, and by their rates of charge, especially by the irregularities and discriminations of such rates, and by their sudden and severe fluctuations. They are also represented, in part, by suddenly developed incompetencies of transporters to meet sudden growths of movement; or to meet, promptly, clearly foreseen increases in demands for track, power and carriage facilities. And they are, finally, also represented, to a large extent, by the evil results of many unwisely conducted struggles for traffic, and for monopoly of position, which are waged between railway corporations, and which, by a curiously weak misnomer, are classified under the title of competition.

It is a consideration of some of these existing obstacles, which bar our way to more effective transportation conditions, that I will now ask your attention.

Perhaps our perception of the evils we suffer from, and of the possible remedies for them, may be quickened and clarified by first making plain to our minds, what conditions of transportation capacities we would like to have—what conditions, which, in the light of present knowledge, will probably be improvements on those we now possess, and yet not be beyond a reasonable hope of practical attainment. To set forth these new and desirable conditions with any approach to adequate fullness, I have found to be quite impossible within the limits of time permitted by a proper regard for your patience. I can, therefore, but hint at a few of their outlines; and, indeed, I have been obliged to restrict these hints to the subject of property movement only, and that by railway within the United States.

First, then, we must have reasonable rates of charge, and reasonable stability in such rates, so that the great interchanges of traffic will not have possible ruin always impending over their owners, through sudden and violent changes in tariffs. To-day all traffic is so exposed, and many severe and costly demonstrations of this truth have made the boldest commercial minds timid and halting in their movements, excepting when they can procure, in advance, and from competent authority, assurances against such risks. Communities which possess two or more really competitive routes, equally effective and far-reaching, are less exposed to this danger than others. It is indeed a frequent practice for a transporter to maintain high charges to or from points which no other transporter can reach, while making low rates to and from other points which are in competition with rivals. There are few practices more tempting to the transporter, but none more ill-judged, nor more permanently harmful to both transporter and locality. It is an abominable evil, which should be absolutely suppressed.

Stability must be attained, however, by means that will not stifle improvement. Destructive competition has, as its one good effect, the betterment and cheapening of methods; but surely our civilization is not at this day so crude that progress in method cannot be won in better ways than by the destructiveness of the savage.

Next: we must have a greater approximation to uniformity in rates of charge, and absolute freedom from inequitable discrimination between shippers. The big shippers must not be charged so much less than the little shippers, that the little ones shall perish and the big ones find their business increasingly swollen. It is proper and necessary to have a wholesale rate and a retail rate of charge; but the basis of the wholesale rate must, both for the public benefit and the interest of the transporters, be small enough to be attained by the many, and not so large that it can only be reached by the few.

THE RAILROAD PROBLEM. 35

Again: we must have a separation of terminal and transfer charges from the road charges. Terminals and transfer facilities are costly, and their expenses cannot be easily cheapened. The great future economies will be made in the movement between terminals, and it is this movement which the individual members of the public cannot provide cheaply, each for himself. It is here that the main usefulness of the great transporter is found. Many shippers prefer to provide their own terminals and do their own terminal work. When they can do so they should have the right to do so, and they should not be charged for what they do themselves.

Again: we must have a separation of road charges into charges of a certain amount when cars are furnished by the road owner, and charges of a less amount when cars are furnished by others. Many prefer to furnish their own cars, and should be allowed to do so, and such division of the total road charges should be made as will fairly apportion them according to the relative capital and risk of each interest. This should apply, whether the car owner carries traffic for himself or for others. Under this regulation, shortage in car supplies will become less frequent, and the railway will approximate the character of a common highway; a result much to be desired.

Again: we must have, within defined limits, a practical blending, for the movement of cars and property, of all the railroads of the country, as they are now, and as they may be hereafter, into a single effective system. That is, the rates of road charges should be on a mileage basis and should apply to the total mileage any shipment they make, regardless of the fact that it may, in its transit, pass over many roads differently owned. This will be easily accomplished if the divisions of the road charges already suggested be made, and if every road be compelled to move, with impartial promptness, over its tracks (but not into its terminals) every suitable car which may be offered to it.

Proper rules as to such interchange of cars, including also just requirements as to the character of the cars, should, of course, be established.

Again: railroad-owners, as one of their duties, should be under compulsion to be suitably supplied with tracks and power. This is a question of difficulty, and ought not to be adjusted inequitably; but it should not be left, as it now is, wholly to the degree of providence or foresight, financial skill or commercial courage, possessed by each such road-owner.

These leading changes impress me as absolutely essential to be made, and made as speedily as may be consistent with equity, legal power practicability and good judgment. They will constitute, I believe, a set of fairly effective remedies for the main imperfections yet developed in our present system of inland traffic movement. There are, of course, other difficulties needing cure, including difficulties local to cities and to all closely-settled communities, which I cannot touch on now.

If what I have said be correct, we have then to consider the equities involved in these changes; afterward the legal power to make them; and, finally, the practical method, if any can be found, of accomplishing them.

And first, what equities are to be considered? I take it no American, in his movements of sober thought, will feel that any readjustment of conditions can stand, or ought to stand, or will produce permanently useful results, unless they be founded on equity.

When, early in this century, the movement began among civilized nations, looking to inland transportation upon a scale beyond all precedent, each large community turned naturally to its governments, municipal, provincial, state or national, as the only available organizations competent to provide for a common need; the cost and apparent risk of which were so much beyond the range of individual power. Moreover, the idea of a common highway was properly a dominant one. Hence states built canals and railways, and, later, lesser communities joined interests with individuals in constructing like works. The national government of the United States built a great macadamized road. European governments embarked largely in the improved form of highways. Certain disadvantages in many cases were soon developed under governmental ownership and operation. Political necessities often took precedence of commercial necessities, and the governmental management became frequently incompetent and tainted.

Most communities in this country grew satisfied that the element of individual interest must be introduced to secure transportation efficiency, and avoid governmental deterioration. The introduction of such an interest soon became, with a few exceptions, the general rule here, and forms of corporate organization were evolved, in which, under restrictions for the public protection, thought at the time to be sufficient, but which have often since proved inadequate, the private interest of the transporter became the leading motive, and the convenience and interest of the public subordinate considerations, excepting when and as it became clear to the transporter that deference to the latter motives would contribute to his own prosperity.

Vast amounts of individual money have been invested in this form of public service, under the belief that this relation of interests would always continue.

It would be unfair to sacrifice to any proper degree these individual interests, thus authoritatively called into existence; but the time seems to have arrived when through the processes here suggested, or such other processes as may seem to be wiser, but in any case by processes which shall be mutually just, the public service must take the front place as a motive, and the private interest of the transporter an equitable, but a secondary position.

THE RAILROAD PROBLEM. 37

The next point, that of legal power, is one which I think need hardly be considered at present. Under our form of government, whatever a sufficient number of the people ultimately, and after full consideration, decide shall become the law, will be made the law, and the present moment is the time for discussion and for experimenting, and not for much law-making. We, therefore, come, finally, to the consideration of methods of reformation.

Railroad owners are clearly unable to introduce such methods unaided. They have tried to harmonize in various ways ever since the dawn of competition among them, and their efforts have been but a continuous succession of short-lived pacifications, alternated with longer periods of mutual reproaches, impartially distributed breaches of faith, and bitter and destructive rate wars, track wars, and wars over every other species of difference between them. The public look with disfavor upon peace conferences between railroad companies, and in fact have now made pooling unlawful. The pool was, perhaps, the most nearly successful form of traffic combination, on a great scale, ever made in this country; but it was only imperfectly maintained; and when its provisions seriously pinched the prosperity of any member, the pool was only preserved because those members whose interests it was aiding, winked at the secret remedial methods resorted to by the member whose interests it was harming.

The public disfavor would not have been unwise had the pool been perfect. Such a huge combination of almost unchecked power over the fortunes of citizens would have certainly been unwholesome, and might easily have grown dangerous. But the natural existing conditions make pooling substantially harmless at present, and its illegality is, therefore, at this time a needless safeguard.

The separate states are clearly incompetent to establish efficient regulations. Their jurisdiction is limited to their own boundaries, while the controlling traffic is continental.

There is but one power which can deal with the subject effectively, and that is the government of the United States. This power has made a movement in this direction by enacting, and to some extent, enforcing, the interstate commerce law. The movement has been useful, but less so than was hoped for. It has cured something, and has probably tended to prevent more harm than it has discovered or punished. The commission created under it has labored under a radical disadvantage in not having among its members either trained transporters or capable merchants or manufacturers, and of being loaded with duties which entirely overtax a single tribunal. If it was confined to the duty of interpretation, and if the duty of enforcement was divided among a number of other tribunals, the results should be better. The power it claims, of determining absolutely the rates of charge, is a dangerous power, which transporters are naturally contesting, and which, if it exists, should doubtless be modified.

The precise relation which the national government should adopt toward this question is very uncertain in the public mind. Government ownership and operation are urged, but I think this view is not held by those who have carefully studied the subject. Such a course is open at present to many objections, some of which seem vital.

Probably the wisest relation it can now establish is that of a controlling regulator. Tariffs of charge and tariff conditions cannot be made with good judgment, excepting by trained experts, and such experts are to be found almost wholly engaged in performing the active duties of transporters; therefore such tariffs should be primarily framed by the transporters themselves.

Railroad owners can be forced by suitable national legislation to wholly forego participation in foreign or interstate business, unless they unite in certain prescribed relations.

These relations should comprise proper regulations and agreements for the proper conduct of all their business, and proper conditions and rates of charge; all upon the bases finally determined upon. Such agreements, after formulation, should be subject to the judgment of a national tribunal composed of capable lawyers, transporters, and shippers. In cases of irreconcilable differences between that tribunal and the transporters, such differences should be controllingly passed on by the supreme court of the nation. Variations in form or essence from such rates and regulations while in force, should be punishable by heavy penalties, both corporate and individual; and the detection of such offences and their punishment should be done at the national cost, and before any one of a sufficient number of national courts to insure convenience and prompt results. A few important convictions and punishments would probably make the subsequent legal business of this sort quite limited in quantity. Changes in either rates or rules thus established should be made only by the same authorities, and through the same formal processes as the originals.

These suggestions, and perhaps all suggestions having similar purposes, will hardly commend themselves to the existing railway owner. No curtailment of privilege or power ever seemed wise at first, to him who suffered such loss. But it should not be forgotten that this power is, in the aggregate, greater over the fortunes of the people than any ever before possessed, even by governments in times of peace, if the governments were free. The people of several of our states have already grown so restless under the existence of this power and some of the evil results, that laws bearing a painful leaning toward confiscation have been enacted. Such laws, of course, hurt both sides, as all inequitable action always does; but they have been made, and will probably have worse successors, unless enlightened and competent remedies, consistent with peace, be established.

THE PUBLIC AND THE RAILWAYS.

By the Hon. Shelby M. Cullom,

United States Senator from Illinois.

The history of railroads in the United States is very interesting, exhibiting as it does the growth and development of a system superior in all respects to that of any other country. In a little more than sixty years the railroad mileage in this country has increased from 23 miles, in 1830, to over 170,000 miles, in 1892. Railroads have been regarded as public highways; but their present relation to the public has greatly changed from that which existed when they were first being built. For a time they were regarded as public highways in the broadest sense, subject to use, upon paying toll to the owners, by all who desired to avail themselves of them, and who could furnish their own motive power and vehicles of carriage. It was not long, however, before this idea became obsolete, and railroad charters were granted to associations organized for the purpose of building railroads, and such privileges and grants of power were given to corporations as made the roads monopolies instead of highways to be used by the people generally. These corporations were given control over their railroad lines as against all the world, except as the States might insist upon controlling their action, and, finally, except as Congress might provide for their regulation under the National Constitution.

Railroads in this country have been built almost entirely by private capital. True, a few railroads have been assisted by the Government, by the donation of lands, and by the issuance of bonds in aid of their construction; and some have been aided by the States and municipalities. But whether built by private capital or aided by the Government, the States in which roads have been constructed have for many years claimed the right of controlling or regulating their conduct. When the doctrine that the States had the power of regulation or control over railroads was first asserted, especially when the attempt to declare such control by provisions in constitutions and statutes was made, earnest resistance was shown, and the lawyers of the country generally denounced such assertion of authority as subversive of, and in antagonism to, all the settled principles established by the courts in

---

Reprinted by permission from the Independent of October 6, 1892.

the earlier history of the country. There is now, however, no dispute as to the right of the States within their respective jurisdictions and of Congress within its constitutional jurisdiction, to regulate commerce; and the power to regulate commerce, carries with it the power to regulate railroads, as common carriers doing the business or carrying on the commerce of the country.

Some one has said that the ownership of railroads is private; the use is public. Railroad corporations are called public corporations, and as such are granted special privileges. They are granted the right of eminent domain. In order that they may the better serve the public they are granted powers more enlarged than are those given to private corporations. They are called common carriers, and are required to carry passengers and property for all alike, and are entitled to reasonable compensation therefor. Under the common law, common carriers have no right unjustly to discriminate between persons or places in the conduct of their business for the people. The railroad corporations of the country are the creatures of legislative power; as such they are subject to control or regulation by their creator; and yet any act of a State Legislature or of Congress, by the terms of which a railroad company would be authorized to impose upon the public, would be set aside by the courts.

Mr. Choate years ago said that the railroads were made for the people, not the people for the railroads. Notwithstanding this manifest truism, before any regulation of common carriers was attempted, either by the States or the National Government, a condition of things grew up in this country which seemed to indicate that those engaged in operating railroads believed that the people were made for the railroads; and apparently there are men still engaged in that business who do not seem to comprehend the true legal status of railroad corporations. They are said to be at common law quasi-public servants, as it is expressed by some writer. The State has no right to exercise an arbitrary power over railroad corporations unrestrained by principles of right and justice; it has no right to pursue a policy of regulation or control which will destroy the value of the property. A stockholder in a railroad corporation owns his stock as fully, and is entitled to as much consideration in respect to his rights, as if he were a stockholder in any other enterprise; and the State is bound to respect those rights.

There are, as has been intimated, two jurisdictions over railroads in this country; first the State, next Congress. The States exercised control over railroads many years before Congress attempted any substantial regulation of commerce *among* the States. The States are confined to their respective jurisdictions; but in the absence of Congressional regulation of commerce among the States the courts decide that the States may pass laws requiring railroad corporations to perform certain acts, even though the transportation is not wholly within the State, especially if such action is a police regulation.

With the exception of two brief acts, regulation by Congress is of recent date, the National Legislature never having attempted any general regulation of commerce until the Act of 1887. The people who lived under the old Confederation of States became dissatisfied with it, because under that system of Government they could not secure a uniform regulation of commerce. Every State set up for itself. The necessities of trade, however, demanded a different form of government, a government by the people in one union. Hence, the adoption of the Constitution of 1789, which contains a provision expressly giving to Congress the power to regulate commerce with foreign nations and among the several States. This power carries with it the power to regulate railroads, inasmuch as they are the instruments or means by which commerce is carried on. Courts say that cars and railroads are the vehicle and means by which commerce is moved; and, in fact, they become a part of commerce itself.

We have in this country, therefore, a dual system, the States regulating commerce or railroads within their respective jurisdictions as to domestic or State commerce, and the National Government, under acts of Congress, regulating the commerce among the States, including the means for carrying it on. The efforts of the States alone to control the operations and conduct of railroads failed to meet the necessities and to prevent the railroad corporations of the country from dealing with the people unjustly, because the States could only exercise control of such corporations within their respective jurisdictions and doing business within the State. A much larger portion of the commerce of the country has become interstate, and under the Constitution of the United States the several States have no jurisdiction over it. Therefore, finally, after long years had elapsed, in which the commercial clause of the Constitution had never been appealed to by the legislative power of the Government, the Act of 1887, to regulate commerce among the States, was passed; and it may not be amiss for me briefly to refer to it. It provides that all charges in connection with the transportation of passengers and freight shall be reasonable, and declares unlawful and prohibits discriminations of all kinds, and undue or unreasonable preference or advantage. The Interstate Commerce Law does not seek to change property rights, but simply to enforce common law principles. The act declares the law and provides for its better enforcement by providing for a Commission with certain powers—they are limited—and while many able men believed when the act was under discussion in Congress that greater power was given to the Commission than it ought to possess, yet I think that the general judgment now is that even greater power should be conferred upon it. The great reason for the law was to provide a system of law by which the people dealing with the railroad corporations doing an interstate business should have a remedy for wrongs committed within easy reach and one that would be inexpensive. The findings or decisions of the Commission are not final. They may be appealed from to the courts, and unless some way is devised by which the findings of the Commission shall be conclusive the elements of dispatch and cheapness will prove a delusion. This is the problem now under consideration by the Senate Committee on Interstate Commerce. There has been much discussion as to the wisdom of the fourth and fifth sections of the act, the former known as the long and short haul provision and the latter as the anti-pooling section. The practice which obtained prior to the act to regulate commerce of charging more for the shorter than for the longer distance constituted one of the worst evils in connection with the transportation business. I will not detail the many hardships and the gross injustice that this form of discrimination worked. Suffice it to say that freight was frequently carried for the same or a less rate a longer haul by several hundred miles than the same commodity was carried the shorter distance.

Referring to the anti-pooling section, the most glaring abuses known to railroad management occurred during the existence of pooling and prior to the passage of the Interstate Commerce Act. The impression grew in the minds of the people that pools were not only used as a means of preventing competition, but to increase and maintain high rates. On the other hand, the railroads claim that their sole object was the prevention of rate wars, disastrous both to shippers and roads alike, and that their tendency was to maintain stable and uniform rates. There are wide differences of opinion on the question of pooling. Men engaged in conducting railroads generally favor it, business men differ, while students of railroad problems generally believe that pooling is necessary in the interest of stability of rates. The great majority of people do not believe that pooling should be allowed even though under the supervision of the Commission.

Having briefly defined the relation of the Government to the railways and the nature and extent of Government supervision, I shall next speak of the public reasons for Government regulation.

The failure of the courts to afford prompt and inexpensive relief to the complainants; the inability of state agencies to cope with interstate traffic, by reason of the power given congress by the Constitution to regulate commerce among the states, and the apparent disposition of railroad managers to regard carriers as a law unto themselves, were the chief causes of the act to regulate commerce. The magnificent railroad system of the country had grown up without legal restraint. The rights of private citizens and of localities were as naught compared with the will of rich and powerful corporations. State charters of railroad corpora-

tions were secured and sold or bartered; and the obligations to
the public were disregarded, and discrimination and extortion
followed. Soulless corporations, of insatiable greed and rapacity,
of immense strength financially and politically, regarding themselves as superior to all law, could not forever go unchecked and
unrestrained in their course of selfish aggrandizement. Those
roads which attempted to conduct their business on sound business principles, with due recognition of their public functions,
were driven into bankruptcy by the methods of their competitors
or compelled to conform their course to that of their unprincipled
rivals.

It is not for me to say what would have been the ultimate result of the lawless course of the majority of the roads if allowed
to go unhampered by legislative restrictions. To-day we are informed that the railroad interest represents a capital of ten billion
dollars, employing on June 30th, 1890, an army of seven hundred
and fifty thousand persons. It will not be an exaggeration to say,
I am sure, that such a system, with common interests, and of rapidly increasing proportions, would have rivalled the Government
in power in a little time longer, and it is not strange that such a
power would resist any positive governmental regulation and control. It did not come too soon, and has not come yet with sufficient power.

Looking now at the advantage both to the public and to the
railways of a wise system of regulation, what can be said? The
present legislation, while unquestionably imperfect in many ways—
and certainly it is faulty—is formulated on correct principles, and
in my opinion, it is destined to remain in active force. Future
amendatory legislation, as time and experience disclose the defects
and weaknesses of the present act, will strengthen the law and
increase the possibilities of its beneficent results.

As showing the advantages which the people have derived from
the tentative enactment of 1887, and amendments thereto, it
would be interesting to recall some of the many cases of discrimination, extortion, etc., decided by the Interstate Commerce Commission, where the railroads complained of having ceased their
unlawful practices without going to the courts; but the limited
character of this article forbids. The act, in a measure, protects
the roads against each other.

Many men engaged in business on a limited scale have found in
our system of regulation an even opportunity to do business with
larger and richer competitors, and small towns which heretofore
sought to encourage the establishment of manufacturing industries
in their midst by liberal bonuses of land and money, only to see
them driven to the wall by favored competitors, a further distance
from the market, being given a better rate, or by competitors in
a neighboring town equi-distant from the market being given a
rebate, now have busy factories among them, and prosperity has

come to their people. The consumers have thus been benefited, and the gain to the whole country cannot be measured in dollars.

When the railroads come to a complete realization of their duties to the public, and recognize the further fact that governmental regulation is a fixed determination of the people—as I believe it to be—the advantages of such regulation will be greatly increased; and with a more cheerful disposition on the part of the roads to obey the strict letter and spirit of the law, one great point will have been gained in the settlement of the railroad problem. Law breaking in all its phases will continue until the millennium; but when governmental regulation shall be fully recognized, accepted and obeyed, it will mark an epoch in the history of the United States which cannot be regarded but with gratification by all law-abiding citizens; and such obedience to law will place the railroad business in a safer and better position in every way than it has ever before occupied, and will result in vast good to all the people of our common country.

Springfield, Ill.

THE RAILROADS AND THE PUBLIC.

By Frank J. Firth.

Under this borrowed title, it is proposed to consider a very important, often discussed, but not yet exhausted question.

The Railroads and the Public! The title appears to be peculiarly appropriate as an introduction to the present article. It permits us to consider the railroads in a physical way, consisting of roadway, rails, depots and equipment. Monuments of a past expenditure of brain and capital, but dormant, needing something to vitalize them. They stand as an unused turnpike road may stand with its gates open, no vehicles in motion upon it, of no public service.

The object in asking that the railroads be, for the moment, considered in this dormant state, is that "the public" may be made, for once, to include all its properly constituent parts. "The public" is a sort of will-o'-the-wisp. It is never present. It is almost incapable of definition, as it is popularly conceived. It matters not how large may be an assembly, the public is always conceived, in a vague sort of way, to represent those who are absent. The politician declaims about his duty to the public and the public being accepted as meaning the absent and unheard from members of the body public, is but a shadowy sort of task master. It is time to call a halt on this wrong use of the term "the public" and to demand that the fact be clearly and at all times recognized that "the public" in the United States of America consists of every member of its population in any way interested in any public question that is to be considered.

We therefore have the dormant railroads on the one side and all of the people of the United States upon the other; and what are the proper relations of the one to the other; what is necessary or desirable action to be taken by those members of the public body who have been selected from its number to act as legislators in the interest of all?

It is believed that more equitable conclusions will be arrived at if we thus consider our question, than would result if we considered it under the conditions that attach to the railways in motion, as we then find one section of the public arrayed in seeming opposition to another, and we of necessity side with one party or the other.

Reprinted by permission from the Railway Review of January 23, 1892.

The dormant railroads exist as monuments of a past expenditure of brain and capital. They have been made possible by legislative acts. The early railroad legislation was no doubt, much of it, faulty, lacking in intelligence, corrupt; it no doubt granted large powers to the corporations created to provide the capital to construct and operate the railroads; land grants, immunity from taxation and other special privileges were freely given. Restrictions as to charges that might be made for service were uncommon.

While these are all facts, it is not believed that any of this class of legislation with all its sins of omission and commission can be justly held responsible for the present difficulties that are presented by the railway problem. The railroads could not have been called into existence at all except under grants of the right of eminent domain and of an aggregation of capital under conditions of limited liability. This much must be granted by the most intelligent and pure legislation. Freedom from taxation, grants of land, etc., may enrich the corporations and operate inequitably in many ways, but they are not the conditions responsible for the relation of the railroads to "the public," so called, that occupies such widespread attention, and that is thought to demand remedial legislation.

It is a fact that the early legislators often omitted to exercise a rate limitation control, but this is not thought to be an omission of great present importance. No set of rate limits inserted in any of the older charters operate as any restraint upon the railroads of to-day. The immense and continuing increase in the volume of the carrying business; improved and economical methods, resulting from the natural ingenuity of our people, stimulated by the necessities of a competition unmatched in any other business or in any other part of the world, have led the carriers to voluntarily adopt rates for their service that no sane legislator would have dreampt, a few years since, of exacting by law.

Whatever inequities have existed, or may still exist in the treatment of "the public" by the railroad corporations, will be found to be the result of honest or dishonest selfishness on the part of individual railroad managers, a selfishness made powerful for harm by a practically unrestrained control of capital and patronage. By honest selfishness is meant effort intended to be in the interest of the corporation. By dishonest selfishness is meant effort in the private interest of the individual manager, regardless of his corporate obligations.

Selfishness, often unintelligent selfishness, is not peculiar to the railroad business, and it might as well be recognized that the operating of railroads is a business, and is carried on with the same end in view that any man or body of men seek in conducting any other business. There may be a peculiar duty owing by the railway corporations to the people, but notwithstanding this the carrying service is and must be conducted mainly with the idea of securing a business profit from its operations. All of the methods that are found necessary to obtain a profit from other business operations conducted upon a large scale and under competitive conditions, will be found necessary in the railway service. The railway management of the country controls no short road to success, and has no patented processes that ensure its receipts exceeding its expenditures.

Let us return to the dormant railroads and the public and consider the action that our legislators should take in our interest. It is clear that these railroads to be useful must be operated. To bring about this result brain and capital must be applied to them. The first duty of legislation is to afford a proper protection to the brain and to the capital that are to be induced to undertake this important work. The capitalist who may step forward from the ranks of the public and undertake to serve its remaining members is entitled to a fair opportunity to benefit from his voluntary action. He is entitled to protection for his property and to an assurance that the necessary distribution of competitive traffic, and of its resulting revenues, shall be made between parties interested in the simplest possible way and the one that involves the least needless waste of revenue. If capitalists deem it to their advantage to adopt pooling methods, so called, in distributing their traffic receipts they should be permitted to use these methods, subject always to the right of the public to protect itself against any possible monopolistic results. Distribution is a necessity, and unintelligent distribution works a public calamity. In the interest of capitalist and the public, equally, the legislation proposed should protect and prevent the creation of unnecessary carrying facilities. A needless duplication of carrying facilities lessens the volume of traffic obtainable by each, and the smaller the volume of traffic the greater the cost of performing the service. The public must, in the end, pay the cost of the carrying service. It is clearly to the interest of the public to confine the traffic to as few lines as can satisfactorily care for it, and thus secure the low-priced service that is made possible by a large volume of business.

Having obtained the capital needed to vitalize the dormant railroads, and drawn upon a share of the public to supply it, there is now a need to employ this capital in hiring the brain and sinew to place the vitalized body in active, wholesome motion. Here we draw again upon the public, and in doing so we must consider the legislative protection to which this share of the public is entitled. The brain and sinew devoting itself to railroad operation is the peer of that found in any other occupation in the land. It is as much entitled to legislative protection. It represents millions of industrious men and women, all of them workers in the true sense of the word, none of them drones in the hive. To them we unhesitatingly commit our property and our lives, and our confidence is rarely abused. The brain and sinew operating the railroads of the country are full partners with the capitalist in the results of these operations; in fact, they are special or preferred partners. They must receive their share of the results of the business before anything can go to the capitalist. They are deeply interested in having their chosen legislators enact laws that may permit such a distribution of railway earnings as will prevent wasting rate wars, from which they, the laborers, suffer. The railway laborers of the country may well demand legislative protection from the pernicious effects of that unrestrained competition which is popularly, but ignorantly, believed to be the life of trade. The needless duplication of carrying facilities and the unintelligent distribution of competitive carrying results are made at the expense of the laborer on the railway lines, whether it is a labor of brain or of sinew. Rate wars waste the carriers' revenues and force reductions in the numbers of employes and in the wages of those who are retained. The wage earners suffer from an evil that legislation should eradicate. Intelligent distribution, which in its present state of advancement is represented by pooling, so called, should not only be authorized, but it should, perhaps, be enforced by legislation. It is marvellous that organized labor has not appreciated its vital interest in this question of rate wars, and insisted, with all its united power, upon equitable legislative protection against the consequences of wasteful railway management. If a tithe of the time and money wasted by organized railway labor in "striking" against wage reductions had been devoted to demanding legislative protection against the ignorant and frequently unlawful competition between carriers that has reduced revenues and forced the wage reduction, much more of practical benefit would have been realized by organized labor. In all of the legislation for the regulation of the carrying business of this country there is yet to be seen anything that considers in the remotest degree the wage interests of that vast class of the public employed in carrying on the railroad service.

We have now drawn from the public the railway capitalist class and their vast army of employes. Let us consider another portion of the public in its relation to the railways. Every man or woman carrying on or interested in any occupation connected with the supplying of material to the railways to be used in their business operations and every man or woman similarly supplying material or service to anyone in the employ of the railways, may be embraced in the class of the public it is now proposed to consider.

This class, or some of them, may occupy another relation to the railway question, that of passengers or shippers or receivers of freight on the railroads, but these relations will be considered later. As supplying service or material this class has a vital interest in preventing the waste of railway revenues. Poor railways are poor buyers. They are also, as has been before said, poor payers of their employes, and this makes the employes of necessity poor buyers of material and service. The supplying class is, therefore, as much interested as the railway wage earners in demanding legislation that shall protect them against the needless waste of carrying revenues. The railroads of the country constitute a vast clearing house. The one thousand millions of annual revenue they collect is all disbursed among the people. It is not hoarded. Something over ten per cent of this vast revenue is all that goes to the railway shareholders as a return for their capital. From the remaining ninety per cent the wage earners are paid the money with which they purchase the service and material used by themselves and their families; the factories are paid for all of the great variety of material that enters into the daily repair and operations of the railroads. Prosperity for the railway means prosperity for the country. When the railways are liberal buyers and wage payers the farmer, miner and manufacturer are alike benefitted

Again let us return to the public and see what class or classes we have left demanding our consideration.

The producers of the country, whether farmers, miners or manufacturers, constitute a very large and important class and in their relation to this question, as passengers on the railroads or shippers or receivers of freight carried upon these roads, they are entitled to legislative protection. The protection they may naturally demand is in safety of service, and reasonable charges that do not unfairly discriminate between persons or places. This class is as greatly interested as any of the others in demanding that there shall be no needless duplication of carrying facilities with its attendant lessening of the volume of traffic on each line and increase in the cost of the service. This class is also entitled to demand uniform and stable rates of freight, and freedom from rate wars, whether such wars result from dishonesty or inefficiency in railway management.

The public may be further differentiated but there is neither time nor space now available for the work and it is perhaps unnecessary for the purposes of this article. All of the bankers, brokers and middle men, constituting as they do an important and aggressive class, should perhaps be considered as a portion of the producer or consumer class. They stand between the producer and the consumer and their interest in the railway problem, important as it is, appears to be an interest in which they properly represent the producing or consuming class.

When the public is spoken of in its relation to the necessity for remedial railway legislation let it be understood that in the United States of America the public consists of all of the men and women who constitute its population, and that the legislators chosen to

4

represent them all must be required to equally regard all of their respective interests.

Legislation on this important question should be thoughtfully worked out by the best minds in the country acting with absolute freedom from prejudice. That some legislation is necessary and right is a fact beyond dispute. It is a further and equally apparent fact that this necessary and right legislation is not yet to be found in any of the existing statutes either state or national.

Philadelphia, January 18, 1892.

THE FUTURE OF THE RAILROAD PROBLEM.

By A. B. Stickney,

Chairman of the Board of Directors of the Chicago, St. Paul and Kansas City Railway.

You have invited me to speak on "The Future of the Railway Problem." There seems to be an Evil Genius besetting and controlling this problem. This malign spirit has two names and two faces. When the people hear one of its names and look upon one of its faces they are filled with admiration and love, and cannot believe or understand that it is the same evil spirit which under its other name they so thoroughly detest, and whose other face is so hideous.

The beloved name of this uncanny existence is "Competition in Railway Rates." Its detested name is "Discrimination in Railway Rates."

In my judgment the future of the Railway problem depends upon the fate of this Demon.

"Competition in trade" is a phrase which has a peculiar charm in the ears of a commercial people. It implies freedom of thought and action and a fair chance. For generations the children at school have been taught that "competition is the life of trade;" and so it is, as between individuals on approximately the same footing. It sharpens the wits, awakens inventive genius, and stimulates good manners. But that competition which is "the life of trade" can only exist between parties occupying substantially the same plane. It cannot exist between "Big Fish" and "Little Fish" in the same pool. The little fish must keep close to shore, be contented with what the the big fish don't want, or be swallowed.

The practice of railway companies of making unreasonably low rates from important junction points, while maintaining high rates elsewhere, has been improperly named "competition," and the name has given it a certain amount of popularity. But, in fact, it has not been competition but "discrimination." Discrimination, instead of being "the life of trade," is the death of that fair competition as between individuals and localities, which so long and justly has been styled "the life of trade." The city in whose favor discrimination is practiced becomes the "big fish" and at

---

Reprinted by permission of the Northwestern Railroader, November 9, 1890.

once begins the process of "swallowing" the trade and population of its unfortunate neighboring cities; and the individual tradesman who receives rebates quickly devours those who do not.

It is as though the Government should make rebates from its tariffs to some importing houses which it refused to make to others. It would be absurd to suppose that as between such favored houses and houses not so favored there could be any competition. If houses which paid the full tariff continued to exist it would be by permission of the favorites. Their existence would be by grace, not by good works.

To judge correctly of the effect of railway discrimination requires the possession of certain commercial information. For example, it should be known that when corn is worth 25 cents a bushel in the Chicago market, at the railway station west of the Missouri River it would be worth from 12 to 15 cents; the difference between its value in the Far West and in Chicago being made up of cost of transportation, and the expenses of buying and selling, and a profit to the middle man. A clean profit over all out-of-pocket expenses of one-half of one cent a bushel is a satisfactory profit to the middle man, and a sure guaranteed rate of transportation of even so small a sum as one-quarter of a cent a bushel less than any other middle man can get, will give the man possessing it the monopoly of the business of handling the corn in the district covered by the guarantee. That is to say, if it were possible to give one middle man the absolute, permanent advantage in respect to rates over all others in this business to the extent of one-quarter of one cent a bushel, it would be a weapon of warfare sufficiently powerful, under present commercial conditions, to drive every other middle man out of the field and to secure to the fortunate individual the whole corn traffic. Why? Because a clean profit of one-quarter of a cent per bushel would be sufficient to pay an enormous interest on the necessary capital, while it is evident that, if he contented himself with that profit, no other man could get any profit at all.

Such are the facilities of trade by means of bills of lading, drafts, telegraph, banks, &c., that to do an enormous corn trade the middle man requires only a comparatively small capital to use as a margin. A capital of fifty thousand dollars is ample to thus handle, say, 15,000,000 bushels, and, with activity, double that amount, *per annum*. One-quarter of a cent a bushel profit on 15,000,000 bushels would amount to $37,500—equal to 75 *per cent per annum* on the capital employed. As a matter of fact, such discrimination to the extent of one-thirty-second of a cent a bushel in the hands of a Rockefeller would accumulate in a short time the wealth of a Vanderbilt, because it would create a monopoly; and after all other buyers were driven out of the field, he might not be contented with one-thirty-second. He would then have the power to exact more. So in the coal trade, 15 cents per

THE FUTURE OF THE RAILROAD PROBLEM. 53

ton is a satisfactory miner's profit, and an absolutely sure, permanently guaranteed discrimination in rates of 5 cents a ton would be sufficient, in the hands of a competent man, to create a monopoly and drive all other miners out of the business.

A like profit, from the same source, of 5 cents a barrel on flour would pay the shareholders of the great milling corporation at Minneapolis satisfactory dividends and give it a monopoly, if it cared to increase its plant sufficiently.

With these facts fresh in mind, who is willing to say that the power to discriminate in freight rates ought to be lodged in the absolute control of one man or of a few men? Under such conditions what business is safe? The average business man feels strong enough to cope with his competitors on equal terms, but here is a power against which it is useless to contend, but which cannot be evaded. This power, like a Government, has authority to make a tariff and enforce its collection. It claims a right which no civilized government claims, and no sovereign has dared to exercise for centuries, of rebating a portion of its tariff, and thus discriminating between its subjects in the collection of revenues. It is safe to say that if the Congress of the United States should enact a law which established, on any commodity, one import duty for the city of New York, and a different duty for other cities, or one duty for one firm and another duty for another firm, no matter how slight the difference, the people would resort to arms, if need be, rather than submit.

Railway transportation, under present conditions, is to the industrial world what the atmosphere is to the physical world. It pervades and is essential to all industries. As in the physical world no man, nor beast—no plant, nor shrub, nor weed—can refuse to breathe the air, without death ensuing, so in the industrial world no branch of business can refuse railway transportation except under like penalties. It pervades every article of commerce. When one buys food, clothing or fuel, he buys railway transportation. When he builds houses or stores or manufacturing establishments, churches or school houses, he buys railway transportation. When he buys horses, carriages, jewels or statuary, paintings or books, theatre or lecture tickets, or indulges in the luxury of doctors or lawyers, he pays for railway transportation.

Who would consent that a few men should have the power to dictate upon what terms the air should be breathed? It is idle to talk about railway transportation being a mere article of commerce owned by the company, "which, as such owner, may sell it or not as it may see fit, or if it elects to sell, may demand such price as it chooses or can obtain." It is nonsense to call that "merchandise," which no one can refuse to purchase.

Looking at the subject from the standpoint of the owner of railway property, this absolute power in the hands of managers, who after all are but human, with limited knowledge and capacity, seems quite as dangerous to that interest as to the interests of the people. It is evident that in order to keep railways running, sufficient revenue must be collected to pay operating expenses; and fairness requires an additional amount as compensation for the use of the capital invested. So large is the tonnage that a slight change in the average rate a ton a mile makes the difference between a profit and a loss, and the whole revenue is made up of an almost infinite number of comparatively trifling individual collections. An average difference of one-tenth of one cent a ton a mile on the tonnage of the Chicago & Northwestern Railway in 1888 would have made a difference in its aggregate revenues of $1,939,044 10, a sum more than sufficient to pay a six *per cent* dividend on its common stock.

A mill a ton a mile is about equal to two cents a hundred-weight between St. Paul and Chicago. These figures show how delicately a tariff must be adjusted to produce the proper revenue, and how slight a variation may result in wiping out the dividends for a year.

And yet, upon each road, one man with autocratic power, and his many subordinates—acting separately, without consultation—are making rates varying in amounts, from day to day, and as between different men and different localities; without rule or principle as a basis, simply guessing in each individual case, with the expectation that the average of their guesses for a year will come within the fraction of a mill per ton per mile of the proper amount.

This appears to be the present basis of the value of railway property. If the people need a fixed rule or law establishing rates, the companies need it even more. If there should be vouchsafed to the American people a man with the genius to produce such a rule, which shall be just to both the people and the companies (for no other can become effective), the future of this great problem will then look bright. Every citizen will then have a fair chance. That fair competition between persons which is the "life of trade" will again be possible. Individual enterprise and judgment and genius will again have scope. And that prosperity which always goes hand in hand with the privilege for every man to look out for himself, will follow.

If, on the other hand, paternalism in railway management is to continue and increase, if these companies keep on discriminating in favor of certain towns and business houses, all the business of the country sooner or later will fall into the hands of the few. Later on discrimination, as between these few, will reduce their numbers, and so on, till finally the prospect would seem to be that in addition to the Standard Oil Company, which we already have, there might be one Standard Mercantile Company, one Standard Manufacturing Company, one Standard Railway Company, four Presidents, four General Managers, a score of Directors, and the rest of the then probable population of 100,000,000 of people will be poor grangers, clerks and employes, all mere "strikers" and impotent "kickers," living, packed like sardines, in enormous tenement houses at "competitive points," sucking their daily food through one of Bellamy's tubes, from the common pot in the company's perennial soup house, until the "boss" chooses to turn the valve on them. O happy day!

Then those who are not Presidents or General Managers or Directors will be like the two urchins who were only stockholders in a Joint Stock Company consisting of three, who had each contributed a cent towards its capital, which was invested in a cigar which the President smoked. As the little fellows saw the cigar disappearing they began to clamor for their turn. The larger boy, who was President, exclaimed that in all corporations it was the proper thing for the President to smoke the cigars. But said the boys, "Where do we come in?" "Well," said the President, deliberating, "let me see, you are only stockholders, I suppose you may be allowed to spit."

Let us hope that in that "sweet bye and bye" the common people may be allowed to spit.

Of course, gentlemen, I do not wish to be understood as even indirectly implying that I apprehend such a future. I fully believe that the time will come when the evils of discrimination in railway rates will be done away with. I fully believe that the time will come when these rates will be so adjusted that the people will have an opportunity to compete fairly in business matters between themselves without the interference of railway companies. Then the railways will be free to compete with each other, not by discrimination in rates, but by exercising the ingenuity of their managers and employes in discovering and putting into effect improved methods, which shall cheapen the cost of transportation and improve the service to all alike. Then the railways will become in fact what they are in theory, *great highways of free trade.*

Then the companies will devote themselves exclusively and impartially to transportation. Then there will be no attempted competition between an individual on the one side and an individual with a railroad corporation combined on the other, nor between one locality on the one side, and another locality with one or more railways combined on the other side; but there will be actual, fair competition between individuals alone, and actual, fair competition between railways.

But let the people and the companies remember that "cutting rates" in favor of individuals or localities is not competition between railways, but unjust discrimination. And let the nomenclature of railway parlance be reformed. Hereafter, instead of "competitive rates," let them be called "discriminative rates," and instead of "competitive points," let them be called "points of discrimination."

And let the people and the companies also remember that "discrimination" prevents "competition" and tends to establish monopolies in the hands of the few.

Lest those who have hitherto prospered by discrimination should be prompted by selfishness and self-confidence from giving heed to the lesson, let the people of St Paul and Minneapolis, and Sioux City and Omaha, and St. Joseph and Kansas City, understand that their cities are now becoming what the cities of La-Crosse, Dubuque, Clinton, Davenport and Burlington became twenty years ago, midway stations (instead of terminal stations) on great through lines of railways. Let them remember that the latter cities, twenty years ago, were in respect to commerce and manufactories as important, *relatively*, as are now the former cities, which were then mere frontier trading posts; that for twenty years these Mississippi River towns, through the influence of the malign spirit of discrimination, have practically stood still in point of commerce and population, while the then frontier trading posts have grown into important cities of national reputation.

Let the people of these cities consider what assurances they have that this mischievous spirit will continue true to them.

Has it a soul, has it love, which will make it forego the "long haul?" Or will it for the next twenty years be playing its pranks in favor of the "long haul" to the terminal cities, as it has done in the past?

On the other hand, let the companies remember that by discrimination they have built up some manufacturing and mercantile concerns so big that they are now more powerful than the companies inasmuch as they are able to dictate the rates that they will pay—that monopolies in trade are as dangerous to railways as uncontrolled monopolies in transportation are to communities. And let all remember that it is dangerous to "play with fire," and that no business can be permanently properous which is not founded on principles of justice.

UNITY OF RAILWAYS AND RAILWAY INTERESTS.

By the Hon. A. Schoonmaker.

Ex-Member of the Interstate Commerce Commission.

"Distinct like the billows, but one like the sea," is a figure that applies to more things than the States of the American Union. It applies with emphasis to the railways and railway interests of the country. The roads are distinct entities as regards their corporate existence, their ownership of property, their internal management, their capitalization, and in some other respects. But as regards their public uses and duties, their relations toward each other, the principles that should govern their conduct, the business in which they are engaged, the methods they should employ in their business, and the conditions of usefulness and business success, there is a unity that admits of no distinct or independent action.

This unity is the groundwork of public regulation of railways. Regulation is an exercise of sovereign power through general laws and administrative agencies. The primary object of regulation is to secure fairness and impartiality on the part of railways to the public; but obviously no system of regulation can be complete that does not provide for fairness and impartiality between the roads themselves.

All railroads are creatures of the Government. The Government may be State, Territorial or Federal. They come into existence by some public authority exercised in some sovereign form. Theoretically, at least, there is a public necessity for their existence, and this is a conclusive presumption in their favor. They are public agencies organized and operated by private hands. The State thus performs its duty to the public to furnish highways of commerce and intercourse, because this duty can be better done in this way than directly by the State. The incentive of private interest in every such enterprise is added to the public duty involved, and advantages of economy, efficiency and adaptation to changing conditions secured, that are never attainable under the ponderous machinery of governmental action with its endless fric-

---
Reprinted by permission from the Independent of October 6, 1892.

tion and tardy motion. Economy in construction and management, superior ability in the service generally, direct accountability to the public for losses and injuries, the stimulus of competition among roads, the avenues opened to individual enterprise and employment apart from dependence on Government, are some of the strong reasons for private ownership and operation of railways. Probably in a country like the United States, where everything involving patronage is more or less partisan, there could be nothing more dangerous or eventually disastrous than Government ownership and operation of some ten billions' worth of railway property, with about a million of necessary employes, and an incalculable amount of traffic handled. To say nothing of the incapacity of Government for so huge and intricate a task, the political, financial and economical perils of the undertaking should forever forbid its assumption. Government supervision to secure justice and fairness and redress for wrongs, is as far as governmental authority can safely extend or ought to venture in meddling with the pursuits of citizens.

The inducement to private citizens for the construction and operation of railways is the profit arising or expected to arise from the business, and this is legitimate. If, however, the profit is expected to accrue from manipulation of stock and bonds, or from forcing some competitor to purchase the property, it is wholly illegitimate, and opens up a field where governmental authority might very properly be exercised in regulating the construction of new roads. This is only part of the duty Government owes to existing roads. Every new road of considerable importance constructed and put in operation is a disturbing factor. It must have business, which in the main must be diverted from other roads. It competes for business, generally by reducing rates; and just to the extent that it acquires business other roads suffer. And they suffer in a double sense—loss of amount of business, and reduced charges on the diminished amount. And a road once in the field is there to stay. It cannot be put to another use. It cannot be abandoned, for that is a total loss. The old law maxim, slightly changed applies: Once a railroad, always a railroad. It is then a part of the railway system of the country, which, for business purposes, for its uses and its revenues, and for the rules that govern its business, or regulation, is a unit.

The unity of railways in respect of their mutual obligations and interests is fully recognized by railway managers. No railway manager at all fit for his post considers his road independent of the system of which it forms a part. Cut off from that system his road would be practically useless. It would have no outlet or inlet. It could have no rates beyond its own line. It could receive or forward no traffic, but everything would be local on its own line. It could meet none of the necessary conditions of modern transportation and business requirements. It would be an isolated and aggravating nuisance.

Every road, therefore, owes allegiance to the entire railway system. It is part of it, and must contribute to its success and usefulness. It must interchange and receive and forward cars and traffic. It must bill goods and ticket passengers and check baggage over other roads. It must have suitable connections with other roads, both as to times and places. It must, in short, recognize the fact that it is simply an integral and inseparable part of one connected system, and govern itself accordingly.

The unity of railways applies, in the first instance, to their physical structure and the connections they form between the remotest points. The expanse of continents, the channels of rivers and mountain elevations, do not interrupt these physical connections. Even national boundaries and foreign jurisdictions present no barriers, but the tracks of steel penetrate all territorial dominions, regardless of flags or forms of government, and unite for business purposes the most diverse peoples and countries. Thus the Canadas, the United States and Mexico form one theater of operations, with a prospect of an early extension to South America.

Other conditions of unity are found in gauge of tracks, the character of the motive power, the passenger and freight equipment, the use of air brakes and couplers and other appliances. These naturally result from the nature of the business and the conditions necessary for its transaction. A business that ramifies everywhere, that is conducted by almost numberless distinct but cooperating agencies, that requires both dispatch and safety, must have substantial unity in the means and methods by which it is carried on. Every separate agency, therefore, finds it necessary to conform in essentials to whatever conditions are found best for the successful working of the whole connected system. For example, only a few years ago there were disparities in gauge. Different roads, even connecting lines forming parts of one proprietary or operating system, had a difference in gauge, involving vexatious delays and no small expense in changing trucks for continuous journeys. Now, under the compelling force of the unwritten laws that control business operations, substantially all important roads are of uniform standard gauge.

The unity of railways also applies to the traffic they carry, whether passengers or freight. There is no specialty in railroad carriage, though here and there a particular commodity like coal, or cotton, or lumber, may furnish the chief freight business; but their business is almost universally the same, and includes all varieties of freight, and all passengers offered. The traffic seeks numberless destinations, and moves from line to line, and from road to road, over main lines and branches, and large roads and small ones. The right to the use of railways for transportation, both of persons and property, is mandatory, and cannot be refused. The condition of railway franchises is to carry whatever transportable traffic is offered. And in this respect all roads are alike. They are common carriers, and can apply no limitations to their business, nor upon the patrons they serve. The nature of the traffic transported being the same, all roads have a common interest in whatever relates to the movement of the traffic and the recompense for the service.

Another element of unity is conspicuous in the charges of service. In no respect is the fact more distinct or the compulsion more arbitrary than in the matter of charges. Competing lines must carry at substantially the same rates. There may be slight differentials, founded on length of haul, conditions of route, character of road, and the like; but such differentials are only intended to equalize advantages and disadvantages, and to place competitors on a fairly similar basis. This rule is illustrated all over the country, wherever there are groups of roads carrying between the same or dependent points. The trunk lines carrying between Chicago and the Northern seaboard, the Northwest lines between Chicago and St. Paul, and between Chicago and Missouri River points, and the Transcontinental lines, are all examples of this law of uniformity in charges. A rate made by one line on a particular traffic must be the rate of all the other lines in order to share in the business. This is also illustrated, in another way, by the effect of charges for water carriage upon railway rates. For example, water carriage of grain, flour, lumber, provisions and other articles by the Great Lakes and the Erie Canal, forces down the railway charges in direct competition with the water route, and these again depress rates on other rail lines all over the country. Upon the article of sugar carried by rail from San Francisco to the Missouri River the rates are largely influenced by water carriage around Cape Horn to New York and thence by rail to the same destinations. Then again, sugar from Louisiana must be carried at such rates as will enable dealers to compete in the markets at the points mentioned. Tea, coffee and a variety of other articles might furnish similar illustrations. The postulate is that there can be no independent rates upon any road which is part of the general railway system, and inasmuch as there is no road which is not part of the system, all rates are related and dependent, and must substantially conform to one another. Rates and revenues are not synonymous. Revenue, of course, arises from rates; but the same rates that may afford net revenue to one road may leave a deficiency for another. More expensive operation, want of judicious economy in general management, larger fixed charges and other causes may exhaust revenue and leave no margin of profit. Volume of business alone, as in the case of the Pennsylvania Railroad or the New York and New Haven road, is the most important factor of all. The fact that over 60 per cent of the roads in this country pay no dividends on stock, although carrying at proportionally similar rates, is evidence that rates alone do not determine the profitableness of a railroad.

But out of the interdependency, or, in other words, the unity of railways, and railway interests, arises the necessity for harmonious action in respect to all their common duties and their charges for service. The prosperity of the system means, in a degree, the prosperity of all roads in the system. Adversity to the system affects nearly every member of the system.. For mutual protection, therefore, and to prevent general disaster, as well as separate loss, roads enter into agreements to maintain specified rates, and support elaborate and expensive associations to establish rates, adjust rate questions, and protect revenue to make the properties remunerative. The power of independent rate making is an abstract corporate power of every road; but, like the power to commit suicide, it can only be exercised for self-destruction. In its consequences it is worse, and works destruction to others. As in the social body absolute liberty exercised by any individual is chaos, so in the railway world the liberty of a road to act as it pleases, in disregard of the rights and interests of others, is general ruin. Society is only made endurable when liberty is regulated by law. The restraints of law upon individual liberty are no more indispensable to society at large than to the whole subject of railways, their construction, their use, and the exercise of their corporate powers. The common welfare always demands certain limitations upon individual rights, and sometimes their surrender. It is only in this way that public order, stability and safety can be assured. Among railways, voluntary association undoubtedly is of considerable value, but in the main is entirely inadequate; and the exercise of a power that can compel respect for the rights of others, enforce fair agreements, afford redress for violations of mutual duties and breaches of obligations, is essential. This is the power of government—through its legislative and judicial branches—a power held in trust only for the public good.

The close relationship existing between railways, and the far-reaching consequences of independent action by one or more roads upon all others, are the moving causes for the voluntary associations to preserve harmony of action among roads and guard against the evils resulting from every road doing as it pleases. The lack of affirmative legal authority for such associations, the bad faith often exhibited by some of their members, and the inability either to restrain or punish delinquency, have operated as potent causes in another tendency which has grown stronger as railroads have increased in number and the system become enlarged. This is the tendency toward consolidation. The consolidation in some form of connecting lines to form extended through lines has gone on from nearly the earliest period of railroads, and has been an obvious necessity of transportation. But the consolidation of lateral and sometimes parallel or divergent lines is a tendency of later date, and has attained extraordinary development. Such great systems as those of the Pennsylvania Company, the Union Pacific, the Southern Pacific, the New York Central, and some others, are striking illustrations of this tendency. The New York Central system, which began in 1853 by the consolidation of nine small roads between Albany and Buffalo and Niagara, with about four hundred miles of road, now has upward of 2,270 miles of road in New York State alone, traversing the State in all directions, and more than 15,400 miles of affiliated and controlled lines in the country at large, equal to two-thirds of the whole railway mileage of England.

The same argument that has been used against agreements between railroads to prevent fluctuations and discriminations in rates has been urged against consolidation—namely, that it may deprive the public of the advantages of competition. The misleading argument, which is mostly theoretical, has largely lost its force in the light of actual experience. Scarcely an instance can be named where agreements, respecting rates have prejudiced the public, and the instances are very rare where consolidations have harmed the public. On the other hand, the benefits, alike to the railways and the public, in both instances generally far outweigh any actual injuries. To the railways consolidation secures large economies and stable and uniform management; and to the public, far more efficient and better, and often cheaper, service. A railroad must derive its sustenance from the public, and therefore, must, as far as practicable, please and satisfy the public. It is the servant of the public, and must as a condition of its employment render an acceptable service.

Under the supervisory and regulating powers of Government, long held in abeyance but at present vigorously exercised by Commissions both Federal and State pursuant to laws rather tentative as yet but likely to increase in vigor and efficiency, there is no valid reason to apprehend any serious or long-continued prejudice to the public either from rate agreements among roads or from limited consolidations. Whenever the public interests are jeopardized, correction can be speedily applied by commissions and the courts. The recent action of the Chancellor of New Jersey in respect to the Reading Railroad leases is an illustration of the potency of judicial authority in such cases. It may be that the rights of coal producers and of rail carriers did not in that case receive the consideration to which they are equitably entitled. The decision rests mainly on local statute law forbidding leases to foreign roads, and upon a theory of public policy in favor of unrestricted and unregulated competition. It is questionable, however, if sound public policy requires any business to be carried on at a loss. For example, it is not conducive to the public welfare that coal producers shall consume the entire price of their product in cost of production and transportation, nor that carriers shall receive no remuneration above cost of carriage to them for their service. An inquiry, therefore, into these features of such combinations, underlies the question of public policy.

In 1823, before the era of railroads, DeWitt Clinton, to whom is due the glory of New York's commercial supremacy by the creation of its most potential factor, the Erie Canal, condensed a volume of wisdom in a single sentence:

"To countenance commerce is to countenance cheapness of transportation and goodness of market; and to promote the wealth of any member or section of the Union is to enhance its ability to use the fabrics and to consume the products of the others."

One of the profoundest thinkers of this country, S. J. Tilden, twenty-five years ago, in an address delivered in the Constitutional Convention of New York, used the following language:

"I do not think there is any just ground for the jealousy which appears to be felt in some quarters toward the railway system of the country. It certainly has served the public with great efficiency and with incalculable utility. A new mode of intercommunication, whereby the products of different soils and climates and capacities of supplying human wants are more rapidly or cheaply interchanged, adds as much to the productiveness of human industry as increased geniality of the climate or increased fertility of the soil. The Convention of 1846, by provisions which it fell to my lot to report, provided, first, in favor of a system of incorporation under general laws; and, secondly, for a supervisory legislative control over the chartered powers and privileges of all corporate bodies.

"In my judgment these two provisions were and are perfectly adequate to secure every public object, however, freely we may grant to private enterprise all the powers necessary to enable it to create these great machines of travel and transportation, and to the management of them by corporate bodies, which can serve the public with more skill and economy than the State can. . . . Experience has shown that the tendency thus far of railways has been, not to overcharge the public, but rather, through excessive competition among themselves, to serve it more cheaply than they could afford. They do not now, taking the country together, reserve to their stockholders and for their bondholders much, if anything, over 25 per cent of the cost of carriage to the public. . . . The people of this country ought to know that whenever they pay a dollar for any transportation or for travel, not less than 20 or 25 cents of that dollar, is not the cost of the service they receive, but taxation unduly imposed on such subjects in our time. If one-half of the net earnings of railways goes to their creditors, the bondholders, then not more than 12½ to 15 per cent of their gross earnings are received by the proprietors of these great works, the stockholders. This includes all interest on the investments of the proprietary class, and all indemnity for the risks of their enterprises, and all compensations for a supervisory attention to their administration."

As early as 1846 Michael Hoffman, one of the ablest, broadest and most far-seeing men of this century, said in the Constitutional Convention of New York of that year:

"Neither in form nor substance do I accede to the doctrine that the canal tolls shall be taken for general purposes. I deny it. The right of way is the right of the million. The sovereign holds it in trust and can exercise it only for their benefit, and has no right to make a revenue out of it. Such a course must endanger the worst oppression and the worst corruptions, and soon realize the worst vices of the worst governments; taxation on all we consume, which will allow nothing to go to or from the markets without tribute to the State."

This was said of a State highway of commerce, the Erie Canal, the greatest monument of practical wisdom in the Empire State. It was not until November, 1882, that Hoffman's conception of a free highway for commerce was realized by the adoption of a constitutional amendment providing that "no tolls shall hereafter be imposed on persons or property transported on the canals."

How far the powers of Government can be wisely exercised in relieving the commerce and its instrumentalities from burdens is an interesting question beyond the scope of this paper. Manifestly, free wharves for shipping, and ample terminal facilities for railways, at minimum cost, are among the most important elements of commercial prosperity.

The conditions existing twenty-five years ago, so strongly depicted by Mr. Tilden, have, through "excessive competition" and other causes, become steadily worse for the railways; and at the present time about two-thirds of the "proprietary class" receive no increment whatever on their investments. The argument, therefore, for relief from unwise taxation, and in favor of reasonable methods for mitigating the effects of competition, and preserving revenue, has been greatly re-enforced by the lapse of time.

One other particular remains to be mentioned in which the unity of railways is important. This is in respect to governmental regulation. Regulation is a duty of Government, and in some form it will be continued. But regulation, to be effective, must cover the whole subject. Divided regulation, like divided authority of any kind, can only lead to confusion and embarrassment. We have now our systems of Federal regulation and of multiplied State regulation. Collision and friction are to a greater or less extent inevitable. Uniformity under such circumstances is practically impossible. An instructive instance of this character is furnished by recent events in Texas. Certain regulations of the Commission of that State, which seemed to proceed upon the theory that the railway business of the State could be isolated from the general commerce of the country, have been enjoined by the Federal courts because they were unduly prejudicial to railways as carriers, and because local judicial redress was prohibited. This could not have happened under Federal law or a Federal Commission. Considering that railways and their business are so unified both within State lines and interstate, there cannot be just, uniform and efficient regulation except under one authority, and that must necessarily be the Federal authority. As has been often said, the business of a railway, whether within a State or interstate, is so blended and mingled, both with respect to the traffic and the agencies by which it is carried, that separation for purposes of regulation, or even taxation, is impracticable. The traffic all moves on the same tracks, is carried in the same cars, handled by the same employes; and all is managed by the same

UNITY OF RAILWAYS AND RAILWAY INTERESTS. 65

officials, and the same treasury receives and disburses all moneys. How a part of this business can be segregated for one system of regulation, and part for another system, is a problem that has not yet been solved. It may be said that the country is too large, the railroad system too great, and the transportation business too vast for one central regulating body. But however this may be, there can be one plan and method of regulation, with general powers in the central tribunal, and auxiliary agents or boards in every State or specified territorial division, and all working in harmony. Whether a constitutional change may be required to bring about entire regulation under Federal authority, or whether the Federal courts may evolve the necessary power under existing provisions, from the nature of the business, are questions that need not be discussed. It is sufficient at present to refer to the facts of the situation, and to invite attention to the logic of the condition.

Some important practical suggestions flow from a sober consideration of the unity of railways and railway interests. One of these is the popular conception concerning railways. As viewed by the public, railways stand as a class or body. There is no separation of the body into good or bad, strong or weak members. And this conception is shared generally by the various orders of society, by citizens at large, by shippers, by lawmakers and the courts. As a natural and almost inevitable consequence, the morals and conduct of railway managers as a class are estimated by the behavior of the worst among them. The faults and misconduct of a few reckless and unprincipled managers (and happily they are comparatively few) are imputed to the class and to the business. The public omits, or does not care to discriminate between the innocent and the culpable. The whole body is held responsible and shares in whatever odium may be justly due to only a few. And the retributions of public sentiment, of legislative bodies and of the judicial tribunals fall with equal severity upon all.

Another of these is the importance of a higher standard among railways than has yet been attained. Like individuals, they must deserve public confidence and respect in order to enjoy them. Manifestly it is greatly to the interests of railways that the highest standard possible should be maintained by all. Railroads ideally managed would need no law to regulate them. Law is intended only to prevent and punish wrongdoing. Law for railroads is the intelligent judgment of society with respect to what is best for itself and for the roads as part of the social organization. This is the point for the railways to apprehend and apply to themselves. In the past, overlooking too often their essential unity and their indivisibility from the public standpoint, they have in the main recognized only one principle in their relations toward each other, the heathenish notion of retaliation. If wrong was done by a road, retaliation was at once resorted to by others; and too often frightful sacrifice of property rights has been the result. This eye for an eye and tooth for a tooth policy, a barbarous application of lynch law methods to great property interests, society has made up its mind shall cease. It is prejudicial to great and varied public interests, a savage anachronism in an enlightened age, and the public good demands its abatement. Prevention by lawful means must take the place of retaliation. Equitable principles embodied in statute law now regulate the conduct of railways. A faithful observance of these principles, and compliance with prescribed rules of conduct, would of themselves correct most of the faults charged against railroads as a class, and leave little just cause of complaint. But if offenses should still come offenders should confront the majesty and authority of Government, and be dealt with by the civilized codes to which offenders against other laws are subject, and not by the barbarous code of private retaliation. It rests largely with the railroads themselves to elevate their body in the public estimation by substituting legal remedies for destructive warfare. They can magnify the law and make it honorable. If in a case of bad faith, infractions of agreements, and violations of established schedules, present laws are not sufficient, additional legislation can readily provide summary remedies to restrain offenders and punish their derelictions. Then, if well-disposed roads shall cooperate with the public authorities, they can remove most of the reproaches charged upon the system as a whole, and confine reprobation to actual culprits, who would be left to face the law, the courts and public sentiment single-handed.

Kingston, N. Y.

THE RAILROADS AS ONE SYSTEM.

By Joseph Nimmo, Jr.

Out of chaos—cosmos. This suggests the generally accepted law of evolution—a natural tendency of forceful elements toward organic life and organic unity. It is a law which asserts itself not only in nature, but in the social, industrial and commercial progress of the age. It voices the inevitable and therefore carries with it its own sanction. Men submit to its decrees without question and with an instinctive faith in their beneficence. It is the glory of the common law that in the domain of justice it proclaims the best results of the evolutionary experiences of mankind under democratic government.

Although we live in a phenomenally statute-making age, and one in which the human mind seems to be more prone than ever before to project lines of development, yet the widening thought of men is coming to the faith that there is an unobserved onward movement in the affairs of the world above all human prescience or control, and that unless men build better than they know they will build in vain.

It is the object of this paper to trace in rapid lines the evolution of the American railroad system with special reference to its relations to the social, industrial and commercial interests of the country. An attempt will also be made to present certain practical lessons which the subject suggests at the present time.

The American railroad system is the most wonderful product of human invention, adaptation and enterprise of this the most progressive of the centuries. It correlates the arts and sciences of the age in one grand utility. Conformity to its possibilities and to the peculiar exigences of its physical characteristics has revolutionized the commercial methods and the social habits of the world. This has been accomplished mainly within the memory of persons now living, some of whom even at this day would regard it as an unkindness to be designated as old men.

The railroads built in this country up to about the year 1850 were crude affairs and gave but slight intimation of the commercial characteristics of the railroads of the present day. For many years after Stephenson's locomotive made its famous competitive

---

Reprinted by permission from The Railway Age and Northwestern Railroader of January 27, 1893.

trial trip the people of England and of the United States clung to
the idea that the railroad must become a free highway of commerce in the sense in which that expression is applied to wagon
roads, canals, rivers, lakes and the ocean; and yet the fact is
clearly recognized today that there is nothing which prevents the
railroad from being in the most absolute sense of the term a common or impartial carrier, subject to all the economic and commercial restraints which the law of the common carrier imposes upon
carriers on free highways of commerce. Although the most
marked characteristic of the railroad—its pathway no wider than
the wheel of the vehicle which moves upon it—forbade that it
should become a free highway of commerce and gave to it an inevitable aspect of monopoly, yet it has done far more than all the
free highways of the world toward creating and setting in motion
competitive forces whose interaction has been irresistibly reducing
and equalizing prices and transportation charges. In truth carriage by rail has so intensified competition in transportation and
in trade as to create disorder and at times to threaten a general
collapse in the business interests of the country. Hence the necessity which has arisen from self-restraint on the part of the
companies in connection with supplemental governmental restraints.

From the year 1830, when the first railroad was opened for
traffic in this country, until about the year 1850, each railroad in
the United States was, as a rule, operating independently of all
other railroads. The bare idea of connecting the tracks of different companies having a terminus in the same town was repelled
by railroad managers as something in the nature of an entangling
alliance fraught with complications and administrative difficulties
which had better be avoided. Besides, the drayman and the forwarding merchant asserted their right to live, and the railroad
companies had respect for such opposition. Different gauges were
adopted in many instances for the express purpose of preventing
"the carriage of freights from being, and being treated as one
continuous carriage from the place of shipment to the place of
destination," a practice now treated by the interstate commerce
act as a public offense. (See section 7.) One of the largest and
perhaps most notable instances of the policy of breaking gauge
for the specific purpose of securing to a city the commercial advantages which that expedient was supposed to afford was that of
the Cincinnati Southern railroad, an important line, 336 miles in
length, built by the city of Cincinnati, and completed about the
year 1880.

But the social, commercial, postal and military necessities of
the age rapidly brushed aside all obstacles to the formation of
that great American railroad system which is today unto the
traveler and the shipper as one instrumentality of transportation,
embracing nearly 200,000 miles of track, administered and oper-

ated as though by one central authority. This wonderful organic development has involved connected tracks, a common track gauge, union depots, through rates, the uniform classification of commodities, rate agreements, prorating, through tickets, related time schedules, the unimpeded passage of freight, passenger express and postal cars and of locomotives over the tracks of different companies, and to a considerable extent the employment of operatives in the pay of one company, upon the lines of other companies. Each company has also become, in ten thousand instances, the agent of many other companies for the sale of tickets, the collection of freight moneys, and the procurement of traffic. This practical unification of the great work of transportation by rail came about not advisedly, or as the result of design or forecast on the part of the companies, but as the outcome of an evolution resisted by them at every stage of its progress. Obstacles to this union of lines and traffic interests which at first appeared insuperable were swept aside by an imperious force of circumstance. During this entire period railroad managers were divided into two schools in regard to this new development, the majority opposing and the minority favoring it. Some of the stronger companies attempted to resist the movement by the consolidation and extension of their lines, assuming that thus they might be enabled to remain a law unto themselves. But in time they too were forced to acknowledge the compulsions of the interdependent relationships which were slowly but surely evolving one vast national railroad system. The peculiar environment of each road of course had much to do with the detail of forming connections with coterminous roads but above every consideration of economy and convenience there arose an imperious commercial and social demand for a united American railroad service. To this was added a more coercive demand, upon the outbreak of the war, which was to determine the question of maintaining our national unity. Military necessity then demanded through cars and through trains over the lines of different companies. The tracks of railroads having terminals on opposite sides of cities were connected by lines constructed through or around such cities in order that men and munitions of war might pass unimpeded. The military demand for an expedited postal service also gave rise to the post office on wheels, in which the work of assorting and distributing the mails is done on trains in motion. Then the sleeping car came into vogue with a rapidly developed and imperative demand for connected tracks and through service over the lines of two, three and four or more different companies. It was in vain that conservative railroad men protested against the loss of independence and the inconveniences and vexations incident to forced partnerships with companies and with railroad officials whom they would gladly have shunned. The most serious difficulties arose in the establishment of a through or interchanged freight car service. Sometimes cars, when thus employed, far from the road upon which they belonged, were left standing for days and even weeks on side tracks or kept in use without any authority or compensation for such service. In many instances cars were thus lost, and in certain cases actually stolen by being repainted with the name of the appropriating company substituted for that of the company to which they belonged. But despite all these inconviences the effort to prevent a common use of freight cars was futile. In time the difficulties just alluded to were cured by car service associations and auditing arrangements of various sorts. Finally, in the face of untold opposition, frauds and frictional resistances incident to the imperfect methods of conducting joint traffic, the American railroad system emerged in its present form and magnificent potentialities for good.

The social, commercial, industrial and political forces of the country have beckoned the companies on to this unity of transportation facilities, as absolute and as imperative in its manifestations as is the political unity which binds towns, counties and states into a nation which is one and indivisible. State governments also have extended solicitous invitations to railroad companies to construct their lines across state boundaries in order to form such connections, and in so doing to exercise freely one of the most sacred attributes of governmental sovereignty, the right of eminent domain.

At last a concensus of the social, political and commercial forces of the country led to a statutory enactment by the national government which legalized the physical combination of railroad interests just described. I refer to the act of Congress approved June 15, 1886. This statute, the most important concerning the internal commerce of the United States which has ever been enacted by Congress, was simply a legal recognition of something already existent as an organic characteristic of the transportation and commercial interests of the country. In a word, it was nothing more or less than the statutory approval of an institution and of usages which had become expressions of the commercial and social life of the nation. The act in question reads as follows:

An act to facilitate commercial, postal and military communication among the states.

WHEREAS, the Constitution of the United States confers upon Congress, in express terms, the power to regulate commerce among the several states, to establish post roads and to raise and support armies; therefore,

Be it enacted by the Senate and House of Representatives of the United States in Congress assembled, That every railroad company in the United States whose road is operated by steam, its successors and assigns, be, and is hereby, authorized to carry upon and over its roads, boats, bridges and ferries all passengers, troops, government supplies, mails, freight and property on their way from any state to another state, and to receive conpensation therefor, and to connect with roads of other states, so as to form continuous lines for the transportation of the same to the place of its destination.

*　　　　*　　　　*　　　　*　　　　*　　　　*

Section 2. *And be it further enacted*, That Congress may at any time alter, amend or repeal this act.

This act of Congress fully and explicitly authorizes all the railroad combinations and co-operative arrangements which I have just described. In form and substance it is permissive and clearly in the nature of a grant of power. It also expresses an implied contract, viz: a duty to be performed in consideration of a privilege granted. Therefore it may be properly regarded as the charter of the American railroad system.

That it had this significance in the minds of its framers is clearly indicated by the fact that out of abundant caution it was provided in the second section "that Congress may at any time alter, amend or repeal this act." This provision was apparently prompted by a fear even then entertained by many, that such intimate combinations among the railroads might, in the course of their development, prove detrimental to the public interests. That apprehension, however, no longer has place in the minds of the American people.

But the American railroad system has a higher charter even than this statutory enactment, and that is the very charter of the government itself—the will of the people, for this act formulates at once the public needs and the public sense of what is necessary and proper concerning railroad transportation in this country.

THE FEDERATION OF THE RAILROADS

No organization of human devising can exist as a forceful entity in the absence of an intelligent directory. The American railroad system was not a thing which could run alone. Its existence involved conventional agreements touching almost innumerable matters of detail and co-operative arrangements for the maintenance of such relationships. Hence the federation of the railroads by means of associations of various sorts followed as a necessary step in the processes of that evolution which was to bring them all into practical unity. Certain of these organizations are based upon the idea of managing the traffic of great geographical areas, while others take cognizance of great traffic currents. There are also associations which have for their object the management of through cars, i. e., car service associations; other associations have the management of through tickets, of baggage and baggage checks, etc., etc. There are besides claim associations and local associations of various sorts. These associations constitute the mind or administrative thought of the American railroad system. Their function embraces the classification of freights, joint rates, traffic facilities, the apportionment of traffic, receipts from traffic and a thousand matters of detail involved in the administrative management of a great transportation system.

The agreements thus entered into by the companies cover two entirely different subjects—agreements in regard to joint traffic over connecting and co-operative lines, and agreements between rival lines in regard to competitive traffic. Traffic associations also embrace the enormous work of adjusting joint traffic accounts; that is to say, they are clearing-house establishments.

Thus the law of organic efficiency was to a very great extent substituted for the law of unrestricted competition. This of course involved a considerable sacrifice of independent corporate power. But whenever men organize for the accomplishment of any great work they most always surrender something for the purpose of gaining something which eludes disassociated effort.

The thing of chief interest attained by the federation of the railroads was the maintenance of order in the conduct of the internal commerce of the country. The time had come when the alternative confronted the people of this country—the maintenance of order or the maintenance of the absolute freedom of competition. Order is not only heaven's first law, but it is a vital condition of all living. Competition on the other hand is only a manifestation of living under favoring conditions. And yet much of the reasoning of the day would place the maintenance of a wild and destructive competition above the maintenance of order. That is a great mistake. When competition becomes so fierce that it degenerates into disorder it passes the acme of its possibilities and becomes the very swoon of existence—the syncope of effort.

The practical reforms which the federation of the railroads accomplished through the restraints imposed upon reckless and destructive competition cover the following subjects: (a) The classification of freights; (b) the rates which shall be charged; (c) the maintenance of agreed rates; (d) the publication of rates, and (e) due notice of changes in rates. Each one of these conventional arrangements is now recognized as being in the nature of a just and proper regulation of the internal commerce of the country and absolutely necessary to its orderly conduct. For this reason such self-imposed regulations on the part of the companies have been legalized by the act to regulate commerce. As such statutory provisions formulate what had already been evolved by usage, they may be regarded as expressions of American common law.

But even as thus organized railroad traffic associations exhibited a fatal infirmity. The reforms which they proposed were beneficent, but the spirit of the reckless and uncontrolled competition survived. No company was satisfied with the share of the traffic which it secured. In order to secure that, each company employed soliciting agents who were stationed far and wide at the principal centers of traffic on connecting lines. That lead to confusion worse confounded. In the case of a loss of traffic by any one company, the order was issued to its widely scattered soliciting agents to secure the desired traffic at any rates which might be necessary in order to secure it. That involved not only a violation of rate agreement, but it was essentially an abdication of the rate making power of each company into the hands of an army of agents acting without the caution which attaches to ownership, and relieved of all responsibility for results. The inevitable tendency of this condition of affairs was toward commercial disorder—widespread and disastrous. For example, a contest between the lines connecting Chicago and Boston at one time so beat down rates between those points that for weeks traffic moved from New York to Chicago via Boston. Even Philadelphia and Baltimore traffic to and from Chicago began to move by the way of Boston. This of course inaugurated confusion into the commercial affairs of the country.

Rates reasonbly remunerative to the carriers, common to all shippers and steadily maintained are found to be infinitely better for the general good of the country than much lower rates, unjustly discriminating and wildly fluctuating, which inevitably run to disorder.

But a trouble even more serious arose from an external source. The larger shippers made constant efforts to induce particular roads to grant them discriminating rates as against other shippers, by throwing their entire traffic on lines which would enter into such unjust arrangements. This was demoralizing not only to conduct of transportation, but also to the commercial interests of the country. It went in the face of all right and all justice. It seemed for awhile as though the evolution of the American railroad system had proceeded up to a certain point and then chaos had come again. And yet it was too absurd for serious thought to assume that the men of this generation had created a vast and potential system of transportation which they lacked the virtue or ability to administer. It was therefore clearly perceived that some new expedient must be adopted in order to keep this great system of transportation in harmonious action. The root of the difficulty lay in the fight by each company for a larger share of the competitive traffic than any other company was willing to grant it. Hence was evolved out of the fierce interaction of forces the new law of self-restraint—agreements as to the share of the competitive traffic which should be carried by each line. This expedient, although abhorrent to independent common carriers in the narrow sphere in which such carriers compete on disassociated free highways of commerce, was seen to be a necessary feature of administration upon sharply conditioned highways of commerce constituting by their enforced relationships one vast and closely connected American railroad system. In a word, it was seen that competition upon such a system of transportation must be placed in a harness of self restraint not applicable to common carriers on turnpikes, canals and rivers.

The agreement as to the apportionment of traffic is the corollary of the rate agreement. The former is no more in restraint of competition than is the latter. Both restrain destructive competition, which runs to disorder. This is not theory, nor can it be refuted by theory. It is fact, inculcated by the hard lessons of actual experience. When the people of this country come to realize this important truth, as they certainly will, and to impose upon their representatives in legislative assemblies the duty of conforming the laws of the country to this natural law of the American railroad system, then, and not until then, will that system become an orderly and self-regulated institution.

THE COMMERCIAL ENVIRONMENT OF THE AMERICAN RAILROAD SYSTEM.

It is impossible to appreciate the full force of what has been said in regard to the interaction of forces whereby the American railroad system has been evolved without at least some reference to the influences which have been exerted by the commercial forces of the country in the course of that evolution. This wonderful system of transportation brought every center of trade and of industry into close competition, and provided a means whereby the product of every farm and of every mine may be speedily placed at the gates of commerce. Besides, the physical combinations which have been described had corresponding and co-ordinate commercial expressions in through bills of lading and other commercial arrangements connecting transportation in vitally important particulars with trade and with the finance of commerce. All this, in connection with the facilities for quick commercial intelligence afforded by the telegraph and the public press, has directly and indirectly created a competition of commercial forces, the intensity and coercive force of which was never before experienced on this planet. The tendency of this far-reaching and instant competition has been irresistibly toward a parity of values and toward a constant reduction in prices. This has reacted upon the railroads as an absolute limitation of rate-making which no traffic manager can resist. For example, if the price of wheat in Chicago is ninety cents and in New York one dollar and ten cents a bushel the cost of transportation must be less than twenty cents in order to insure the movement of wheat.

There is no popular fallacy more misleading than the assumption that the railroad managers of the country exercise a very wide range of discretion in the matter of rate-making. In spite of every expedient rates have fallen while traffic has increased. This is illustrated by the fact that the average charge per ton per mile on eighteen of the principal railroads of the country fell from 1.896 cents in 1872 to .926 in 1888, a decrease of 50 per cent, while the tonnage carried more than doubled during that period.

The influence which commercial forces necessarily exert upon transportation charges may also be inferred from the fact that the value of goods transported on railroads each year is about three times the value of all the railroad properties of the country, and at least thirty times the total railroad receipts each year from freight traffic. Then there is the fierce struggle of rival cities for trade, which expresses itself in constant efforts to secure unjustly discriminating advantages. When to this is added the struggle of the large shippers for rates discriminating unjustly in their favor, it is clearly seen that the companies are constantly between the devil of unjust discrimination and the deep sea of popular indignation which such discriminations naturally evoke. These are the most formidable obstacles to the harmonious operation of the American railroad system. Agreements between rival carriers as to the share of the competitive traffic which shall be awarded to each has been found to be the only effective means of removing the temptation to accede to such demands for unjustly discriminating rates, which not only disturb the orderly conduct of commerce, but also greatly deplete the revenues of the companies.

And now I think I have in a somewhat hurried manner presented facts and considerations which may be regarded as an answer to the question: Why the railroads should be treated as constituting one American railroad system.

This statement would however be incomplete without some brief notice of what has been accomplished in the direction of

GOVERNMENTAL REGULATION OF THE RAILROADS.

It was impossible that such a mighty evolution of commercial and transportation interests as that already described could have taken place in this land of liberty, regulated by law, without giving rise to some manifestations of governmental power. It became necessary not only to impose restraints upon evils but to give legal effect to practices and usages established through the interaction of forces and proved by the lessons of experience to be beneficial and necessary. This political solution of the so-called "railroad problem" has for a generation harassed the legislative and the judicial mind of this country. Many carefully wrought out plans and expedients for correcting real and supposed evils have been devised. A large proportion of these measures has resulted in failure. But under all the difficulties which surrounded the task that was not a strange thing. As the explorer approaches the harbor of a strange coast he finds where the channel is by running aground.

When the act to regulate commerce, commonly known as "The Interstate Commerce act," took effect, April 5, 1887, the constitutional power conferred upon Congress of regulating "commerce among the states" had been practically dormant for a period of 98 years. Prior to that date the American railway system had been evolved, and it had become the grandest system of transportation ever seen on this globe in point of speedy carriage, the facilities afforded for the distribution of freights, regularity of movement, safety, cost of transportation and general efficiency. The practical difficulty which confronted the legislator in any general scheme of regulation was the betterment of this splendid system of transportation.

The interstate commerce act is from beginning to ending based upon the idea of an existent American railroad system, its needs and possibilities. It is probably true that the legislator had not clearly in mind this particular significance of the statute, but that inadvertence seems to illustrate the fact that in the processes of an evolution men build better than they know. That the interstate commerce act was based upon the conditions imposed by the law of the American railroad system is clearly indicated by sections 2 and 7 of that act. The language of section 2 is as follows:

> Every common carrier subject to the provisions of this act shall, according to their several powers, afford all reasonable, proper and equal facilities for the interchange of traffic between their respective lines and for the receiving, forwarding and delivering of passengers and property to and from their several lines and those connecting therewith, etc.

Already the railroad companies of the country "according to their several powers" had created the American railroad system, and it was performing all the functions mentioned in this section. Section 7 of the Interstate Commerce act reads as follows:

> That it shall be unlawful for any common carrier subject to the provisions of this act to enter into any combination, contract or agreement, expressed or implied, to prevent, by change of time schedule, carriage in different cars, or by other means or devices, the carriage of freight from being continuous from the place of shipment to the place of destination; and no break of bulk, stoppage or interruption made by such common carrier shall prevent the carriage of freights from being and being treated as one continuous carriage from the place of shipment to the place of destination, unless such break, stoppage or interruption was made in good faith for some necessary purpose, and without any intent to avoid or unnecessarily interrupt such continuous carriage or to evade any of the provisions of this act.

No intelligent legislator would ever have proposed this administrative measure if the practices which it required had not already become firmly established by the railroad companies from motives of self interest, in obedience to the law of commercial intercourse, wrought out by the interaction of forces. This section of the act created nothing, but simply proposed an experimental measure for regulating something already created and set in motion by forces superior to those of legislation.

All that there is in the Interstate Commerce act in the nature of beneficent regulation is based either upon common law requirements or upon usages proved to be wholesome and proper in the course of the evolution of the American railroad system. The provisions of the statute which relate to the prohibition of unreasonable rates and unjust discriminations are simply re-enactments of time honored rules of the common law. The provisions which relate to securing shipments on direct and most convenient lines were already in force as rules of railroad associations. The propriety of this latter rule of conduct was clearly enunciated as long ago as the year 1874 in the report of the investigating committee appointed by the Pennsylvania Railroad Company. That report clearly enunciated the doctrine that railroad companies recognize their true interest in furnishing ample facilities, and by refraining from unwise efforts to defeat the interests of the shipper in the matter of attempting to dictate the route or destination of traffic;

that being determined mainly by elements other than the way of carriage.

The provisions of the sixth section of the Interstate Commerce act, relating to joint rates, the maintenance of agreed rates, the publication of rates, and ample notice of intended changes in rates were already cardinal features of the regulations established by railroad associations. It was also the fundamental object of such associations to prevent all forms of rate cutting now forbidden by the Interstate Commerce act. Outside of these wholesome regulations the provisions of the act to regulate commerce may be described as quasi-judical and quasi-administrative, terms which, however, have no distinct legal or practical significance.

It is unfortunate that in giving the force of legality to so much which experience had proved to be just and beneficent, the legislator should have gone astray in regard to a clearly established law of the American railroad system which had been forced upon railroad managers by the logic of events. I refer to the clearly established fact that the maintenance of rates must be based upon precedent agreements as to the share of the competitive traffic which shall be secured by each competitor. The fifth section of the act forbids such agreements and thereby forces the railroads to the violation of every beneficent provision of the statute.

The specious objection is urged to agreements as to the division of traffic, that they are similar to agreements made by the suppression of competition and for establishing monopolies in commercial and industrial pursuits. This objection ignores the whole object of traffic apportionment agreements and the conditions under which they are made. It is a sufficient answer to such objection to say that combinations of every character which tend to forward almost every beneficent enterprise of the age are also employed for evil purposes. Knives are instruments of great utility, and their use is not to be proscribed because they are sometimes employed to do murder and to commit suicide. It is manifest that if agreements as to the apportionment of traffic shall be legalized, they would be guarded by all the provisions of the act to regulate commerce, relative to the publication and the maintenance of rates—provisions which in the hands of all sensible railroad managers would become efficient instruments of self-government.

The refusal to comply with this evident leading of the evolution of the American railroad system has naturally evoked a fresh manifestation in another direction, viz.: the consolidation of railroad interests, whereby competitive elements are eliminated. That appears to be the only other recourse against destructive competition, which invariably leads to disorder.

THE LIMITATIONS OF GOVERNMENTAL REGULATION.

There is no public question of great moment at the present time than that of determining the proper limitations of governmental regulation of the railroads. It is a question in regard to which the provisions of the act to regulate commerce are obscure and concerning which the Interstate Commerce Commission appears to be at sea. The subject cannot here be discussed in all its commercial and political bearings, for it involves a careful consideration of those fundamental principles which engaged the profoundest thought of the founders of our present form of government. Our political institutions are based upon faith in individualism as opposed to governmental imperialism and upon an abiding faith in the beneficent results of that conservatism which inheres in the untrammeled interaction of commercial and industrial forces. Those political principles had their origin in the deep-seated conviction of our race that one honest and determined effort at self-control is worth a hundred efforts at governmental control. The civil polity which voices this sentiment is recognized in this country as Jeffersonianism, pure and simple. I am free to confess that a somewhat careful study of the commercial development of my country for more than thirty years has brought me more and more to recognize the wisdom of the line of policy which that faith inspires and to make it a cardinal doctrine of my political convictions. It is a doctrine which discards the idea of directing men how to go aright in the management of commercial and industrial affairs and claims that the exercise of governmental powers in such matters shall be confined as closely as possible to the prevention and punishment of wrongs. Governmental administration of the subject of transportation necessarily involves to a certain extent governmental administration of the commercial interests of the country. But that cannot proceed far before meeting the indignant protest of a free people.

Again, the prevention and punishment of wrongs under governmental authority involve the exercise of both executive and the judicial function. Unfortunately the attempt has been made in the act to regulate commerce to unite these two functions in the powers granted to the Interstate Commerce Commission; but the federal courts have steadfastly refused to recognize the asserted judicial character of that body, and I honor the judiciary for its loyalty to the fundamental principle of American liberty enunciated by Alexander Hamilton and adopted by Judge Story, that "there is no liberty if the power of judging be not separated from the legislative and executive powers."

In considering this vitally important matter it is always a pleasure to recall the words of the Interstate Commerce Commission recorded on page 106 of their third annual report:

> There is also in the public mind a sense of incongruity between the prosecuting function . . . and the judicial function.

In this connection I would briefly allude to two other fundamental errors involved in the act to regulate commerce.

First, it embraces provisions which, in a rather vague and uncertain manner, seem to confer upon the commission the power of rate making. Since its organization the interstate commerce commission has been afloat upon a sea of speculation in regard to the question as to whether it does or does not possess that power; also as to the conditions under which it shall be exercised. I maintain, for reasons which it is unnecessary to elaborate here, that the exercise of such a power by the national government is un-Jeffersonian, un-American and opposed to sound principles of public policy. The second error involved in the Interstate Commerce act relates to the equally uncertain function of forcing railroad companies to connect their lines and to enter into those traffic arrangements whereby the American railroad system sprung into existence. This involves the error of rate making as well as that of meddling with the course of the development of the commercial interests of the country—a line of procedure which the lessons of our political and commercial experience repel. Such interference with the industrial interests of the country may respond to the ebullitions of passion and to apparent exigencies in the nature of attempts to circumvent firmly established principles of American liberty, but they can acquire no permanent place in the governmental policy of this country.

In the practical administration of the powers of government it is always a nice thing accurately to discriminate between liberty regulated by law and liberty enchained by law, for we live in a world of imperfect remedies—a world in which the better is oft times the enemy of the good. It is certain that the American railroad system can never become "the faultless monster that the world ne'er saw." It must have freedom of motion—room for development on its own lines.

If the question is ever presented to the people of this country—Shall we have governmental railroad regulation which violates fundamental conditions imposed by the evolved law of the American railroad system and by fundamental principles of our cherished political institutions, or shall we have no governmental regulations of the railroads?—there is not the slightest doubt in my mind that the latter alternative will be adopted. And I reckon that as the years come and go the men who set up expedients in violation of those fundamental principles of government and in contravention of those lessons of experience clearly taught in the evolved law of the American railroad system will be brought to read the history of their inventions in the song of the babbling brook:

"Men may come and men may go,
But I go on forever."

THE FEDERAL CONTROL OF RAILWAYS.

By Hon. S. M. Cullom.

The act to regulate commerce, popularly known as the interstate commerce act, has been the subject of discussion by all classes of men, legislators, lawyers, judges and business men. The act was passed by congress in pursuance of the constitution of the United States which says that "congress shall have power to regulate commerce with foreign nations and among the several states," and "to make all laws which shall be necessary and proper for carrying into execution the foregoing powers."

One of the controlling objects of the convention which assembled at Annapolis and which made our national constitution was "to devise means for the uniform regulation of trade." Therefore each of the thirteen states possessed powers separate and independent, and they could discriminate in the regulation of commerce in favor of the citizens of one state against those of another. By the adoption of the national constitution the power to regulate commerce among the states was taken from the states and lodged exclusively in congress. It remains there.

All fair-minded men will agree that the condition of affairs in this country in connection with the operation of railroads as common carriers prior to the passage of the interstate commerce act necessitated the exercise by congress of constitutional power by enacting legislation for the "regulation of commerce among the several states."

The passage of the act of 1887 encountered stubborn opposition, and its enforcement has been exceedingly difficult. The greed for money and the determination to secure it, impel men operating railroads and those dealing with them to seek an advantage over others in competition with them to the extent even of violating the plain letter of the law and taking the chances of a fine and imprisonment.

Several judicial decisions have been rendered which weakened the statute, and public opinion for a time was that the courts had well nigh destroyed the law. Nevertheless the act is not destroyed and will not be. As weak places are found in the act they will be strengthened by amendment. The people will never relinquish

---

Reprinted from the Railway Age and Northwestern Railroader of April 14, 1893.

control over the common carriers, which are quasi-public corporations representing vast wealth and power. All obstructions thrown in the way of a proper constitutional law regulating commerce among the states will be removed in time.

A great deal of friction in attempting to put into practical operation a new and heretofore untried system of regulation—untried at least as to the interstate commerce of the United States—was inevitable. The questions that have arisen could not possibly have been forseen or guarded against. The requirements of the law against unjust discrimination and favoritism as between persons, places, and particular classes of traffic pinched very hard in a good many quarters. The "big fish" were placed upon an equality with the little ones, or more nearly so, and energetic and vigorous protests from those who have been enjoying all kinds of special privileges and advantages at the expense of the general public was but to be expected. But I have regarded it as the duty of congress to legislate with a view to securing the greatest good to the greatest number, and while the act has not proved a panacea for all the ills connected with commercial operations, it has, taken by and large, proven generally beneficial to the entire country. There is no business question in which the people of the country have a deeper interest, for the reason that there is none which bears more directly upon their financial prosperity. Cheap transportation and equality of rights in its enjoyment are two great demands of the times, and the nation will fail of its duty if it does not do what it can to secure both to the people. The best possible conditions must surround our internal commerce, and we must give the people the best possible advantages, whenever we can, in reaching whatever market may be open to them in any of the nations. The constitution imposes the duty upon congress of regulating commerce among the several states and with foreign nations. That duty must be discharged in the interest of the people without fear or favor, fearing not to do right by all, whether engaged in one pursuit or another, favoring none, whether clothed with corporate power or in the common walks of life. Equality of rights is the watchword in this country, and it applies as well to business transactions as to any other civil right, or the right to vote.

All laws which interfere with the schemes or special privileges of men secured or granted against public policy are difficult of enforcement, but this fact furnishes no valid reason why such laws should not be enforced.

The interstate commerce commission has done great work; no commission or court in this country has ever done a greater work in the same length of time. It has decided very many difficult questions of law touching the transportation question, and has settled almost numberless differences between shippers and carriers without serious expense to either. In the enactment of the interstate commerce law congress intended to give the people a better and cheaper method of settling disputes or differences with common carriers than that provided by the common courts of the country. Congress designed that the commission in the discharge of its duties should take the place of the courts in so far as power could be given it under the constitution in the work laid out for it by statute.

I may briefly refer to one method of the commission. That is the informal investigation of grievances set forth in the correspondence of shippers. The usual course is to verify the statement of the complainant as far as possible to do so in the office of the commission. Then, if the complainant appears to possess merit, the carriers concerned are called upon to make a statement in relation to the matter or to settle with the complainant if the facts so require. This endeavor to adjust differences between carriers and shippers without formality, delay or expense, has been attended with very satisfactory results. The settlement of overcharges is thereby greatly facilitated, for instead of the claim paper being sent first to one carrier and forwarded by it to its connecting road and so on until all the companies whose roads are linked in the through line have passed, and oft-times repassed, upon the claim (as was the case before the passage of the interstate commerce act) by this method all the carriers are reached at once, and their reasons why the matter should or should not be settled are considered by an impartial arbitrator without delay.

The world soon forgets past conditions. Doubtless few now remember the utter disregard by the common carriers of the country (I speak especially of railroads) of the common rules of fair dealing with those engaged in shipping, or with localities, prior to the passage of the interstate commerce act. Extortion was practiced at non-competing points; unjust discriminations were practiced by all manner of devices—special rates, rebates, drawbacks; and concessions were given which enriched favored shippers and bankrupted their neighbors. Men engaged as presidents, managers and superintendents of railroads used their positions to amass fortunes for themselves in utter disregard of the public interest. Many of them seemed to know no law; they were a law unto themselves. A patient people finally determined to endure no longer such a condition. State legislatures and finally congress, as a result, adopted the policy of regulation.

The decision of the supreme court in the somewhat famous Counselman case declared that Section 860 of the revised statutes was not broad enough to protect from prosecution, witnesses who might by their testimony become their own accusers. This decision made it difficult to secure the testimony of any witness identified either with the common carriers or the shippers, and consequently difficult to secure convictions for violations of the law. An amendment has been adopted which broadens the statute, and while requiring witnesses to testify, is intended to give them absolute protection. The decision in this case was heralded throughout the country as a knock-down blow to the interstate commerce law; eminent lawyers freely announced their opinion in the press that the decision so seriously impaired the law that its further usefulness was a matter of extreme doubt, while, as a matter of fact, as I have just said, the decision involved no provision of the act to regulate commerce, but it was a decision announcing that Section 860 of the revised statutes, enacted in 1868, was not broad enough to protect witnesses from prosecution on account of their own testimony. It was a provision of law which had been upon the statute book for nearly thirty years; under it evidence had been procured from witnesses in all classes of cases, including those in which human life hung in the balance, and never until the methods of a great corporation were to be inquired into had the sufficiency of the section to protect witnesses been formally raised in the higher courts of the country.

The decision of Judge Gresham in declining to aid the interstate commerce commission in compelling certain persons to produce books, etc., and to testify, was regarded as a severe blow, almost if not quite destroying the usefulness of the commission. The learned judge however indicated a remedy for the adjudged defect in the law and suggested the character of legislation necessary to enable the commission to compel witnesses to attend, to testify, and to produce books, etc.; *and that legislation has been enacted.* The two decisions, therefore, which have most embarassed the enforcement of the act to regulate commerce have been overcome by new legislation, the legislation following the line of the decision in each case.

Important legislation affecting vast interests, overturning old conditions and requiring new methods is always resisted and subjected to the most critical analysis and the severest tests by the courts. The commerce act has been subject to such criticisms and tests and will continue to be perhaps in the future. The people will finally learn what their rights are, however, and it is to be hoped that when the duties and obligations of the common carriers doing an interstate business are more clearly defined, the laws will be more generally obeyed and greater harmony will prevail between carriers and shippers. The common carriers cannot live and prosper without the aid of the people, and the people cannot afford to do the carriers an injustice. The prosperity of the one is, in a large degree, dependent on the other. No business in a community or a state can be injured by unwise legislation or by any other means without, to some extent, impairing other business interests. Hence in legislation under the constitution, the utmost care should be observed so that only wise laws should be enacted. The vast wealth invested in American railroads, amounting to about $10,000,000,000, must be given an equal chance with investments in other enterprises. No fair-minded man should seek to enforce by legislation a policy which becomes injurious to any legitimate business enterprise whether carried on by individuals or by corporations. The difficulty in dealing with railroad common carriers is to properly enforce just laws. There are good and bad men engaged in the conduct of railroads, just as there are in any other business—men who are not honest and do not enjoy doing even honest things in an honest way, if any other way can be found.

The railroad interest in this country stands more nearly perhaps as one interest than does any other. Legislation affecting it should be enacted in the light of the fact that while there are hundreds of separately chartered and organized railroad companies the combinations and consolidations which have been made have resulted in placing the control of the American roads in the hands of but a few men. If this were not so, that great interest must still be recognized as distinctly one by itself, and legislation in respect to it must be enacted in full recognition of the fact that the practice of unjust discriminations, rate cutting or other schemes of violation of the common or statute law by one common carrier, however remote from the others, has its injurious effect upon the others. This being so, it is pleaded as an excuse by those who desire to obey the law that self-preservation drives them to violate it because other carriers persist in doing so. Railroad companies urge that no law for the prevention of unjust discriminations will or can be enforced as against all the common carriers, unless the anti-pooling section of the commerce act shall be repealed and a law passed legalizing contracts between railroad common carriers authorizing pooling in some form. Opposition to pooling by common carriers is strong in the minds of the people, and it is urged with great force that to legalize pooling of freights and earnings, or either, would result in the carriers being able to maintain higher rates than would otherwise obtain; that whatever power might be given to the commission the charges upon freight and passengers would be increased as the result of the effect of contracts under which competition would cease. Stability of rates is important to the business of the country as well as to the railroads, but fluctuations in rates are less objectionable than a constant oppression of all business by high rates. The men engaged in the railroad business do not regard the repeal of the anti-pooling provision of the law as sufficient to give the relief they desire. Before the law was passed prohibiting pooling the carriers made pooling contracts, but as they were regarded by the people and held by the courts to be contrary to public policy they could not be enforced, and fluctuations in railroad rates were constantly going on as the result of the scramble incident to unrestrained competition.

The passage of the act to regulate commerce checked fluctuation of rates to an extent by requiring publication of any change of rates and by providing penalties for violations of the act. Stability of rates is unquestionably in the interest of the general business of the country, but the people are not willing to permit any legislation that will give greater power to the railroads than they now possess. On the contrary, the people demand of congress and of state legislatures legislation that will protect them from the greed and rapacity of monopolies, trusts and combinations, which, in my judgment, are a menace to general prosperity and to the liberties of the people.

Time will develop proper changes in the act to regulate commerce. Some amendments were pending during the last session of congress, which should have been adopted and which are recognized as wise by managers of railroads, as well as by shippers. I hope they will be adopted at the next session of congress. There is a suggestion worthy of attention which I venture to make here. There seems to be a rapidly growing disposition among those who represent capital in this country to dominate legislation both in state and national councils. Capital has the right to protect itself against unjust legislation or any unjust policy of government, but when great corporations seek to place men in legislatures or other official positions to represent any special interest instead of the interests of the whole people, danger to free government becomes imminent and the people should sound the alarm.

I trust the time may not soon come in the United States when the money power shall be allowed to exercise more than its reasonable influence in shaping the conduct of affairs in America.

REPLY TO THE HON. S. M. CULLOM.

By G. R. Blanchard.

To the Hon. Shelby M. Cullom,
United States Senate:

SIR: Your article in the last *Railway Age* entitled "The federal control of railways," deserves attention because of your long and prominent legislative connection with the question treated, the importance of the subject and your manner of discussing it. It also deserves a frank reply because your printed views of mutual equities have not been advocated by you in the Senate or its committees, where and when frequent opportunities have been afforded you to give them public value.

Your senatorial office and these public utterances justify me in addressing you direct, and I do so with more than the consideration and none of the recent hostile intimations of some of the Chicago press, although I represent a larger constituency, it being computed that nearly one-fifth of the population of the United States derive their support directly or indirectly from its carriers.

I do not gainsay the need of a proper and effectual act. The accumulated irregularities of corporate carriers for 30 years justified national action to protect not more the public than contending carriers against each other's folly under the misomer of competition. It was, however, the duty of the national legislators to remember, like statesmen, that the combined railway abuses of a third of a century were far exceeded by the political, financial, commercial and international benefits which railways had conferred upon the country during their pioneer struggles and development periods.

You well say that "the world soon forgets past conditions."

Nor do railway managements generally contest your premises that the proper "regulation" of interstate commerce is constitutional. They do however allege that regulation in its original and just sense is rapidly assuming oppressive forms of restriction, paternalism and control. Your article, for example, is entitled "The federal control of railways" and you say: "The people will never relinquish *control* over the common carriers." Control embraces

---

Reprinted from the Railway Age and Northwestern Railroader of Aprill 21, 1893

more than both regulation and restriction, meaning, if anything, the decision and direction of all railway affairs, including finances, consolidations, etc., as well as their commercial transactions. The constitution did not assume the right of federal "control" over interstate transportation routes, some of which then existed by water. The title of your article is therefore assumptive, yet it indicates the drift of public purpose. The intent of the builders of our constitution cannot be proven to have been as broad as "control," nor as invasive of private rights as modern public opinion and recent judicial decisions. Happily you quote the Annapolis constitutional convention in proof of my averment. That historical assemblage declared one of its objects to be "to devise means for the *uniform* regulation of *trade.*" Do you regard the interstate act as the "uniform regulation of trade?" Do you believe that had this law been presented to that constitutional body it would have adopted it as an interpretation of its intent to uniformly regulate trade? You are doubtless aware also that the constitutional provision was for both the primary and final purposes of preventing a state (and not a carrier) from discriminating against, or taxing or refusing passage to, or embarrassing the commerce of another state. None of these questions are involved in our present contention, and no railway is attempting such halts or hinderances to commerce. You should not therefore confound trade regulation such as is the interstate act with "the uniform regulation of trade" itself. No railway then existed on earth, and the constitutional convention could not have intended what you intend.

Contrary to the Annapolis dictum and the language of the constitution, the railways now allege and prove that the interstate act did not seek to "regulate commerce," but only one and a minor element of it, to wit: the proportions which railway charges bear to the totals of the commercial transactions involved in their transportation. The railways maintain that the act did not even seek to regulate that moiety uniformly by all carrying routes, because it exempted interstate carriers by lake, river, oceans and canals. All those carriers may still change their rates, discriminate and pay rebates, etc., at will, which is clearly preferential legislation and not the "*uniform* regulation of *trade*" nor the "regulation of *commerce.*" Nor did it regulate the interstate traffic of the telegraph or sleeping car or stage companies, etc. We allege and show that the interstate act did not and could not bind Canadian carriers to all our conditions, inasmuch as the rates within Canada are not legally regulated or measured by the rates through Canada on American traffic. We prove that the act ignored the older legislative transportation experiences and enactments of other great countries, in particulars requisite to the just, equitable and efficient administration of the act. I cite the uniformity of charges by German governmental lines and their machinery for compelling their observance as our own government does its customs tariffs.

Also the territorial distributions of traffic in France, etc., as striking contrasts of national sense and equity in kingdoms when compared with the prohibitions of our republican interstate law in the same respects, although there is greater need for their action in our country of more complex conditions, etc.

For these major reasons it is clear that the law was devised, urged and enacted, not in the spirit you now publish, that railway investors "must be given an equal chance with investments in other enterprises," nor "to regulate commerce" in the old constitutional meaning, but to restrict corporate rail carriers only. It was enacted to curtail the rights of railway companies and to enlarge public privileges. Your article proves this by its tenor and its statements of the causes which not only justified the act but warrant further restrictions. It is no answer or justification of these preferences and inequities of the law, to charge that railways had done unjustifiable things. Clearly when the "regulation of commerce" was entered upon with presumptive impartiality, our railways did not lose their constitutional right to just consideration by the national congress. When that body sought to "regulate" the question, it should have defined, maintained and conceded that which was best for both which harmed neither. It was only because this was not done that the act encountered the "stubborn opposition" you cite. The railways as well as the country were fully prepared for a good and impartial act, but it was a duty to oppose its unfair conditions and omissions then, and is now.

Notwithstanding these cited eliminations of equal justice in the act, a great majority of American railway companies accepted and adopted it in good faith. It required that, between February 1 and April 1, 1887, the transportation methods of sixty years should be changed, and but for the thorough co-operation of the large majority of railway companies the measure would have failed at its outset. In sixty days they conformed their enormous systems to an untried and crude law at large expense. It justified them in advancing many through rates, but they reduced local rates instead. Five freight classifications between the Mississippi and the Atlantic were consolidated into one. The first-class rate, Chicago to New York, of $1.00 per 100 pounds was reduced to 75 cents and all the upper class rates proportionally. Rates were made the same in both directions. Fixed bases of rates generally replaced former inequalities. Parallel waterways were untouched by the act and continued to be the great minimizers of railway rates, and railway tariffs were adapted thereto. Railway associations were re-organized to fit the new law. Pooling was abandoned in obedience to law, not because it should have been prohibited or that it was illegal if the rates themselves were legal and reasonable.

The great change was frictionless and undisturbing to trade, and those who declare that railways did not generally co-operate to fulfill the act speak in surmises. The railways did more to give it due effect than all the combined trade bodies, senators and commissioners who had pleaded for its passage, but your article nowhere recognizes that national fact.

Trade organizations, having secured what they had long sought, owed the law the organized co-operation which they have not yet given it. On the contrary a majority of the largest shippers have continuously sought preferences which would vitiate the act. No railway allows unsolicited rebates. They usually result from shippers' importunities, intimations, threats to divert their business, or illegal devices which secure to them gains and preferences.

In 1892 the Trunk Line Inspection Bureau corrected 130,000 misdescriptions of goods and false weights on westbound traffic from New York City and Philadelphia only, and the association I have the honor to represent collected more than five times its entire expenses in 1891 and '92 by the discovery and correction of shippers' devices to evade legal regulations and tariffs. What would you say of the railroads if they resorted to similar devices to defraud forwarders 130,000 times in one year at two cities on business one way only? Corporations are regarded generally as fair prey for individual aggrandizement, and no board of trade of the United States is known to have taken steps to stop these devices or the receipt of illegal rebates by its members nor to protect those who do not receive them. Each of those bodies forbids cutting its own commission, storage, insurance and other rates, and if they are violated their members are impeached or expelled. Most of the same gentlemen who vote for such expulsions would bestow their tonnage and applause upon the railway agents who, being members of the same bodies, violate the law, and would regard their fellow members as justifiably acute who secured such illegal preferences.

This is a swift review of the conditions under which the law was passed and put in operation and which now exist.

It is well known to the interstate commissioners that in addition to the failures of the law in respects decided by the courts, rebates and preferences have not ceased because of the law. This proceeds largely from inherent defects in the act. No law built simply upon the false theory that all interstate railways and routes can secure equal rates, can be satisfactorily effective. Railways of unequal financial responsibility, terminal facilities, speed, regularity of transit, capacity and connections cannot normally maintain equal rates, because competitive traffic gravitates to the stronger roads and away from the weaker. Travelers will not use all lines alike at equal rates of fare, and the same reasons operate upon their minds in entrusting their tonnage to different carriers.

When therefore a persuasive shipper carries a large tonnage to a competitive weak line it usually results in some grant of those preferences which were made a leading reason for the passage of the act, only they are renewed in new and ingenious but concealed forms.

The public good *the law* has accomplished is therefore found in two principal particulars: The long and short haul clause has corrected many unjustifiable disparities between through and local rates, which was a chief contention for its passage, incidental to which were rate wars, and it has provided, as you state, a tribunal before which shippers as well as railways can seek the mutual interposition of commissioners of whose fairness no question has been suggested.

Thereafter the great fact remains unchallenged that the act has not stopped discriminations and preferences in rates; nor will it do so until competing railways have therein the right of contract to maintain only reasonable rates.

The railway companies, fully appreciating these unassailable facts and conditions, made reasonable, urgent and respectful representation to the last congress, showing the necessity for restoring the right to pool; their propositions being substantially as follows:

1. That competing lines be given the right to divide their tonnage or earnings under contracts, which with the rates and fares were to be submitted to the interstate commission, and that such agreements be enforcible by law.

2. That in effect the interstate commission license such agreement while they were used for the legitimate purposes set forth; otherwise they were revokable at its pleasure.

Can you controvert in any particular the fairness and justice of this plan any more than you can the governmental pools to maintain the equally just customs, postage or internal tax tariffs? And if competition is the shibboleth, why do you not advocate that the custom houses at Boston and New York compete with each other as those cities and their railways do?

The railway companies anticipated your concurrence in these propositions because of your original report, because six years of the law had proven its inadequacy in respects above set forth, etc., and for the following additional reasons:

The honorable committee of the senate which reported the interstate act interrogated 149 persons regarding pools, discriminations, rebates, concessions, uniformity and stability of rates. Twenty-four of them were railroad men, 20 were or had been railroad commissioners, 61 represented mercantile interests, 16 the farmers, 9 the manufacturers, 7 the law, etc.

Fifty-five opposed pooling, 15 were ambiguous, 42 favored pooling generally, 26 of whom favored the legalization of pools, and 41 favored pools governed by law. A close study of the testimony shows that none of those who opposed them offered adequate substitutes, nor have you offered one when the subject was first or recently presented in the senate.*

Furthermore the senate report preceding the act and to which your name is appended did not recommend the abolition of pools, but wisely and justly said:

---

* I am indebted to Vice-President Stubbs of the Southern Pacific Company for this interesting condensation.

REPLY TO THE HON. S. M. CULLOM. 91

"A majority of the committee are not disposed to endanger the success of the methods of regulation proposed for the prevention of unjust discrimination by recommending the prohibition of pooling."

The act itself as first presented to the senate said:

"The commission shall especially inquire into that method of railway management or combination known as pooling and shall report what, if any, legislation is advisable or expedient on the subject."

You were one of that senate and majority and six years' experiences have proved that this majority was right and that "the success of the methods of regulation" has been endangered and largely nullified by the prohibition of pooling. This fact was recently and incontestably laid before a senate committee of which you were still a member, but your ballot was cast against it in apparent reversal of your former views, thereby creating an adverse majority of but one against the just and neutral duty to railway equities which your article lauds. Moreover why do you omit to say that all but two of the house committee reporting in December last favored this amendment?

The fact is that but for your ballot a majority of the commerce committees of both houses would have endorsed it.

Can you reconcile this result with those portions of your present article where you say:

"The public cannot afford to do carriers an injustice."

Also—

"The vast wealth invested in American railroads amounting to about $10,000,000,000, must be given an equal chance with investments in other enterprises. No fair-minded men should seek to enforce by legislation a policy which becomes injurious to any legitimate enterprise, whether carried on by individuals or corporations."

You say that the constitutional duty to regulate commerce among the several states and foreign nations—

"Must be discharged in the interest of the people without fear or favor, fearing not to do right by all, whether engaged in one pursuit or another, favoring none, whether clothed with corporate power or in the common walks of life. Equality of rights is the watchward in this country."

"These be brave words" which stand like silhouettes against your vote when only this "equality of rights" was asked for. You were made fully aware before you cast it that the request for authority to pool was coupled with conditions to secure the public rights by preventing advances in pooled rates and that no such intent existed. You knew also that if the rates were reasonable their maintenance by a pool which would secure the uniformity and stability which your report commended was a desirable public as well as corporate end. You ascertained the views of the interstate commerce commission, whose judgments your article commends, which are well understood to have been that the provisions of the bill presented met their substantial assent, and that they held the belief that its passage would largely assist to stop the causes of many complaints before them. I especially wish at this point to correct your error of statement that "the men engaged in the railroad business do not regard the repeal of the anti-pooling provision of the law as sufficient to give the relief they desire." It may not have afforded all the relief desired, but it was one and a universally desired relief.

Did you not think when the act was being amended in particulars to make its enforcement more practical and just, such as the testimony of witnesses, granting them immunity, etc., that the mutual justice of which you write demanded that railways be given some single privilege somewhere between the first and last lines of the act, especially as the authority asked conduced to the stability of rates much commended by you?

If that was not the time for the interposition of your watchword "equality of rights," under what circumstantes and when do you think it will be proper for senators and other national and state legislators to utter it and give an "equal chance" to the "vast wealth invested in American railroads?" May I respectfully ask, when is it your individual purpose "to favor none, whether clothed with corporate power or in the common walks of life?" When, in your judgment, will be the time when "no fair minded man should seek to enforce by legislation a policy which becomes injurious to any legitimate enterprise, whether carried on by individuals or corporations?"

Can you cite one legislative transportation measure of congress or any state since the granger legislation of 1872, which gave this "equal chance to railway investments?" which "favored none in the common walks" more than railways, or which was not "injurious to legitimate (railway) enterprise?" That you do not believe the time has yet come for theoretical justice to be given practical effect seems proven by your recent votes and by other nullifying words of your article, such as the following:

It is urged with great force that * * * * charges upon freights and passengers would be increased as the result of contracts under which competition would cease.

Taken in the connection in which this is written the reverse of each word has been fully proven. You say elsewhere "the public cannot afford to do carriers an injustice"—yet you do them great injustice by the repetition of such disproven intimations. You know that the railway charges of this country are the lowest in the world and that under the pools existing prior to 1887 railway freight charges were reduced. I proved this in a public letter addressed to you June 9, 1890.

Apropos of railway charges in your own state, an English writer, W. M. Acworth, called attention in a volume published in 1891 to the results of unrestrained American railway competition as follows:

Let this one fact suffice. "Between Chicago and Cairo, a distance of 365 miles, there are 22 railway companies whose lines cross that of the Illinois Central. Eighteen out of 22 passed into the hands of receivers since 1874."

All these railroad bankruptcies occurred while pooling was permissible, and many of the insolvent companies were parties to pools. During the same period land values in the same districts advanced greatly. You knew that the amendment urged last December provided that the pooled rates be more in the hands of the governmental commissioners than now. You knew it was repeatedly averred by the advocates of pools that no advanced tariffs would be issued. Presidents Roberts and Depew and others gave that assurance to the house committee as to rates between the seaboard and the Mississippi, where the majority of the tonnage of the country is handled. They were mainly anxious to maintain the present rates against the conditions I have herein set forth. You well knew also that competition would not and could not cease, for the reasons clearly set forth in your own and in the Windom reports.

The Interstate Commission cordially commended by you said in 1887:

"Excessive and unreasonable competition is a public injury. Competition is to be regulated, not abolished."

That is all the railways sought to do by the proposed law, and if their tariffs are reasonable they are entitled to your aid in maintaining them.

Judge Deady of Oregon said *before* the law:

"It is not apparent how a division of the earnings of two roads can concern or affect the public so long as the rate of transportation on them is reasonable."

Judge Blodgett of the supreme court of New Hampshire has decided *since* the law that if such an agreement be a—

"Reasonable business arrangement which does not cause unreasonably high charges or violate any duty which the companies owe to the public it should be sustained and enforced by the courts."

England legalizes "joint purses," which we call 'pools.

You do not attempt the slightest refutation of these judgments and usages in your dual generalities.

Hon. John H. Regan, after experience as a railway commissioner for Texas, contrasts his equity with yours by saying recently:

"Further study has caused me to believe that the section may be amended so as to benefit both the railroads and the people by allowing railroads to enter into traffic arrangements with one another."

Further study seems to have brought your mind to the reverse conclusion.

I therefore repeat my inquiry: When do you think this much vaunted and little achieved mutual justice should legislatively begin? Could you not have inaugurated it in your article by a public recognition of some of the following uncontrovertable facts?

1. That the railways gave a cordial support to the act and that their subsequent rates averaged a reduction.

2. That there is no general interstate tariff of the country which has been reduced by judicial decree.

3. That upon nearly all the tonnage carried in the United States the rates average greatly less than those charged for similar rail transportation in other portions of the world.

4. That our present rates do not average one-half the charges made 15 years ago.

5. That with this decrease has come increased speed, responsibility, security of transportation, absorption of lateral charges, stoppage of transfers, etc., unequalled elsewhere.

6. That with the lower rates and quicker freight transit we pay railway labor much the highest railway wages of the world.

7. That the basis of railway taxation is being constantly increased.

8. That there were many measures pending in the last congress for the restriction of railways and but one for their relief, which one you assisted to defeat.

9. That in addition to the national discriminations I have shown, there were further countless national, state and municipal measures pending for reductions of passenger fares or freight rates and for pro rata laws, bills of lading, grade crossings, speed of trains, elevated tracks in cities, car couplers, automatic brakes and safety appliances, the better protection of labor, etc., every one of which would have the result to decrease the net revenues of the railways instead of giving impartial protection to railway investments.

10. That the public should as justly pay for the increased railway privileges they seek as they would in any other business.

11. That the cheapest through interstate rail transportation of the world has been achieved without legislative enactments.

12. That to the railways has been due the unparalleled development of the nation itself and the extension of its foreign commerce.

Why not only no recognition of these facts by you, but the repetition of mouldy formulas that "cheap transportation, etc., is a great demand of the times ;" and "we must give the people the best possible advantage in reaching whatever market may be open to them in any of the nations," and that "the nation will fail of its duty if it does not do what it can to secure both to the people?"

Does all this mean to influence courts and that congress is to make or limit the rates? If not, what is its purport? You have the cheapest rail transportation already, and the railways have brought the world's markets to our people.

I come now to the contrary views expressed in your article where you say:

"There seems to be a rapidly growing disposition among those who represent capital in this country, to dominate legislation both in state and national councils.

Capital has a right to protect itself against unjust legislation or any unjust policy of government, but when great corporations seek to place men in legislatures or other official positions to represent any special interest instead of the interests of the whole people, danger to free government becomes imminent and the people should sound the alarm.

I trust the time may not soon come in the United States when the money power shall be allowed to exercise more than its reasonable influence in shaping the conduct of affairs in America."

Logicians will ask, if capital has the right to protect itself against unjust legislation or any unjust policy of government, *how* it is to protect itself when such students of the problem and presumptive representatives of all interests as yourself do not assist to protect them. Moreover, why should they not seek to place defenders of their enormous interests and vested rights in congress and legislatures to contend there against those who bend the ballots rather than to justice, and, denying us any relief, accord all the law to those who under various arguments and political guises are elected to the same bodies upon avowed platforms of corporate hostility? Are our rights of interest, influence and election to be made less than theirs touching the care and protection of our own properties and rights?

Have you sounded any alarm that the interests of the whole people have been endangered by the repeated legislative restrictions upon corporate bodies? Are you aware of any legislative body which is dominated by corporate representatives? Surely no legislation of which I can learn reflects such domination or even a neutralizing influence. The public has a right to expect of men who hold your high office, especially when the tenure has been as long and full of experience and repute as yours, that they shall become teachers of the right and impartial guardians and not pleaders for the specious, under guises of impartiality.

I have scanned your article to find but one suggestion of the actual proposals you would have inserted in the law to accomplish the "equality of rights" which you suggest railways should receive, but I do not find any.

I do find however such sentences as the following:

"The people demand of congress and the state legislatures legislation that will protect them from the greed and rapacity of monopolies, trusts and combinations, which in my judgment are a menace to general prosperity and to the liberties of the people."

Why did you not point out what greed and rapacity interstate carriers now exhibit or practice by charging the world's cheapest carrying rates and fares?

I cannot refrain, in conclusion, from quoting the following passage from Cervantes:

"As they were thus discoursing they discovered some thirty or forty windmills * * * and as soon as the knight espied them * * * cried he: "Look yonder, friend Sancho, there are at least thirty outrageous giants whom I intend to conquer * * * for they are lawful prize. * * *
" What giants?" quoth Sancho Panza.
" Those whom thou see'st yonder," answered Don Quixote, "with their long extended arms."

Finally, I respectfully invite you to a public discussion of these issues before the World's Railway Congress which convenes in Chicago, June 19th, or before the Chicago university, or elsewhere after you shall have resumed private life.

LIMITATIONS UPON RAILWAY POWERS.

Hon. Augustus Schoonmaker,

Ex-member of the Interstate Commerce Commission.

The tendency of all power is in the direction of some form of abuse. This fact is as well known as any truism of human experience. When power is exercised by individuals it becomes despotic and arbitrary. In the case of unrestrained legislative power it expands into waste, extravagance, oppressive taxation, and often selfish enactments for the benefit of a few at the expense of the many.

In the case of municipal power the same abuses are developed. In the case of corporate power the temptations to abuse in its exercise are even greater, for the reason that private corporations are organized for gain, and there is no popular constituency to hold their managers in check by the voice of the ballot-box.

Private corporations are too often like privateers upon the ocean, they become licensed freebooters to the extent of their powers, and as a rule their victims embrace the whole public, even the unofficial proprietors of the corporate property. In no instance of corporate misconduct have abuses been more flagrant and mischievous than in the case of railway corporations. The unjust discriminations in respect to persons, in respect to traffic and in respect to localities; the reckless construction and extension of roads and branches in advance of the demands of business; the organization of subsidiary corporations to absorb the resources of enormous indebtedness impossible of payment and ruinous to credit are subjects familiar to the country, and form a history of unscrupulousness and criminality that brings a blush of shame to the cheeks of a patriot.

On account of the universal tendency of power to divers forms of abuse, society has long found it necessary to impose restraints and limitations upon its exercise in all matters of government. In nearly every State of the Union the fundamental law limits legislative and municipal power within certain prescribed boundaries, beyond which its enactments or resolves are void. In the State of New York, for example, the prohibitions upon legislative

---

Reprinted by permission from The Independent of June 1, 1893.

power make up the greater part of the Constitution. Nearly one whole article consists of restrictions intended for the protection of persons and property. Other articles contain numerous and specific provisions prohibiting legislation upon a large variety of subjects. The power to contract debts is greatly limited; appropriations to run for more than two years are prohibited. Municipalities are also under stringent limitations upon their powers, and in all municipal charters granted by the Legislature there are careful restrictions upon the expenditure of money and the creation of indebtedness.

Under the charter of the city of New York, the greatest city of the western continent, there is scarcely any power whatever in the municipal legislative body, the Common Council. Even the amount of necessary taxes to be raised is determined by another body of men, the Board of Estimate and Apportionment. This is under a provision of the Constitution to the effect that it shall be the duty of the Legislature in providing for the organization of cities and incorporated villages "to restrict their powers of taxation, assessment, borrowing money, contracting debts and loaning their credit, so as to prevent abuses in assessments and in contracting debt by such municipal corporations."

These rigid and manifold limitations have sprung from the danger of unrestrained power, as shown by long years of experience, and their salutary effect has approved the wisdom of their adoption.

The limitations that have been found necessary in representative government to prevent abuses of power, are equally necessary in the case of private corporations. They are especially appropriate and urgent in the case of railway corporations, which are universally recognized as public in their character, and have some of the highest prerogatives of government delegated to them, such as the power of eminent domain, and the taxing power, in the form of tolls and charges. The right of the Government to limit the power of these corporate bodies is unquestionable, and is derived in part from the fact that they are mere creatures of Government, either State or Federal, and in part from the business in which they are engaged which is affected with a public interest and therefore subject to public control. Governments are organized primarily for general defense, and for the protection of persons and property with all the rights and incidents that pertain to them.

Further objects of government of equal importance are the regulation of public or quasi-public organizations or combinations, to bring them under the supervision of public authority and the control of law, and prevent depredations upon the public, and restrain the growth of a power representing vast financial and property interests that may become threatening to the public safety.

The railway interests, which in many respects are a unit, constitute a power of this character, which must either be held in subjection to governmental authority, or will itself control in a large measure the legislative, judicial and administrative departments of the Government.

A careful analysis and truthful account of the extent to which railway influences enter into the action of different departments of the Government would surprise many patriotic people, who solace themselves with the optimistic creed that "whatever is, is right."

Not a few seats in legislative bodies have long been occupied to represent railway interests, and the same influence can be traced in every branch of the public service. In a few States it is said a railway party, or party of railway employes, exists strong enough to control popular elections. The railway interests of this country represent untold billions of capital, and an available voting force of a million or upward of men. If this immense organized and disciplined body with all its vast resources were of a military character, it is probable that it would excite some alarm in even the strongest government on earth.

There are reasons of a general character, therefore, plain to the understanding of every one and apart from the economic reasons that are alone sufficient, why limitations should be placed upon the powers of railway corporations. Special interests will always strive for representation under all forms of government, but particularly in a republic. There is no objection to such representation so long as it is open and avowed, but danger lurks in disguised representation and influences exerted under cover.

The limitations in view in this paper, however, have reference to corporate powers solely, and not to the sphere in which representation is sought and influences exerted in favor of corporate interests.

National banks furnish an illustration of limitations and safeguards upon corporate powers. The Banking Act is full of restrictions upon such institutions and provisions to protect the public who deal with them. No bank can incorporate itself, or issue bills in its own discretion, or transact business not embraced within the objects of its incorporation. There must be governmental authorization of the bank; bill holders must be secured by a deposit with the Government of adequate security; the circulation is limited; a reserve fund·must be maintained; the stockholders are liable to creditors to the extent of the stock they hold; officers and directors are restricted as borrowers; Government officials make stated examinations to ascertain the condition of the bank. In case of impairment the Government takes possession, and if liquidation must take place the Government, through its own receiver, administers the fund. In short, the system of regulation is complete and covers the whole ground, from the organization

of the bank, through all its operations and to its final liquidation.
Suppose some such provisions were applied to railroad corporations, would there be so many unnecessary and speculative railroads? Would two-thirds of the stock and many of the bonds of railroads of the country be worthless as investments? and would more than two dozen companies, representing upward of eighty millions of capital, go into the hands of receivers in one year from inability to meet their obligations?

If it be said that national banks are chartered by the government, and that they are therefore national institutions, and the government may impose upon them any restrictions deemed appropriate, it is a sufficient reply that railroads, whether chartered by the national or the state governments, are also national institutions by reason of the business in which they are engaged.

The doctrine is undisputed that railroads are public highways of commerce, and the Government, instead of constructing and operating them itself, delegates its powers to private corporations to perform this function, because it is deemed better public policy.

The Government having exclusive control over interstate commerce and of all the agencies and instrumentalities by which it is carried on, its authority to require a railroad to procure an authorization to engage in interstate commerce is as full and complete as its authority in the case of a bank to engage in the banking business, and it has equal authority to attach such conditions to the authorization as the governing body may see fit to prescribe.

We are thus brought to a consideration of some of the limitations that public policy seems to require upon railway powers.

The first limitation, obviously, should be upon the organization of companies and the construction of new roads and the extension of existing roads. An authorization should in all cases be necessary for the organization of a railway company, and for the construction or extension of a road. The promoters of a railway should not be the sole judges of its necessity or the propriety of its creation. A common highway or private roadway in a country district cannot be laid out without the action of the public authorities. If a new road is projected for which no public demand exists, and which can only have a precarious career of its own by working harm to established roads, it has no just claim to come into being. And the same principle applies to improvident extensions into territory already adequately served when the necessary effect must be only to divert business from competitors. Competition in such cases is not a benefit, but an injury. It is a sound rule in railroad construction that whatever road is useless is detrimental to existing roads and to the public.

Can any one believe that eight or nine competing lines between Chicago and St. Paul would be in operation, when three are sufficient for the business, if an authorization had been required? Would half a dozen unprofitable trans-continental lines have been brought into losing competition when perhaps two might have maintained a solvent existence? Or would similar conditions exist in any other territory if limitations upon improvident and unneccessary construction were in force?

What enormous losses of capital might have been averted; what disappointment and distress on the part of investors prevented; what unnumbered frauds, violations of law and principles of justice, and' criminal artifices to get business, would have had no inducement; what public and private dishonor would have been avoided, under the working of suitable limitations on construction, can never be estimated; but as cause and effect must always coexist, had not the principal cause of these evils existed, their volume would have been immeasurably less.

If railways were only private affairs and a man could own and operate his own road, as he uses his carriage and horses, the public would have no concern in them; but as they are public agencies, and the public is profoundly interested in them, both as to the service they render with the charges made for the same, and also their solvency, they are matters of the greatest public importance.

Closely allied to a limitation upon new construction is a limitation in the form of authorization to engage in interstate commerce. This simple expedient would accomplish two important objects. It would be the most efficient method of regulation in checking transportation abuses, inasmuch as revocation of a license might follow violation of established rules; and it would bring every important road in the country under the jurisdiction of the Federal authorities, as no such road could afford to lose interstate business.

Another limitation of the greatest importance is a restriction upon the debt-creating power of railways. The chief trouble with railways is the latitude and profligacy with which debts are incurred, whether in the form of bonds or current obligations. The interest to be met upon indebtedness produces a necessity for revenue, and business to secure revenue sufficient for operating expenses, fixed charges and necessary improvements must be had, by fair means or foul. Higher rates are also essential than would otherwise be required, and if established rates will not bring sufficient business, the temptation to invite business by secret or cut rates and other devices is to great to be resisted. If railroads were not built almost exclusively upon credit, if the original debt for construction were not constantly increased for all manner of purposes, good and bad, if the funded debt of the railway were not a permanent part of the enterprise, what a different condition American railways would present! Their rates could be largely reduced, lessening the burdens upon commerce, and their bonds and stocks would have a known and permanent value as investments.

The free and easy methods for organizing railroad companies

and endowing them with prerogatives of sovereignty in most of the States are a public reproach. In New York a subscription to capital stock of ten thousand dollars a mile, and payment on its capital stock of one thousand dollars a mile, are all that is necessary to start one of these corporations on its career as an agency of Government, and to license it as a snare and delusion to the public, a solicitor of public confidence figuratively without "purse, wallet or shoes."

The result is inevitable. A debt-burdened corporation from the outset, speedy bankruptcy, foreclosure, heavy losses to bondholders, wiping out of stock and reorganization with a larger capitalization and greater financial burdens than at first.

If solvency of the corporation were the prime object from the beginning, secured by proper limitations upon the borrowing and debt-contracting power, these results could not happen, and there would be less competing roads, for mere speculative enterprises could not flourish.

Another safeguard against the debt-contracting tendency of railway corporations might be to provide a personal liability on the part of officers and directors, and perhaps stockholders, to their creditors for at least any excess beyond specified limits, as in the case of banks and some private corporations. No measure would be more likely to insure conservative expenditure and management than certainty of pecuniary liability for recklessness and improvidence.

Another limitation upon railway powers can properly be applied to the use of private cars of shippers and special cars for passenger traffic. Illustrations of this practice may be found in the Standard Oil Tank Cars, and the Pullman Palace and Sleeping Cars. These organizations which exact compensation in the form of mileage from railroads for the use of their cars have accumulated enormous wealth, while many of the railroads that served them, and whose pliant creatures they have been, have gone into bankruptcy.

The disadvantages to railroads, the exhaustion of revenue, the inducements for officials of roads to become interested in such outside organizations, and the discriminations and other abuses inflicted on the public from the use of private cars owned by companies of various kinds organized to make a profit out of railroads and railroad patrons, have for some time excited a wide measure of attention and are of serious importance. A railroad should own the equipment it employs in its business, except that freedom of interchange of equipment between roads should exist and should be compulsory. If a railroad cannot afford to equip its line with rolling stock and supply its customers, equally it is not prepared to engage in business as an agency of Government, and is not ready to become a common carrier. It is better that such a road should wait to become a competitor with other roads adequately supplied to meet the demands of the public, than to permit it to enter into partnership with shippers or speculative enterprises from which evils of more or less consequence must result to the public and to the roads themselves.

Another, and one of the most important limitations upon railway powers, is a restriction upon the dangerous and destructive power of unregulated competition in rates. This power, now under no legal restraint, and shielded by popular misconception, is prolific in abuses, and is a terror to conservative roads and more disastrous to all railway interests, perhaps, than any other. Theoretically, every road has a legal right to establish its own rates without regard to the schedule charges of other railroads or of their necessities for revenue. Practically, however, there must be comity between roads and with the long distance that traffic is carried in this country and the interchanges between numberless connecting lines, there must be some uniformity in classification and rate schedules. To this end agreements are entered into and rate associations maintained; but they are in general of little avail, for with the possession of the power, and powerful inducements for its exercise, and no serious penalties for its abuse, the power to act independently will be used.

Volumes have been written upon the evils of competition; millions of dollars have been spent upon compacts between railroads in futile attempts to regulate competition; and millions more are sacrificed every year in the strifes of ruinous competition. But the evil will go on until the power that works the mischief is brought into subjection.

The practical question is how to limit this power of reducing and changing rates at will, and it is the most difficult of all the railway problems. It would seem that a Government authorization or license to a road to engage in interstate commerce, might in some degree furnish a remedy. The license might specify as a condition, maximum and minimum rates, or might require traffic to be carried at rates fixed from time to time by some association or designated authority, to be always subject, however, as to their general and relative reasonableness and freedom from unjust discrimination to the proper public tribunals of the country. Further provision might be made to tax the business of any road attempting to engage in or handle interstate commerce without a Government license to such an extent as to be prohibitory.

If authority were also added for Government agents to examine the books and accounts of railway companies, as in the case of banks, and in sufficiently flagrant cases to take possession of the property through a receiver appointed by some proper authority, a check would seem to be created upon the power in question which might to a large extent prove effectual.

The foregoing are some of the powers of railways upon which limitations would be in the public interest, and be in harmony with the experience of mankind.

How far existing systems of regulation fall short of efficient control of the subject is obvious. Under its broad and sovereign power to regulate commerce, all that Congress has attempted to regulate is transportation, leaving the causes of demoralization and of abuses untouched. A requirement that rates shall be reasonable, that roads shall not unjustly discriminate in respect to persons, traffic or localities, that reasonable and equal facilities shall be afforded for the interchange, receiving, delivering and forwarding of traffic, together with the creating of a commission to make investigations and report recommendations to be enforced or rejected by the courts of the United States in their discretion, and a provision that roads shall make annual reports concerning their condition and business, is the sum of Federal regulation. The whole field of unrestrained and overgrown railway powers, in which the rankest evils have their origin, remains in a state of nature. Regulation will only become what it should be when it covers the whole field, and lays its correcting ax at the root of existing evils. Incidentally the tribunal to pass upon questions arising under the regulating laws should be strictly a judicial body, as in England, without being over-weighted with administrative duties; and its decisions should only be reviewable upon questions of law by the highest appellate tribunal, the Supreme Court.

The administrative duties of regulation are important enough and vast enough to be devolved upon a Cabinet minister charged solely with the performance of that task, and to him all statistical reports should be made, and he in return should report the statistical abstracts for the information of Congress and the country.

If it be objected that much of this paper is the old, old story, the fact is conceded. Iteration is doubtless monotonous, but in the field of governmental and economical reforms, "line upon line and precept upon precept" are as necessary as in the realms of morals. Public sentiment must lead the way in all reformatory movements. Legislation never moves faster than public sentiment, and under our ever changing legislative bodies, the lawmakers of today are mostly different from those of yesterday, and those of tomorrow will again be different. The work of presenting facts and arguments to those who create laws and formulate policies of government, has to be done over and over again with patient perseverance.

Kingston, N. Y.

RAILWAY LEGISLATION.

Hon. Walter D. Dabney.

A correct diagnosis of disease is the first essential to its successful treatment. This truth applies with no less force to disorders and defects in the operation of economic systems, such as a country's means of transportation, than it does to the maladies of the human body. A condition precedent to such a diagnosis is thorough knowledge of the system or body in which the disease is manifested and of the laws by which its workings are governed. If this system is composed of many different parts, members, or groups, the requisite knowledge must extend to the internal structure and arrangement of each group and the local laws governing the same, as well as to the structure and functions of the system as a whole and the laws governing the whole. This is particularly true if the different groups of the system have had their origin and development under conditions of comparative isolation from other groups and under laws, both economic and statutory, peculiar to themselves. As the different and once comparatively independent groups become unified into a homogeneous whole, the local laws applying in each may be found more or less in conflict with the general law which from the accomplished fact of unification has become a necessity.

These remarks have been made as preliminary to a plea for a thorough study of the railway laws of the several States of the Union in their bearing and effect upon the operation and enforcement of the national act to regulate commerce, and also, it may be added, of ascertaining whether the latter may not be susceptible of improvement in certain particulars.

A systematic study of local laws, or, more properly, of the attitude of the different States towards carriers engaged in transportation within their limits—for frequently this attitude is most clearly shown by the absence of any regulative legislation—is the prime requisite to the attainment of what the resolution of March 1889, shows to be one of the leading purposes of this Convention, viz., "perfecting uniform legislation and regulation concerning the supervision of railroads."

Reprinted from Proceedings of National Convention of Railroad Commissioners held at Washington, D. C., April, 1892.

The effect upon national legislation of the attitude of the individual states towards the railway carriers within their limits, I believe, will be found to be far more considerable than is commonly supposed. The States' failure to co-operate may result in practically defeating in many important particulars the objects sought to be accomplished by the enactment of Federal laws upon this subject. Without any such design on the part of the States, their local laws and regulations, or, more usually, the mere absence of state regulations, may operate to greatly impair the effectiveness of the commercial laws and regulations of the Union. The actual situation discloses various instances of unintentional, though no less complete nullification of Federal law, resulting from the action, or rather the non-action, of a single State.

Unlike the doctrine of nullification by a State of Federal laws, once held by some as a political creed, the more important results of this modern anomaly are frequently manifested beyond the limits of the State which actually or passively has occasioned it.

This is strikingly illustrated by the fact that the Interstate Commerce Commission, very soon after its organization, found it necessary to announce the principle, which has been consistently adhered to, that the competition of a railroad carrying traffic between points in the same State might justify its rivals in taking interstate traffic without regard to the general rule of the 4th section of the act in respect to long and short hauls. It cannot be doubted that this ruling of the Commission was wise. Under the existing law, indeed, which expressly excludes from its provisions transportation confined within a single state, the ruling was absolutely essential to the protection of interstate roads competing with the State road.

And yet—without expressing any opinion as to the wisdom of the purpose—it may be confidently asserted that Congress intended by the 4th section of the law to declare as a general regulation of commerce by railroads, subject to as few exceptions as possible, the prohibition of a greater charge for a shorter than for a longer haul.

It could hardly have been contemplated that this general principle of regulation might be nullified, as in effect it sometimes has been, by the attitude of the individual States towards carriers within their own limits; and does it not seem probable that Congress, had its attention been clearly directed to the intimate and inevitable effect upon the interstate commerce of unregulated commerce within state limits, would either have greatly extended the general scope of the Federal law or else have modified in important particulars the provisions of the 4th section thereof?

But the effect produced upon interstate commerce by the action of carriers within a single state in transportation, subject only to the laws of that state, is by no means confined to the case of directly competing carriers, having one or both termini of their routes in common. It exists and is potent and sometimes seriously disturbing under circumstances where yet it may not be sufficiently direct to secure recognition as a justification for departing from the general rule of the long and short haul.

An illustration of the disturbing influence which roads engaged in transportation between points in the same State might exert upon numerous other roads engaged in interstate commerce between points in other States is found on the one hand in the lines connecting St. Louis with Kansas City, both in the same State, and on the other hand in the lines connecting Chicago with Omaha and other cities on the Missouri river, in Nebraska, Iowa, Kansas and Missouri. The pressure of commercial forces operating throughout many years has, after repeated conflicts, resulted in a certain agreed percentage of difference between the railroad rates from eastern points to Chicago and St. Louis respectively, the latter being charged a somewhat higher rate from the east than the former.

In obedience to a commercial necessity which experience has proven to be irresistible, the rates from Chicago to all points on the Missouri river from Kansas City to Omaha, inclusive, are made greater by a fixed percentage than the rates from St. Louis to the same points, and all these points have the same rates from Chicago and the same rates from St. Louis. A disturbance of this adjustment in the rates from either Chicago or St. Louis to either Kansas City, Omaha, or any intermediate Missouri River point has, whenever attempted, introduced serious trouble, confusion, rate wars, and discriminations injurious alike to the interests of shippers and of carriers, through the whole region between Chicago and the Missouri river. No detailed explanation of the causes to this fact need be entered upon here. As a fact it is perfectly well established. The rate from St. Louis to Kansas City, for instance, if these general evils are to be avoided, must be maintained at a uniform ratio to the rate from Chicago to Omaha. Secret rebates from the published rate from St. Louis to Kansas City will, if long continued and applied to any considerable and important line of traffic, inevitably affect injuriously the roads carrying the same line of traffic between Chicago and Omaha. A resort to rebates or other devices to retain their business is forbidden by the interstate commerce act to the latter roads; but the lines carrying between St. Louis and Kansas City, the transportation being confined within the limits of a single State, are not restricted in this respect by Federal law. Unless the State of Missouri forbids by law the use by carriers of rebates and other similar devices to secure traffic, it is plain that the voluntary self-restraint of the Missouri roads can alone be relied on to preserve a status of justice and commercial equilibrium throughout a vast territory wholly beyond the borders of that state. Fortunately through the medium of the railway associations the self-restraint necessary to maintain the proper equilibrium has generally of late years been practiced—at least in the territory which has been referred to in illustration; but it is evident that the absence of state laws in harmony with Federal laws may very likely result, if not in complete nullification of Federal laws, at least in rendering them far more difficult of enforcement than they would be if aided by harmonious state legislation. A railway carrier of interstate traffic is not likely under ordinary circumstances to render other than a compulsory obedience to law when obedience affords the opportunity to other carriers not subject to legal restrictions to take away its business by resorting to devices which the law forbids to it.

Another respect in which state laws and regulations may, though confined in terms to business wholly within a single state, have a decided bearing on interstate business, is through the fixing of maximum rates either directly by state laws or by state commissions.

The reasonableness of a carrier's rates on interstate business must depend to some extent upon the amount of the carrier's earnings from all its business. Where a line of railroad traverses several states, its earnings will be derived in part from traffic within each state and in part from traffic among the several states.

Should one state by legislation or by a commission fix charges at figures deemed unremunerative by the carriers, the attempt would probably be made to compensate the loss by increased charges on traffic beyond the control of such state. The traffic additionally burdened might be either interstate in its character or it may be wholly within the limits of some other state where charges are not limited by public authority. In either case the bearing and effect of the law of a single state upon one, or perhaps several, other states is apparent enough to warrant further inquiry into the matter than has yet been made.

It is also plain that the purpose of congress in prohibiting railway pooling may often be frustrated by purchases, leases, and consolidations of railroad companies under the authority of state laws. One of the principal arguments against the anti-pooling section of the interstate commerce law has' been that it would force competitive lines of railway into the still more intimate relations arising from consolidations and leases.

The unification and subjection to a common control by these methods, of lines formerly independent and sometimes competitive has undoubtedly proceeded to a very considerable extent since the enactment of the act to regulate commerce, though whether this has been in consequence of the anti-pooling section, or whether it would have occurred even had that section not been enacted, has been questioned. But that its effect has been to defeat, in great measure, the object of that section hardly admits of doubt. Whether that object was wise or unwise, and whether consequently the action of the carriers in partially defeating it by resorting to consolidations and leases of competing lines has been detrimental or beneficial to the public interests, it is beyond the province of this paper to discuss. The present purpose is merely to show how national laws and regulations, framed to prevent what congress deems to be a practice detrimental to the public, may be deprived of their intended effect by the action of one or more of the states.

It is conceded by the majority even of those persons who favor pooling as a means of promoting stability in traffic charges and preventing unjust discriminations, that consolidation of railways may be carried to dangerous extremes. The more conservative advocates of pooling also admit that pooling agreements should be, to some extent at least, subject to the sanction and approval of some public tribunal; but where consolidations, purchases, or leases are effected under the authority of state laws there can be no opportunity for the Federal authorities to give any valid sanction or to express any effective disapproval of the arrangement. Yet the effect of consolidations under state authority may extend with equal force to interstate traffic as to traffic within a single state, and may be far more potent in checking and limiting competition in transportation between the states than any mere pooling agreement could possibly be. These brief suggestions show how state action may defeat the policy of Congress looking to prevent restraints on competition in interstate transportation by railroads. Should the policy of the national legislature in this respect be altered at some future time—that is, should it be deemed expedient to legalize pooling, subject to proper supervision by the Interstate Commerce Commission or other Federal authority—it may possibly be found that state constitutions and laws forbidding the unification in any form of the interests of competing lines will be found in conflict with such a policy. Nearly all railway companies owe their origin to state legislation, and are subject only to state laws pertaining to the ownership and management of other roads than their own, either directly or indirectly, through the purchase of controlling interests in stock. The bearing of this fact upon national regulations of commerce is worthy of careful attention. The unification of interests of different railroads, under such circumstances as seriously to affect interstate commerce, usually requires the co-operation of two or more states in legislating to that end.

It is important, therefore, to know what are the laws of each state in respect to the rights of railroad companies of other states to consolidate with companies of its own creation, and this whether the consolidation or other unification of interests apply to continuous or non-competitive or to parallel or otherwise competitive lines.

Consolidations or acquisition into a single hand of controlling interests in several different properties, have usually been found to occur first along continuous lines, and the consolidation of competing lines has generally followed upon and in large measure as a consequence of the first kind of consolidation.

The unification of different but continuous lines into a single through route between distant termini usually means the addition of a new competing line between those termini, where, perhaps, a sufficient number of lines to secure healthful competition and accommodate all the business, already exist.

The opening of unnecessary routes in this way has sometimes been found seriously detrimental, not only to the interests of existing lines, but to the general commercial interests of the country. It therefore suggests another aspect in which a study of state railway laws may be important from a national point of view.

One may at first be disposed to think, when a comprehensive study of state railway laws is suggested, that its chief value would be to bring within a single field of view, for purposes of comparative study and investigation, those provisions of legislation in different jurisdictions designed for the purpose of regulating the traffic charges of railways and providing machinery for adjusting the relative rights of carriers and communities dependent upon them, in cases which the ordinary courts are incompetent to meet; but further reflection leads to the conclusion that this is much too narrow a view. As has already been shown, the attitude of a single state toward its railroads, as manifested by the presence or absence of laws imposing regulations on transportation within its limits often directly affects interstate transportation. But there are statutory provisions in a number of states besides those enacted with the immediate purpose of regulating the commercial relations between carriers and their patrons which have a powerful indirect bearing upon the subject. They have a bearing not simply upon the commerce under the regulative jurisdiction of a single state, but they may very greatly affect that commerce "among the several states" which congress alone can constitutionally regulate. For example, the restrictions or the absence of restrictions in the several states upon the power of corporations to organize for the construction of railways, especially in connection with the privileges or rights conferred by the laws of one state upon the railway corporations of another in respect to leases, consolidations, traffic agreements, &c., have a very powerful and sometimes prejudicial influence upon the efforts of congress to maintain a proper status of commercial rights throughout its wide domain.

A notable and familiar instance may be cited of the construction of new lines and the opening of a new route under circumstances which caused serious disturbance of commercial relations throughout a vast region, beyond, as well as within the limits of the states through which the new route extended.

The free railroad law of New York, where no special act of incorporation is required, enabled the West Shore road to be constructed, paralleling the New York Central from New York to Buffalo, opening up practically no new traffic and responding to no well-founded public demand.

Under the operation of the laws of New York and states west thereof, the new line entered into business connections of an intimate character with lines of the latter states, forming a new through route to Chicago. Over the route thus formed a fight for its "share of the traffic" was at once begun, resulting in a war of rates, with all the attendant evils of unjust discriminations and fluctuating charges throughout nearly the whole territory north of the Potomac and Ohio rivers and east of the Mississippi. The final and inevitable result was the absorption of the new route by the New York Central, and the addition of that much necessary capitalization to the aggregate cost of the great trunk lines. The burden of producing a revenue on this capitalization rests largely upon "interstate commerce."

The history of this transaction has been repeated more than once in other parts of the country.

Where a special charter is required for the construction of a new railroad, or where the permission of some public board must be first obtained for the opening of additional lines, as some states provide, there is some safeguard against the formation of unnecessary new routes and dangerous overconstruction; but the question is so broad and the policy of a single state may be so far-reaching in its effect on other states that it has become one of general national concern.

It is eminently a question for the careful consideration of Congress as well as of the several States.

While uniformity, or at least harmony, in the regulative laws of the several states and of Congress is desirable, it does not follow that it must be attained by conforming state laws to existing Federal legislation. It may be found wise to modify the latter to some extent to meet conditions resulting from the existence of the former.

The question of the constitutional right of congress to take jurisdiction of commerce confined within the limits of the states for the purpose, as could be plausibly urged, of efficiently exercising its power to "regulate commerce among the several states" is one upon which a difference of opinion exists. There appears to be no direct adjudication of the question in the courts, though there are numerous *dicta* of eminent judges denying, either expressly or by plain implication, the existence of any such power. The interstate commerce law clearly excludes all strictly state traffic from the operation of its provisions; yet eminent jurists are known to entertain the opinion that the close interdependence between interstate traffic and traffic confined within state limits would justify congress in exercising the power here referred to. Unless, however, the necessity for congressional interference be very plain and urgent, it would surely be better that this power, even if it exists, should remain dormant. One of the most useful objects to be accomplished by harmonizing state and Federal legislation and bringing them into co-operation toward the same end is to avoid, as far as possible, all occasion or pretext for extending the regulative powers of Congress over transportation confined within state limits.

But as preliminary to determining on a proper course of action in the direction of harmonizing all American railroad legislation, both state and national, it would seem wise to have a compilation, carefully classified, of the railroad laws of all the states. Being for the benefit of all, this work should be done at the expense of all—that is, through the Federal Government.

Such a compilation should include not merely the laws enacted with the immediate view of regulating transportation, such as those creating commissions and conferring powers on them and those forbidding unjust discriminations and unreasonable charges; but it should embrace all that extensive class of statutes which in any way, directly or indirectly, affect this question. A few of these have been hinted at rather than discussed in this paper, which, however, does no more than touch upon a few salient and important points.

Such a compilation as is desirable would be a considerable undertaking; yet its cost to the National Government, should the work be efficiently done, would be trivial in comparison with its value.

THE AMENDMENT OF THE INTERSTATE COMMERCE LAW.

By *Aldace F. Walker*.

Chairman Joint Committee Trunk Line and Central Traffic Associations.

After six years of experiment in the direction of railway supervision by Congressional enactment, during which the practical efficiency of the Act to Regulate Commerce has gradually dwindled away, its progressive decline in administrative force and in the estimation of the public being relieved only by slight biennial tinkerings, which have carefully avoided going to the root of its weaknesses, a movement for its amendment has at last been set on foot, having some promise of valuable results. The act, in its general scope and in most of its provisions, was a Senate bill. It was introduced by a Select Committee of the Senate, after successive investigations and a patient examination of the subject of interstate commerce continued through several years. Following its passage, the special committee was made a standing committee with enlarged membership, and having equal rank in all respects with the other permanent committees of that body. Its special field was to observe the workings of the Interstate Commerce Law and to improve its conditions. The House of Representatives has no precisely corresponding committee. Its Committee on Commerce is of much broader jurisdiction, covering so many topics which require constant legislative action that it is one of the hardest worked committees of the House. Naturally the Senate Committee on Interstate Commerce has been looked to for the origination and prosecution of such measures as might be required to perfect the law of 1887 and to correct its mistakes.

As yet it has done practically nothing. At every session, representatives of leading interests, railroad and public, as well as the Interstate Commerce Commission itself, have applied for urgently needed relief. Many comparatively trivial amendments have been passed, but the most important questions have been hitherto avoided. The double result of this continued evasion of responsibility is that while the railroads have suffered much injury and in many cases have been brought to a point where future operation

---

Reprinted by permission from The Independent of June 1, 1893.

has become financially difficult, on the other hand shippers have learned to ridicule the provisions of the law, and quite universally to ignore its mandates in the business competition.

At last a ray of light appears. The Senate Committee has been reorganized recently and has obtained leave to prosecute during the present recess an inquiry concerning certain alleged weaknesses of the law with a view to their amendment. True, the field of investigation marked out by the resolution of April 15, 1893, is limited; but in introducing proposals of amendment the committee has the broadest powers and is not restricted to the subjects enumerated for inquiry. Those subjects are four: pooling, the short haul clause, Canadian competition, and labor; all important questions, but by no means comprising all the topics on which legislation is necessary.

The repeal of the fifth section of the present law, being the anti-pooling section, and the substitution therefor of some form of legalized and regulated arrangement for the fair distribution of common traffic among competing lines may be fairly expected as an immediate result of this investigation. The impossibility of much longer carrying on railway operations with success in the face of the present prohibition of pooling has at last become manifest to the general public. Little opposition to this change now exists, none among those who have studied the subject intelligently. A large majority of the House Committee on Commerce in the last Congress united in supporting such a measure with at least the tacit approval of the Interstate Commerce Commission; the Senate Committee showed a majority of only one against it. Heretofore the railroads have apparently been regarded as public enemies, to be "controlled" and "restricted" and circumvented in every possible way. A fairer spirit is now apparent on all sides, under which it is recognized that even railway corporations have a right to exist, and to exist successfully, as other business interests are allowed to do; and that the pressure of the present extreme traffic conditions is bearing too hard upon many companies whose financial ruin would produce widespread disaster. It is perceived that with the present unprecedentedly low scale of railway earnings the line of safety for the public in respect of efficiency, and in some cases even of security in operation, is dangerously near. It is also becoming generally understood that the making or "establishing" of railway rates, and the "maintaining" of those rates when so established, are two very different things; that both are absolute necessities to any scheme of governmental supervision; and that the pooling of freights or of earnings is the only practical way known in the history of the world, short of a common ownership, by which such an absolute maintenance of rates as is justly required by law for the prevention of unjust discrimination can be secured. In other words, it is seen at last that the fair division of competitive traffic would be an aid and support to the regulative statute. In the judgment of many it should not only be permitted but compelled by law.

Aside from certain newspapers and politicians that are still found catering to public ignorance in respect to this question, the only objection now heard to the legalizing of pooling comes from the timid, who are still occasionally heard to say that it might afford a basis for the oppression of the public by means of extortionate rates. There are many replies to this fear. It is only a fear, not a fact, as the history of past agreements clearly shows. The object of the railway pool is the maintaining of tariff rates, not the lifting or even making of them. Competition of markets, of producing points and of other carriers will always keep rates low and force them lower. The purpose of the pool is not to extinguish competition, but to regulate it, and that but slightly. The reasonableness of the rate is the point in which the public are interested, together with a just equality of charges for equivalent services, which reasonableness is subject. to control, and which equality is the very object aimed at by the railway pool.

If still there is fear, then let the making and operation of traffic contracts be surrounded by such safeguards as reasonable men may devise; the railroads will not object, for they know them to to be unnecessary and harmless; while the hesitating legislator may thus overcome his fears, or satisfy his convictions.

The next topic on the Senatorial scheme is the famous "long and short haul clause," a bit of legislation which at first filled the public eye so completely that many regarded it as all there was to the law, and believed that its rigid application would accomplish a transportation millenium. Of late it has attracted little attention; its inclusion in the resolution for investigation was on motion of Senator Hoar, perhaps as a reminiscence of the time when he so vigorously opposed its original engraftment upon the Senate Bill. This clause has been very differently regarded by railroad officials; those connected by direct routes and short lines naturally being believers in its justice, while those employed upon circuitous routes and meeting active terminal competition have as naturally regarded its rule as unjust. It seems to have been enacted upon the idea that it was a protection to intermediate points upon indirect routes, and to small communities which did not enjoy competitive facilities; but its value, if any, in that direction has been more than counterbalanced by the unfortunate anti-pooling section, which turned the roads over to the tender mercies of heavy shippers at terminal points, without the possibility of protection against alliances "in the form of trust or otherwise." In this way traffic of great value to the carriers has been hawked about to the lowest bidder, in defiance of law and resulting in great injustice to less potential shippers at less influential points in the interior.

It seems probable that if the fourth, or short-haul section is amended at all it will be in the direction of making more clear and definite the construction of its exceptions. The words "under similar circumstances and conditions" have been construed with elasticity or with rigidity according to the different ideas of those who have had to face this question. Even the Interstate Commerce Commission during the last year has announced a revised construction of the section which very materially differs from its own previous rulings. The courts have not yet had an opportunity to pass upon it in any decisive way. The great point of difficulty has been the determination of the extent to which the competition of other carriers subject to the provisions of the law justifies a departure from the short-haul rule on circuitous routes of traffic; and if testimony is taken by the Senate Committee upon this point many facts will be developed in different parts of the country that, to say the least, will be interesting.

Upon the question of traffic between points in the United States over roads passing through the Dominion of Canada much has been heard of late. It is claimed by the American lines that the law discriminates in favor of Canadian lines and requires amendment in order to put the former upon an even keel with the latter. The Canadian roads strenuously deny this, and assert that there is now a complete equivalence. More than this the American roads should not ask; less than this the Canadian roads should not desire. The question of the justice of the working of the statute in its present form is one of fact, to be determined upon the evidence submitted to the committee, and upon which it is to be hoped that a clear and definite report will be made, and that this subject may be soon forever settled.

The labor clause seems to have been introduced into the resolution, judging from the debate which preceded its formulation, upon the idea that the interpretation given to the third and tenth sections of the act by the courts of the United States in the recent cases decided at Toledo, infringed upon the rights of workingmen; or, as was charged by Senator Voorhees, enslaved them. It is probable that more precise knowledge as to the exact scope of these decisions has since modified the fears at first entertained. It turns out that they only went to the extent of requiring employes to recognize the obligations of the law so long as they remained in the company's service; in other words, holding that engineers equally with directors and stockholders are amenable to the requirement of the law that interstate commerce exchanged with connecting roads must be handled without discrimination; but the right of employes to quit the company's service at the end of any day's run was recognized in the absence of a contract or a law requiring a longer notice. The protection of the public against interruption of transportation service by strikes of employes was not the thought which led to the inclusion of this subject in the resolution; but it is by no means an impossible outcome of the investigation.

A few other points in which the law requires amendment may be hastily reviewed. One is the making of railway corporations subject to its penalties. It seems strange that such is not now the case; and it appears to be true that the purpose to have it so failed through a not unnatural error on the part of the draftsman of the bill. However this may be, a United States Court has held that under its present phraseology an indictment will not lie against a railway company, but only against its officers, agents and employes. In the same connection the fact may be noticed that the penalties now standing against the latter include a possible imprisonment in the penitentiary, for offenses which are only statutory misdemeanors and are not infamous crimes, the excessive severity of which punishment has been a most serious obstacle in the way of the enforcement of the law. If one corporation could complain against its rival corporation for infractions of the statute, and not as now only against its servants with the chance of their imprisonment for acts in which they were not principals but agents merely, the operative efficiency of the statute would be increased a thousandfold. As the law now reads no such complaints are ever made. Amendments to cover both these points passed the House in the last Congress, with the active support of many railway companies, and might have passed the Senate also if the bill which included them had not been side-tracked in order to give the right of way to what was called the Coupler Bill.

Another topic which deserves the attention of the committee is found in connection with the fact that the title of the bill passed in 1887 was a very serious misnomer. It was called an Act to Regulate Commerce. In fact it was only an act to regulate certain common carriers by rail. It does not undertake to regulate commerce at all, but only a single one of the agencies of commerce. Even considered as an act to regulate transportation, which is by no means the equivalent of commerce, it is only partial in its scope. It fails to regulate carriers by water, the volume of whose transportation approximates that of the railways. It does not attempt to deal with other transportation agencies by land, such as draymen, stagecoaches, elevators, etc., or even with subordinate carriers making use of railway facilities, such as sleeping car companies, express companies, livestock transportation companies, and private car companies of all kinds. It even excludes in set terms all railway traffic which is conducted within the boundaries of individual states. It is altogether partial and incomplete; and its partiality and incompleteness in these respects are unjust and unfair, because conditions are imposed upon one set of carriers to which others are not subjected.

Undoubtedly it was considered wise, six years ago, to leave vessels and steamboats carrying traffic upon the numberless lakes, rivers and canals of the country as well as upon its seaboard, free from restrictions, while the railroads should be bound, to the end that the unbridled competition of the former might have full scope to pull down the charges of the latter. This purpose was distinctly set forth as an excuse for not giving a broader jurisdiction to the law. But has not the time now arrived when such an important question can be approached with less prejudice and with more of justice? After the experience of the last six years, with its continued object lesson of the "vanishing profit," so far as railways are concerned, with a constant struggle on the part of railway managers everywhere to reduce expenses by improved facilities, and to attract business by improved service, while the future dividend is either a known impossibility or an unknown speculation, is it not clear that the Act should now be amended and enlarged to conform to its title, or that the title should be re-defined into correspondence with the provisions of the Act, and at the same time the unfairness of the present conditions be so far as possible eliminated?

Another question which should be settled and settled soon, is that of the rate-making power. The Interstate Commerce Commission at first disclaimed power to make rates generally under the law, but has since inferred from the present statute that Congress intended to confer power upon that body to establish maximum reasonable rates upon all interstate traffic. It is admitted that the law in terms says no such thing; but its first section declares that all charges must be reasonable and just; many complaints have been made to the Commission that rates were relatively too high, and it has frequently advised roads of its opinion to that effect; the Commission argues that unless it is authorized to say what rate shall be considered reasonable and just, there is no way by which the first section can be made effective; hence Congress must have intended to confer that power upon the Commission.

In some cases the arguments of the Commission touching the reasonableness of the rates in question have commended themselves to the carriers, who have conformed to the recommendations made. In other cases their reasoning has appeared to the roads to be strained and their findings arbitrary, and in some cases the result has been found impossible of application by reason of the position taken by other lines not parties to the controversy heard. Several suits have been brought to enforce the rates named by the Commission under this claim of authority, many of which are now pending and some of which involve the demand that a rebate be paid during a period antecedent to the naming of the rate by refunding the difference between the tariff published under the law and that afterward awarded as the view of the Commissioners. None of these cases have been decided by the courts, and the question whether Congress conferred any such power upon the Commission in the law together with the further question of the authority of Congress in the premises, are constant sources of uncertainty and irritation. These difficulties should be laid at rest. There is very great doubt whether the constitutional grant of power " to regulate commerce " conferred upon Congress a right to fix the rates which shall be charged for transportation, or whether by that clause anything more was in fact originally intended than that interstate commerce should be forever free from State restrictions; whether, if Congress has the power to make tariffs on railroads—not of Congressional charter, but existing under State laws—it can delegate that power to a commission; whether, if it can empower a non-judicial and semi-political body to nominate maximum rates all over the land, it is a part of wisdom to do so, rather than to leave the establishment of tariffs to the natural and persistent play of competitive forces, universal in their nature and omnipotent in their strength.

Experience in this and in many other countries has shown the impossibility of establishing transportation charges by rule of thumb, or by any kind of procrustean rule. Natural conditions have uniformly proved too strong for such laws to overcome; and when those forces have produced a scale of rates as phenomenally low as that which the American public quite generally enjoys, the policy of attempting to introduce a new authority may be, and is, very seriously challenged.

But if Congress is of opinion that it is to go into the business of making railway rates, it should face the question deliberately, and confer the power in set terms, leaving nothing to implication, either as to the extent of authority intended, or as to the methods of its use. The rules for deciding what shall be a "reasonable rate" should be fixed in the law; it should afford to the carriers who may feel their just revenues imperiled, the protection to which they are constitutionally entitled, by establishing a right of appeal to the courts, which does not now exist. It should include the rates of all common carriers, especially of carriers by water. It should also confer upon whatever body may be deemed the trustworthy recipient of the rate-making power an authority to raise rates as well as to lower them; there is as much public danger in rates too low as in rates too high; and the cases are frequent in which the desired relative adjustment can be better reached by advances than by reductions in tariffs.

One point more demands attention, and it is a point of supreme importance. I refer to the standing of the Interstate Commerce Commission and its relation to the law. In this respect the act was inexcusably crude. The idea seems to have been to lay down certain general principles, under which common law rules against unjust discrimination, undue preferences and unreasonable charges were accepted as applicable to interstate commerce, and then to appoint a commission to work the problem out. That was a very plausible evasion of responsibility on the part of Congress, but was also exceedingly unfair to the Commission. So loosely was the work of drawing up the statute in this respect performed that it was soon perceived that while the Commission was required to administer and enforce the law it had no administrative powers whatever; and while it was required to decide questions under the law, it had no judicial qualities; and while it was both semi-administrative and quasi-judicial, it was neither a prosecuting officer or a court. In fact the law created a composite body, part detective, part state attorney, part statistician, part rate bureau and part court, with no actual power in any single direction. The inconsistency of appointing the same men to act at the same time as prosecutors and as judges does not seem to have occurred to any one; yet it is an actual fact that the Interstate Commerce Commissioners are in one section required to hold the scales of justice impartially in the decision of traffic questions between shippers and carriers, and in another section are required to keep their eyes open for every breach of the law on the part of either carriers or shippers, and see to it that due punishment follows.

Of course this scheme is not worked, and it never can work. The fact is that the present status of the Commission is an impossible one, a fact which sufficiently accounts for its inability to effect results. It either should be a court, or it should be an administrative body; one or the other; it is ridiculous to try and make it both judicial and administrative, being at the same time neither. It would be much better if its powers were simply advisory, as in the case with some of our most useful state railway commissions.

If that idea is not acceptable, then the Commission should be either a branch of the Department of Justice, with power to employ special agents in ferreting out crimes and supervising prosecutions in detected cases of violation, leaving the settlement of civil controversies to the courts; or it should be a part of the Judiciary, with no further demands upon its attention than to adjudge controversies submitted by parties, leaving the enforcement of the penalties of the law to the Bureau of Justice, which enforces other penal statutes. The statistical and recording duties now imposed, and the tariff bureau, might well be attached to the Department of the Interior; they have no relation to the determination of causes, or to the enforcement of the law, except as they may be drawn upon for evidence.

In England the Railway Commission is a judicial body of high standing. Its duties are clearly defined and its powers are carefully conferred. If such a body could be organized in the United States its field of usefulness would be a grand one; its decisions would have legal sanction, and the results of its investigations would command universal respect.

The attention of legislators has frequently been called to this subject in a quiet way; and it was somewhat discussed before the

Senate Committee two years ago, in connection with an amendment proposed by the Commission designed to assimilate its status more closely to that of a Master in Chancery. The time has come when the situation should be frankly and publicly stated, to the end that if the present condition of affairs is to continue, it may be prolonged intelligently, and for some good reason.

During the last Congress a bill (S. 3,805), was introduced so late in the session that it received no consideration whatever; but if the name of its author could be given it would now command immediate attention. It was entitled "A Bill creating Circuit Courts of Interstate Commerce." It proposed to create such a court in each of the nine judicial circuits in the United States, consisting of one justice for each circuit, to have original and exclusive jurisdiction of all cases arising under the Interstate Commerce Act, with full powers; also a circuit court of interstate commerce appeals, consisting of the same nine justices, five to be a quorum; the Supreme Court to review finally questions of jurisdiction and of constitutional right, and the present Interstate Commerce Commission to be abolished.

Whether or not this plan or something like it shall be adopted; whether new administrative power shall be conferred upon the Commission, or whether some other method shall be devised for the enforcement of the law and the prompt determination of controversies arising under its provisions, presents, perhaps, the most important question that will confront the committee of the Senate. Certainly the plan proposed in the draft above referred to has much at first blush to commend it; and if the present intelligent and sincere members of the Commission could transfer their trained experience to a veritable judicial position, like that suggested, their services would be of far greater value to the country than can be possible under the present law, while parties, whether shippers or carriers, having grievances arising from breaches of its provisions, would be assured of a tribunal to which such questions could be submitted for immediate and effectual adjudication.

Chicago, Ill.

THE LEGAL ASPECT OF RAILROAD STRIKES—
THE ANN ARBOR DECISION.

By General Wager Swayne.

An act of Congress, which became a law March 2, 1889, provides that if any common carrier (which, of course, includes the railroad companies) shall fail or refuse to move and transport the traffic or to furnish cars or other facilities for transportation for all parties, upon equal terms, so far as interstate commerce is concerned, the Courts of the United States, upon a proper showing, shall make a peremptory order requiring the common carrier complained of to abolish the inequality and furnish to the party complaining equal facilities in all respects so far as the circumstances themselves are equal.

A rule of the Brotherhood of Locomotive Engineers provides that it shall be recognized as a violation of obligations for a member of the Brotherhood who may be employed on a railroad running in connection with, or adjacent to said road, to handle the property belonging to said railroad system in any way that may benefit said company with which the Brotherhood is at issue, until the grievance, or issue, of whatever nature or kind has been amicably settled.

These two rules are in plain conflict. One of them provides that under no circumstances shall a railroad company refuse to haul all freight offered by other companies, upon equal terms. The other provides that no member of the Brotherhood shall assist in enabling the company by which he is employed to perform this duty, thus required by law, in any case where the company offering the freight is one with which the Brotherhood is at issue.

Such an issue arose between the Brotherhood and the Toledo, Ann Arbor and North Michigan Railway. Thereupon, four engineers of the Lake Shore and Michigan Southern Railway Co., ordered to move trains which contained cars destined for the Ann Arbor Company, simply quit the employ of the Lake Shore.

The United States Court pronounced this action not unlawful A fifth engineer did not quit the service of the company, but simply refused to move his engine until the Ann Arbor Company's

---

Reprinted by permission from The Independent of June 1, 1893.

cars should be withdrawn from the train to which it was attached. As the Lake Shore Company was already under an order from the court, directing it to make no difference between the Ann Arbor Company's cars and those of other companies, and this order was known to the engineer, the court held him guilty of contempt, and imposed a fine upon him, declaring that, while the men remained in the service of the company, they should assist the company to perform its whole duty as required by law, but holding, also, that they were free at any time to quit the company's service.

This was the first issue decided, and was decided by Judge Ricks, of the District Court.

A larger issue arose from the action of the Grand Master of the Brotherhood of Locomotive Engineers in issuing an order to all the engineers upon the Lake Shore road to refuse to move trains which might contain freight destined for, or received from, the Ann Arbor lines.

An Act of Congress, which has been in force for many years, provides that, if two or more persons shall conspire to induce a breach of any law of the United States, they shall be deemed as conspirators, and may be punished.

The Circuit Court of the United States, whose jurisdiction is superior to the District Court, and which was, in this instance, presided over by Judge Taft, held that the action of the Brotherhood in directing its chief engineer to issue such an order, and his action in issuing it, was a conspiracy under the statute above quoted, and peremptorily required the Grand Master to revoke the order, on peril of contempt.

In each case the action of the court seems to have been plainly such as was required by the law. Therefore, the question of the propriety of the court's action is really a question of the propriety of the statute.

The legislation in the United States differs apparently, in this regard, from that of England, the final result of which seems to be that it shall not be unlawful for two or more persons to act together in doing that which it would not be unlawful in them to do, acting separately.

It will be seen, however, that the right of the individual to quit the company's employ at pleasure is not drawn in question by either of these courts. On the contrary, it is expressly held inviolate by the District Court. It is obvious, however, that situations are always present in daily life where the right to forsake an employment at pleasure cannot be freely exercised. A nurse, for example, cannot abandon her employment while in charge of an infant on the highway, and the situation of an engineer in charge of the motive-power of the train upon a railroad highway may sometimes be much the same.

The real question, however, is that involved in the conflict between the rule of the Brotherhood and the conspiracy laws of the

United States. It brings squarely up a question between the claim of organized labor to assert its collective power, and the public need that the railroad shall be operated freely at all times in the service of the public.

If this were simply, or even mainly, a question between the Brotherhood and the railroad companies, it might safely be left to its logical outcome of united action by the companies against the united action of labor, and to the conservatism natural to interests so large as would then be involved. The difficulty is that this leaves the unoffending public to be chief sufferer, as it has been, in all the struggles and contentions which must necessarily precede this equilibrium. The public, as has been seen, has already taken action, and, through the courts, it requires that the engineer do his whole duty, or quit, and inhibits collective action taken with a view to disabling the railroad as a public servant. Probably the best relief lies in the direction of time contracts, prohibiting alike the men from forsaking their engines and the company from discharging them, except on a few days' notice; but any such contract involves the question of "involuntary servitude" which, by a clause of the United States Constitution is prohibited "throughout the United States, and in all places subject to their jurisdiction."

In an article in the current issue of *The North American Review*, Mr. Sargent, Grand Master of the Brotherhood of Locomotive Firemen, insists that any such obligation, if enforced by law, would be not only contrary to this constitutional provision, but also in effect would weld the man to the machine and make him a helpless slave. The obvious reply is that human law deals only with extremes of human conduct and the precept against involuntary servitude, and every such law, has to be enforced with due regard to other laws and necessary situations. The case of the nurse, above cited, the soldier under arms, are familiar illustrations; others are supplied by every situation in life.

I am told that Mr. Arthur, of the Brotherhood of Locomotive Engineers, has said that if you take away the privilege of the boycott from organized labor its fight against capital will be futile. If by this statement he means that engineers shall be free to compel railroad companies to boycott the railroads of other companies, it may be said in reply that the peremptory question here is not the success or failure of organized labor, but the indispensable protection of the public.

It has been said in some quarters that this disagreement between the railroad and its engineers will lead to and hasten the Government ownership of the railroads. I do not share in that opinion, because it is easily possible for the public to protect its commerce, as has been done already by legislative enactment. I do not think the Government will resort to the larger measure when the smaller is sufficient. The question whether the Government will ever own and run the railroads is too large to be answered here. The present tendency of all industrial affairs is to larger and larger organization. Under the Government is the final and comprehensive organization; but I am no prophet, nor the son of a prophet. It is quite as much as I can do to comprehend in a faint way what is going on today without predicting what will occur tomorrow.

The case of Lennon, the engineer, who was adjudged guilty of contempt in refusing to obey the orders of the court in regard to handling Toledo, Ann Arbor and Northern Michigan cars, is now before the Supreme Court of the United States. Lennon was sent to jail for contempt. An application was made to the circuit court at Toledo for his release on a writ of *habeas corpus*, which was denied. An appeal was then taken to the United States Supreme Court. It is not probable that the motion made to advance the case will be decided at this term of the court. The case will then go over to the October term.

The questions certified to the Supreme Court for its decision are the following questions of jurisdiction presented by Lennon's petition, filed at Toledo:

"*First*. Is the suit in which the order is made against Lennon one arising under the Constitution or laws of the United States?

"*Second*. Did the court have jurisdiction of the person of the petitioner by reason of his having had sufficient notice of the proceedings and order in the Ann Arbor case, set out in the petition?

"*Third*. Was it beyond the jurisdiction of a court of equity to issue the orders made in the case?"

In connection with this question of the attitude of the law toward strikes and strikers, it may be interesting to recall the great Missouri Pacific strike in 1886.

The Missouri Pacific Railway, including leased and operated lines, comprised four thousand five hundred miles, extending from the Mississippi river at St. Louis and at Hannibal, Mo., northward to Omaha, Neb.; southward across Arkansas to Texarkana, and across Indian Territory to Fort Worth; and, with various central ramifications, westward in two or three directions from St. Joseph and Kansas City into southern and western Kansas.

At ten o'clock in the morning of March 6th, 1886, at a preconcerted signal, given by steam whistle or otherwise, at points along the line, the yardmen, trackmen, and the men in the shops and freight-houses of the entire system quit work.

They not only simultaneously ceased to work, but also seized the company's shops, engine-houses, freight depots and yards, proclaiming that no freight should be moved until terms were made with themselves. They enforced this position by removing from great numbers of engines indispensible pieces connected with each cylinder, "killing" the engine, as they term it, and by threats and violence intimidating and disabling substitutes employed by the company. The movement of freight they entirely prohibited The movement of passengers and mails they allowed to go on in a disturbed and limited way.

The men who did this numbered about three thousand seven hundred, out of a total of about thirteen thousand four hundred employes of all classes at that time in the company's service. The remaining employes, engineers, firemen, conductors and trainmen generally took no part in the movement. They not only rendered to the company such service as its circumstances allowed it to require, but from time to time, by formal resolution, expressed their disapproval of the strike.

It may be fairly said, indeed it cannot be fairly said otherwise, that but for acts of violence done by the strikers to the property of the company and to persons who attempted to go to work in its employ, the mere quitting of work by yard and shop men to the extent of one-fourth of the whole number of employes would not have broken up commercial traffic even for a day, though it would have delayed repairs and put the company to inconvenience and expense. Complete resumption of business would have come so much earlier as to make the inconvenience to the public comparatively trifling. As it was, the resumption was gradual.

The direct loss to the employes of the company in wages, was estimated by the general superintendent at one million dollars. The greater part of this fell upon those who took no part in the movement, who, being paid by the mile or for the work actually done, lost money by failure of employment. The direct loss to the same company the same officer in his testimony computes at twice the sum above mentioned.

The direct loss to the communities affected—a large portion of the citizens of Missouri, Kansas, Arkansas and Texas—is beyond approximate statement. Individual estimates in great numbers compute the actual loss of business at an average of perhaps one-third of the whole, while the many references to the bright business outlook before the strike contrast almost mournfully with the uniform statements of the loss of credit and confidence caused by it. Public expense was, moreover, enhanced by large necessities for police and by an increase of crime.

The employes who were examined on that point say they quit work simply because of an order which they obeyed. This order was given by Martin Irons, a machinist of Sedalia, Mo., who was not at that time in the company's employ.

The testimony of Irons showed that four days before, he had issued a like order addressed to the employes of the Texas Pacific Railway Company, then in the hands of receivers appointed by the circuit court of the United States. This order had resulted in a stoppage of freight traffic on that railway; and it conclusively appears that the order addressed to employes on the Missouri Pacific was conceived and executed solely as a means of enforcing concessions on the Texas Pacific through an assumed connection of the two which, in fact, did not exist. It appears also that Irons was Master Workman of District Assembly No. 101, of the Knights of Labor, a secret organization, and that it was in this connection that the orders above mentioned were issued and obeyed. Control of the situation was a few days later asserted openly by the chiefs of this organization, and their testimony and appearance abundantly identified the organization itself with the inception and management of these labor troubles, as also with their results.

I summarize some suggestions I made at the time in reference to this strike:

The most instructive exposition of what has been done, and perhaps also of what may be done, in one direction to inhibit strikes is found in Stephen's "History of the Criminal Law," Volume III, pages 202 to 207, in which is reviewed in the history of English legislation and jurisprudence on that subject from the passage of the statute or statutes (for there were two) of laborers, enacted in 1349 and 1350, to the Conspiracy of Protection Act of 1875, in which last it is provided:

First. That an agreement or combination by two or more persons to do or to procure to be done any act in contemplation or furtherance of a trade dispute between employers and workmen, shall not be indictable as a conspiracy, if such act committed by one person would not be punishable as a crime; that is, an offense for which a man may be imprisoned.

Second. That every person who, with a view to compel any other person to abstain from doing or to do any act which such person has a legal authority to do, uses violence to or intimidates such persons, follows him about, hides his tools, watches or besets his house, or follows him through the streets in a disorderly way, shall be liable to three months' hard labor.

Third. That every one who willfully and maliciously breaks a contract to work under a person who is to supply gas or water, or any contract of hiring or service, when he knows or ought to know that such breach of contract is likely to endanger life, cause serious bodily injury, or expose valuable property to destruction or serious injury shall be liable to three months' imprisonment.

This net result of more than five hundred years of judicial and legislative experience in England suggests, first, that it is probably not practicable in this country to make punishable by law agreements simultaneously to quit work when there is no violation of a previous agreement to continue working.

Next, that where the public service and convenience are involved with the maintenance of an agreement to continue working so that the consequences of a breach of that agreement will fall primarily and principally on the public, it is in such a case in harmony with precedents that rest on long experience and are found consonant with English liberty, which is the same as ours, to declare that the willful inflicting of this result on the public shall be deemed an offense against the public and punishable as a crime.

The practical application of this would be an enactment that the employe of a company engaged in interstate commerce, who had made a contract terminable only upon say one week's or ten days' notice, should, upon willfully breaking that contract, be deemed guilty of a misdemeanor. If this were done and if, on the other hand, the company were required to employ their men upon contracts of that character and forbidden to discharge except upon such notice, one practical step at least would have been taken toward the avoidance of such results. Of course this does not mean that an insubordinate or unsatisfactory employe should be continued at his post, but only that unless for flagrant cause discharge should be either on reasonable notice in advance or else accompanied by payment of wages for such period as the notice required by law would cover. Something like this has been for a long time in England the law of domestic service.

The effect of such a system of time contracts upon the liability of a common carrier for failure to receive and carry persons and property upon demand is also worthy of attention. It is obvious that in every instance of a strike there arises a multitude of instances in which the carrier is liable for damage for such refusal, or for delay or damage, unless the plea of interruption by the strike can be successfully interposed.

In the one case known to me in which this question has been tested, the case of the People *vs.* the New York Central and Hudson River R. R. Co., 28 Hun. 544, decided January, 1883, it was held that under the circumstances in that case, which was a combined refusal of freight handlers to work for less than a given price, the defense was insufficient. But it was intimated by the court that if it had been shown that the strike of the New York Central laborers had been caused or compelled by some illegal combination or organized body which held unlawful control of their action, and which sought through them to enforce its will upon the company, and that the company had used all the means in its power to employ other men in sufficient numbers to do the work, a very different case for the exercise of the discretion of the court would have been presented.

In other words, the question whether or not the company was pecuniarily responsible to individual sufferers by the interruption of commerce, was held, as seems obviously just, to be simply a question of whether the company had made all proper efforts to carry on its business.

If it were made plain in such cases, as would be the result of such a law, that the company had reasonable notice that the men would quit work at such a time if their demands were not complied with, and was therefore without excuse and was liable for damages for all persons and goods delayed or injured; and if the companies furthermore were restricted from discharging a man except upon a week or ten days' notice, and from filling the places of men who quit or were discharged except with men whom the company was willing to keep in its employ, or at least to pay wages to, for some such length of time; this apparently would furnish a good and sufficient counterpart for any disadvantage to the employes from a statute making it a misdemeanor to quit work before the expiration of their contracts.

In other words, if common carriers engaged in interstate commerce and their employes were forbidden by law, the one to discharge and the other to quit, except upon notice given by one to the other a reasonable time in advance, no one could be materially prejudiced, while a salutary check would be imposed upon both against those evils which the commerce of the country has experienced. The company, if it received notice from a great number of its employes at once that they proposed to quit would refuse no reasonable demand for fear of liability in case of failure to forward goods and persons as required by its duty to the public; the men, on the other hand, would shrink from any unreasonable demand, as that would stimulate the company to extraordinary efforts to supply their places within the time that must elapse before they would be free to quit.

Add to this an amendment of Revised Statute, No. 5,519, giving to persons and carriers employed in commerce among the states the same protection which that section was originally meant to give to civil rights, and in the same way enlarge the statute with reference to obstructing or hindering mails, so that it shall protect also interstate commerce equally with the mails; then commerce and mails will be alike secure—crime only will be under increased penalties, while neither carriers, nor their employes, will have yielded of their liberties anything beyond the power to break off without penalty from a contract freely made where the public good is involved with its performance.

New York City.

SERVICE OF A BUREAU OF RAILWAY STATISTICS AND ACCOUNTS IN THE SOLUTION OF THE RAILWAY QUESTION.

By *Prof. Henry C. Adams,*

Statistician Interstate Commerce Commission.

A rapid survey of the history of internal communication in the United States shows that four distinct views have been held respecting the relation of public highways to government. Previous to 1830, it was commonly accepted as the proper function of the Federal government to supply the public with turnpikes and canals, the only important public work undertaken by a state prior to this time being the Erie canal. With 1830, however, the sentiment of the country entirely changed. The constitutional right of Congress to build and manage public highways within the boundaries of the sovereign states was questioned. The veto by President Jackson of the Maysville road bill transferred the center of activity from the Federal government to the several states, and from 1830 to 1850 the question of internal improvements brought state governments prominently into view. I need not speak of the financial disasters which resulted from this endeavor on the part of the states to build railways and canals. Suffice it to say that by 1850 public sentiment experienced another radical change, and the people of the states adopted numerous amendments to their constitutions which forbade the use of public credit for commercial purposes. At present there are a large number of provisions of this sort in the state constitutions.

The third phase of public opinion, which may be said to have been entered upon by 1850, regarded private corporations as the proper organizations for building and controlling railways. It will be remembered that at this time the extreme ideas of English political economy respecting the narrow functions of government were quite prevalent, and it is no occasion for surprise to notice that when ownership and control of railways was handed over to private corporations, the governments of the several states did not

---

Paper read at National Convention of Railroad Commissioners held at Washington, D. C., April, 1893.

consider it necessary to retain any voice in their management. It was believed that competition would work with regard to this industry in a normal and satisfactory manner, and that consequently there was no necessity for government to provide for the exercise of any control or supervision.

This sentiment prevailed until about 1870, when it was found, especially in certain of the western states, that an irresponsible administration of the transportation industry had led to many evils of which the public might justly make complaint. Finding no redress at the hands of railway managers, appeal was made to the sovereign power of the states, resulting in the passage of those laws known as the "Granger Laws," which asserted the right of public control over internal commerce. This brings us to the fourth phase of public sentiment referred to. I do not, of course, mean to say that no laws attempting to regulate railway business existed previous to 1870; but rather that the sentiment favoring regulation was not, prior to this time sufficiently strong to be regarded as the prevailing sentiment of the country.

The necessity for regulation being established, the question respecting the proper method of regulation came to be one of importance. Without rehearsing the various opinions upon this point, it may be said that the country at the present time seems to have accepted the idea that the railway problem is to be solved through the medium of railway commissions.

I have called your attention to these changes in public sentiment for the purpose of impressing the fact that the control of railways through commissions is an experiment rather than an established policy. As sentiment has changed in the past, so it may change in the future. The people of this country do not grant their support for any considerable length of time to an idea which fails to justify itself when put on trial, and it may be well for the members of this convention, representing as they do the various railway commissions of the United States, to hold in mind the fact that unless their work is aggressive in character and decidedly beneficial in result the support of public sentiment will sooner or later be withdrawn. It is therefore pertinent to inquire if every means which the law places at the disposal of railway commissioners is now being used for the solution of the railway problem. It is of the utmost importance that a political experiment when once undertaken should be thoroughly tried, in order that, should it prove unsuccessful, it need not be recurred to again in the future. There is no other guarantee that change will be progress.

Without entering into a general discussion of the efficiency of commissions when compared with the powers bestowed by legislatures, I desire to call attention to one instrument of control which the law has placed in their hands, of which adequate use is not made. I refer to the power bestowed on every railway commission in this country to secure statistical returns from railway

SERVICES OF A BUREAU OF RAILWAY STATISTICS. 131

corporations over which they have jurisdiction. The control of railway corporations through the medium of a bureau of railway statistics and accounts may seem at first an idea which none but a pedant would entertain; but I am sure you will grant me your candid attention while presenting a few considerations in its support.

The railway problem is capable of quite a number of definitions, according as it is regarded from a technical or from a general point of view. I shall confine my consideration for the present to the definition of the problem implied in the laws creating the various commissions. It is true that legislative enactments do not contain any formal definition; they do, however, if we consider the acts by which these laws are declared to be illegal, clearly indicate the nature of the railway problem as it lay in the minds of those who framed the laws. From this point of view, we may say the railway problem consists in securing to all shippers equality of opportunity in the use of railway facilities at just and reasonable rates. Our question, therefore, resolves itself to this: How can a bureau of statistics and accounts aid the commissions in establishing and maintaining equality of opportunity and just rates in the use of railway facilities? In endeavoring to answer this question, I shall confine myself to three points: First, the enforcement of the law against discrimination. Second, the determination of just rates; and third, the maintenance of stable rates. If I can show that a strict control over railway accounts is necessary in order to do away with discriminations and to provide for just and stable rates, it must certainly be admitted that a bureau of railway statistics and accounts is an essential part of the machinery by which the commission idea is to be realized.

HOW MAY A BUREAU OF STATISTICS AND ACCOUNTS ASSIST IN THE ENFORCEMENT OF LAWS AGAINST DISCRIMINATION?

Laws which declare certain things illegal are of two sorts—those which rely upon police power to insure compliance with their requirements, and those which are so adjusted to the prejudices and interests of the persons whom they concern that they are self-executory in character. A factory law, or a law which provides for safety in mines, is of the first class; a law which provides for the enforcement of commercial contracts by legal procedure, belongs to the second class. The distinction is that in the first class the interests at stake are of a general character, and the persons whom the law directly affects are not immediately interested in its enforcement; whereas in the second class, the guarantee that the law will be enforced is found in the direct and personal interests of the parties concerned. One can not determine from reading the various acts creating railway commissions to which class of laws these acts belong. Holding in mind the strong commissions, like those of Illinois and Iowa, rather than commissions which are supervisory in character, like those of Michigan and Massachusetts, commissioners may render opinions in cases presented to them, or they may themselves originate cases; they may act as an administrative court, or they may exercise visitorial powers and assume the functions of a prosecutory agency. The character of the laws in this regard is determined by the policy which commissioners see fit to adopt in their execution.

Now, it is no secret that under present conditions it is exceedingly difficult for the shipper whose rights are invaded by a railway corporation to secure quick and speedy relief; and on that account shippers conceive their interests to depend upon the good will of railway managers rather than upon commissions or courts, and consequently refuse to bring their cases, with all the evidence necessary to secure conviction, to the attention of commissioners. Under such circumstances, a sufficient number of cases do not arise spontaneously to enable commissioners to exercise a controlling influence over the administration of railway affairs, and the result is, they feel themselves obliged to undertake the enforcement of the laws by the exercise of visitorial functions, or by the direct instigation of cases. It is not necessary to discuss the wisdom of this policy. It is adopted as a temporary expedient, and, I doubt not, with the expectation that the necessity for it will, sooner or later, pass away. The real purpose of commissioners must certainly be to sit as a tribunal (I will not say court), deciding cases which are presented to them, rather than to seek out cases in which the law is disregarded.

The question, then, naturally arises, what can be done to create those legal and commercial conditions under which this end may be attained. How may the railway laws of the United States be made self-executory in character? Under what conditions will shippers appeal to the commissions, bringing their evidence with them rather than suppressing evidence, use it as a lever to force special favors from railway managers? The establishment of such conditions is essential, in my opinion, to the solution of the railway problem by commissions, for it goes without saying, that a law against discrimination by common carriers cannot be enforced so long as both carriers and shippers are interested in the law's defeat.

I do not, of course, undertake to state all the conditions necessary for the self-enforcement of our railway laws, but I may call your attention to one step which must be taken for the realization of this end. In order that the law against discrimination in rates may be self-enforced there must be a uniformly organized and uniformly administered railway system. Managers cannot be allowed the liberty of adopting unusual methods of business, nor attorneys the right of urging before the commission peculiar policies of management, as defense for unusual methods. All orders pertaining to transportation must be clear, simple and easily un-

SERVICES OF A BUREAU OF RAILWAY STATISTICS. 133

derstood. Under these conditions shippers would come to know their rights, and in case their rights were disregarded by carriers, they would undertake to secure redress or to prove their claims for damages. Now the easiest way, indeed the only way, or at least the first step toward the way, by which uniformity of management may be secured is to establish uniformity in accounts and to take from railway officials the right of adjusting their accounts in an arbitrary manner. Accounts, if they be honest, are true records of administration, and he who controls accounts can, in a large measure, control the policy of management. Should the form of bookkeeping be determined by commissions, and all railways be obliged to adjust their accounts to uniform rules, the commissioners would be in a position to impose their ideas, in a very large measure, upon the management of the roads. And what is more important, they would be in a position to secure evidence against a carrier guilty of discrimination more easily than at the present time. And more than this, uniformity in accounts and strict supervision over them provides a new way of testing the compliance of the carriers with the rules of the commissioners. Statistics properly used and adequately guided are the surest means of detecting any general departure from established rules of management, and, if commissions must continue visitorial functions, will indicate where it is worth while to undertake special investigation.

It is unnecessary to develop this thought further, for by these suggestions you will at once see how far it goes. The railway laws in this country are not, at present, self-executory in character, because of the difficulty of securing evidence against discrimination. And this, in a large measure, is due to the numberless and complex methods by which railways do their business. My claim is that, in order to enforce a law which makes discrimination illegal, it will be necessary to crystalize the railways of the country into a common system so far as principles of control are concerned, and to oblige them to follow uniform rules in business management. This, it is believed, can be the most easily accomplished through the agency of a well equipped and well directed statistical bureau, which shall impose upon the railways a uniform system of accounts. In many of our states it is not necessary that additional power shall be asked from the legislators, for the Interstate Commerce Commission, as also eleven state commissions already have the right to determine the form in which railway accounts shall be kept. The propriety of enforcing these provisions is a question properly debatable by this convention.

HOW MAY JUST RATES BE DETERMINED?

It is not too much to say that the kernel of the railway problem lies in the establishment of a policy for determining rates that shall be generally accepted as based on justice and reason. This is implied in the laws so far as they touch the question. To this end the Interstate Commerce Commission and seventeen state commissions are clothed with the power of adjusting rates. If the commission idea finally breaks down, it will be because commissions are unable to deal with this vexed question.

At present they are not in a position to deal with the question, for there is no generally accepted theory respecting the basis of railway rates, and consequently, there can be no uniformity in their decisions. It is doubtless the consciousness of this fact which makes commissioners so reluctant to exercise the power of adjusting rates in those cases where the law grants them that power, and which makes the legislators, in those states where the rate-making power is not granted to commissioners, hesitate in conferring the grant. Commissioners are in no position at present to judge clearly with regard to the respective claims of shippers, stockholders, and the public, for they have no facts to work upon at all adequate to the magnitude of the problem. If there be any generally accepted theory it is that rates should bear some relation to cost of service. But commissioners are in possession of no information respecting the cost of service that is of the slightest assistance in the application of this theory. It is, however, absurd to speak of determining a just price with regard to any commodity whatever without having first determined the conditions of production. For the purpose of avoiding an extended discussion of the theory of rate-making rather than because I conceive my views to be of especial importance, I may perhaps be permitted to suggest what, in my opinion, is a practicable policy for the adjustment of railway charges.

The rule that specific railway rates should be determined by specific cost of service, appears to me to be wholly untenable, and the practice of charging "what the traffic will bear," as applied by railway managers, to be incapable of defense. Provided, however, it be applied in such a manner as to assign total of cost of carrying traffic to the various classes of freight carried, and not to the determination of a rate which will secure the largest aggregate income, I see no reason why it cannot be accepted as a safe rule for commissions to follow. The process of rate-making, according to this idea, would be as follows: Determine, in the first place, the income which a railway corporation actually needs. Determine, in the second place, the business which rightly belongs to the corporation by virtue of its relation to the source and destination of freight. In the third place, classify all freight according to a uniform classification. The process of rate-making would then be to adjust rates to the various classes of freight in such a manner that the required gross income may be secured to the company and the burden of payment rest as lightly as possible on the customers of the railways. The principles which lie at the basis of just railway schedules arise from a study of the theory of taxation.

As in taxation payment for the support of government should be in proportion to the ability of citizens, so the contributions of shippers to the fund necessary to meet the legitimate demands of railways should be made from various classes of goods in proportion to their ability to bear the charges. If this theory of rate-making be accepted, or indeed any theory which regards the problem from the standpoint of public interest, the determination of rates comes to be a purely statistical problem, or at least, a problem that calls for decisions that can only be given on the fullest and completest information as to facts. Railway commissioners do not have at their command the range of facts which are the common property of railway managers. How, then, is it possible for commissioners to exercise a controlling voice in railway management, or indeed to decide justly and wisely on such questions as are presented to them?

Should this general view of the case be accepted, the next step in the further development of statistical work lies very clearly before us. It consists in perfecting a uniform classification of freight throughout the country and in securing from railways a statement of the amount of freight carried in each class and of the amount of revenue which each class of freight yields. Such an investigation, if carried on so as to permit territorial localization of freight by classes, would place the commissioners in a position to judge what industrial, or, indeed, social results, would follow from changing any special schedule of a particular railway.

It is considerations such as these, and many others that might be mentioned along the same line, which lead me to assert that no commission can safely undertake the adjustment of railway rates except upon the basis of a thorough and somewhat extended statistical investigation. A just rate does not mean a rate which a particular shipper can pay for particular goods, but rather a rate which, when enforced and maintained, entails in a community just and commendable results. The question involved in this controversy is not simply commercial in character, it is at the same time a question of public policy, and as such, like all questions of a political character, demands the fullest and completest knowledge respecting it. A statistical bureau is not an ornamental decoration. It is an essential part of the machinery for the control of railways.

If the commission idea is to retain the confidence of the public, it is, in my opinion, essential that the commissioners recognize the service which a bureau of statistics and accounts may render them in the performance of their duties, and for legislatures to grant such appropriations as are necessary for the development and extension of statistical work. We cannot evade the conclusion that the public has no guarantee that rates will be just and reasonable, whether made by commissioners or by the managers of railways, except they be made after a full investigation into the conditions under which the service is rendered.

136 SERVICES OF A BUREAU OF RAILWAY STATISTICS.

HOW MAY RATES BE MAINTAINED?

It is recognized that rates must be stable as well as just and reasonable The question therefore forces itself upon us, under what conditions may stable rates be secured? The remarks which have previously been made respecting discrimination in rates apply equally well to this question, for rates are rendered unstable through discrimination; and commissioners may regard it wise to postpone a direct consideration of the means by which stability of schedules may be maintained until it is observed whether or not fluctuations in rates will continue after discrimination between shippers and places is done away with. I should not, however, make a complete statement of the service of a bureau of statistics and accounts in the solution of the railway problem were I not to say that in all probability something more will be required to secure stablity of schedules than the elimination of personal discrimination from railway practice. There are many who believe that stable rates cannot be secured so long as railways are prohibited from entering into legal agreements respecting the conditions under which their business shall be managed. It is asserted that the railway industry from its very nature tends toward consolidation; that concentration of power is inevitable; and that the only question for the public to consider is how to use this power for the public good. In railway consolidation there is at least the possibility of cheaper and better service, and providing that they who control it are held to strict responsibility, there is no reason why it should be feared by the public. This, of course, means that great reliance must be placed upon the principle of publicity, for there is no other way by which trustees of a public power may be held to account.

In working out for my own satisfaction the conditions under which pooling might be safely permitted to railways, the fact which has been most forcibly impressed upon me is that no traffic agreements could last for any considerable length of time, except under the application of what is technically known as the principle of territorialization. The strongest argument for this conclusion is found in the outline maps for competitive roads, published by Rand, McNally & Co. When, for example, the Michigan Central Railroad is permitted to compete for freight between New York and New Orleans; of what avail would it be for the roads to which that freight naturally belongs to enter into an agreement as to the manner in which it shall be divided? No pooling contracts could possibly be stable while such conditions existed. Pooling means the limitation of competition, or what amounts to the same thing, an agreement respecting the conditions under which competition shall take place. The first step, therefore, toward the establishment of stable rates through the legalization of pools would be a scientific classification of railways by which each company may know what freight it can legitimately carry. This is doubtless an extension of public authority beyond any which has thus far been contemplated by our laws, but there is no other way of bringing the matter under control so as to adequately guard the public interest. It follows, therefore, that if pooling be forced upon government by the continual wars of railways the government must establish and support well-equipped statistical bureaus; for it is inconceivable that a scientific classification of railways can be made and maintained, except upon the basis of careful and exhaustive statistical investigation.

It seems, then, whether we consider the question of railway discrimination, of just and reasonable rates, or of stability in rates, that a bureau designed especially for investigation and for imposing upon the railways uniform methods of management is essential to the realization of the commission idea. This has not been adequately recognized in the past, and it rests very largely with the members of this convention, whether it shall be recognized in the future.

I have presented the above considerations favoring maintenance and development of the statistical branch of the service of railway commissions, holding in mind the definition of the railway problem as implied in the laws creating the commission. But this definition is not as broad as the problem itself, and I see no reason why commissioners are not justified in taking the most comprehensive view of their office and in administering it in such a manner that incidental, as well as general, benefits may be secured therefrom to the public.

Looking at the matter in the light of history, railways, as administered, have destroyed the conditions under which the principle of competition can work for the great rank and file of business in a normal and satisfactory manner. In theory, competition is the central principle of our industrial structure. Both legislators and courts assume it to be present in the great majority of cases, and because of their confidence in its potency they deny the pertinency of socialistic arguments. In fact, however, competition has degenerated into a struggle for existence between great corporations, or a struggle for special favors at the hand of great corporations, or it has ceased to exist altogether. In this lies the explanation of most of the industrial complications which perplex the nineteenth century. According to the common law of industries, competition is potent; but, in reality, competition is rendered impotent by the arbitrary manner in which railway managers administer their trusts. If this be true, and that it finds adequate support in the history of the nineteenth century lies beyond reasonable controversy, the railway problem comes to be a problem of civilization. It is a question of keeping open the avenues of opportunity. There is involved in its solution the broad question of industrial liberty, and the technicalities of railway legislation take upon themselves a new meaning when one considers the true character and the industrial influence of railway transportation. As equality before the law is a canon of political liberty, so equality before the railways is a canon of industrial liberty. A solution of the railway problem means the reintroduction of those conditions under which competition can control industrial forces and deal justly as between industrial agents.

Such considerations as the above are pertinent at the present time when the question of granting increased power to railway commissions is before the public. It would be impossible for a Bureau of Railway Statistics and Accounts to perform the service which has been assigned to it, except it be clothed with ample authority and provided with adequate facilities. Without doubt the railway corporations would assert that in the exercise of its functions such a bureau would be inquisitorial and encroach upon the established rights of privacy. But if it be clearly apprehended that the question of industrial liberty is involved, that the freedom of opportunity which our common law asserts to be the right of every citizen is jeopardized by the manner in which railways do, as a matter of fact, manage their affairs, there comes to be a reason for the extension of powers which commissioners demand from legislators. One thing certainly is clear—in an industry which touches at every point the life and the prospects of all citizens, there ought to be no question respecting the right of government to make the fullest and completest investigation.

ENGLISH AND AMERICAN RAILWAYS—A COMPARISON AND A CONTRAST.

Mr. W. M. Acworth, of England.

I am asked to institute a comparison between English and American railways in their leading features; and so far as limits of space permit I will endeavor to do so. The first point of difference which strikes one is the vastly greater attention paid to railway questions with you than with us. "Whatever can you find in railways to write about; it is such a dull subject," has been remarked to the present writer times without number. Various causes are accountable for this neglect. Journalistic ignorance of the subject, which makes newspaper men shy of dealing with questions of which they know their own profound ignorance, may be put down as either effect or cause. Another reason is to be found in the fact that politics with us are more generally interesting than with you. You have more than forty legislative assemblies, and they all do the bulk of their business in committee rooms. We have but one Parliament; it does the bulk of its talking in public, and the whole nation listens. Then the political subjects of discussion take a wider range; the army, the navy, foreign policy, are all with us subjects of the utmost importance. It is these professions accordingly, the army, the navy, diplomacy and political life, which absorb the bulk of our ablest men—at least of those who can afford to choose their own careers. Our conspicuous men are, first and foremost, politicians, then soldiers and sailors, lawyers and diplomatists, leading divines, *litterateurs,* or actors—anything rather than the heads of the railway service. Probably there are few Americans who could not give the name of the president of the Pennsylvania Railroad or of the New York Central; it is questionable whether one Englishman in fifty could say who is the chairman of the Northwestern or the Great Western.

Then again, our railway politics are much less exciting than yours, because they are so much more stable. The London and Northwestern ranked as the premier English company twenty years before America had ever heard of either Scott or Vanderbilt. It remains the premier company to-day, and is likely to

---

Reprinted by permission from The Independent of October 6, 1892.

remain so till the New Zealander comes to England to sketch the ruins of St. Paul's. Within a dozen years the New York Central dividend has fallen from 8 per cent, to nothing, and recovered again almost to its former point; but within the memory of the present generation the Northwestern dividend has only varied between the narrow limits of 6 and 7½ per cent. As for the preference stocks and debentures of our leading English railways they are probably among the safest investments in the world. A man can buy them to-day and put away his certificates in a safe, with entire confidence that they will be worth to his grandchild fifty years hence all that they are worth to him to-day. Our leading companies raise millions of fresh capital every year; they might raise ten fold as much without reducing the price at which they can place their securities. That price is a fraction under 3 per cent for debentures, a fraction over for preferences, and somewhere between 3½ and 4 per cent for ordinary stocks. The normal dividend, for example, of the Northwestern may be taken as just about 7 per cent, and the normal price somewhere between 170 and 180.

The railways of America do not owe much to Government aid; but the railways of England and Scotland owe to it absolutely nothing. In Ireland the state has given or lent a few millions to railway companies, with results which cannot be claimed as over satisfactory. But, if our government has not helped, at least it has controlled from the very outset. No railway can be made without an act of Parliament; for it is with us a fundamental principle that no authority short of Parliament itself can condemn private property for public uses. Before sanctioning such an expropriation Parliament inquires with great minuteness into the leading features of the proposed undertaking. Plans of every yard of land to be taken, with the name of every owner and occupier upon it, a list of the promoters, with the exact amount of capital required, and the form in which it is to be raised, are laid before Parliament and receive its formal sanction. To an outside inquirer it might seem strange to learn that, tho' minute details have to be given of the span of a bridge or the depth of a cutting, stations are completely ignored, and the railway company is left free either to omit them altogether or to construct them where and in what form it pleases. The explanatiom, as of most English anomalies, is an historical one; being found in the fact that the Parliamentary regulations were laid down in days when the original theory that a railway was a road on to which each passenger or each carrier would drive out of his own private yard at whatever point seemed good to him, had not been proved to be practically unworkable. One further function of Parliament in connection with new railway undertakings must not be forgotten, and that is the fixing of a maximum scale of rates and fares. Hitherto this scale has been copied, in the main unchanged, from acts passed

ENGLISH AND AMERICAN RAILWAYS.

possibly half a century old, and consequently has been entirely out of touch with the facts of modern commercial life. But the maximum scales of all the existing railways have within the last two years undergone a thorough revision by Parliament, and henceforward, both for old lines and for newly projected ones, the maximum will act as a real limitation on any attempt to impose excessive rates.

In addition to the initial restraints imposed by Parliament, there is also the control of a special department of the executive government, the Board of Trade. A long series of statutes, the earliest of which is the railway regulation act of 1840, has conferred upon the Board of Trade a large number of disconnected but important powers. No line can be opened for public traffic till a Board of Trade inspector has certified that its viaducts and bridges, the masonry of its tunnels and the ballasting of its permanent way, the construction of its stations with their elaborate machinery of interlocking and block signalling, the pattern of its engines and rolling stock, all have reached what might be called an almost ideal standard of safety. Then again, each year the Board of Trade must be furnished with statistics, almost as exhaustive, tho' drawn up in a form far less practically useful than those which are called for by your Interstate Commerce Commission, giving particulars of capital and dividend, of operating expenses and traffic receipts, of mileage maintained and train-mile earnings. Returns are also called for of the working of safety appliances, such as block signals and continuous brakes. Every accident involving injury, however trifling, either to passenger or employe, must be reported forthwith, and in serious cases an investigation is immediately conducted on the spot by a Board of Trade official. Up to the year 1889, the Board of Trade had no power to order—it could and did recommend, and public opinion usually enforced its recommendations—the introduction of new safety appliances on lines whose opening it had already sanctioned. In that year public opinion was excited by an accident in which eighty persons lost their lives, and the Board of Trade was hastily armed with compulsory powers. Like all public departments, in this country at least, it has executed these powers not with discretion applied to each individual case but by general orders, and has, broadly speaking, prescribed for lines in remote rural districts with four or six trains a day the same standard of working that is in force, and rightly in force, on the main through routes of the country. If an American reader will imagine the accident in the tunnel outside the Grand Central Station in New York last year made a pretext for legislation compelling the Missouri Pacific to adopt over its entire system the latest devices of the Hall or the Union Switch and Signal Companies, he will have a notion of what a government department is doing for us in England at the present moment. As far as can be seen, new railways in poor districts will only be constructed in future by millionaire philanthropists.

In addition to Parliament and the Board of Trade, we have also the control of the courts of justice. Your Interstate Commerce Commission was largely modeled on our railway commission, which has existed, tho' with some change of form, since 1873; and the undue preference clause of your act to regulate commerce is copied almost verbatim from an English act passed as long ago as 1854. It is, of course, impossible to summarize the decisions which are collected in the fourteen volumes of English Railway Law Reports; but two points may just be glanced at. Personal discriminations have been so sternly dealt with, that, tho' they never were of much account here, seldom apparently amounting to more than 2 or 3 per cent of the total rate, of late years they have—so at least it is believed—absolutely and entirely disappeared. In dealing with alleged undue preferences as between competing trades and competing localities, the tendency of our courts has always been to have regard to the interests of the individuals before them rather than of the public at large for whom no counsel appeared. For if a rate has been decided in any case to create an undue preference as between two competing interests, our English companies have always been careful to redress the inequality not by leveling down but by leveling up, and so the average of charge to the public has been increased. It should be added, however, that quite recently the broader economic side of these questions has not been without weight in the decisions of the courts. Within the last few weeks, for instance, the endeavor of the Corn Trade Association, of Liverpool, to crush the competition of the Severn ports in the markets of the Birmingham district, has been successfully and apparently finally repulsed.

But Parliament, the Board of Trade, and the law courts, all put together, have not at the present moment as great a share in the control of English railways as has public opinion. It has been profoundly remarked that, in a country whose government is organized on a democratic basis, nothing does its work as well in practice as an institution which is entirely indefensible in theory. For it is only on condition of the practical excellence of its work, and so long as that excellence continues, that such an institution is suffered to survive. Now railways as private undertakings may not be actually indefensible in theory, but unquestionably they are opposed to the absorbing and centralizing tendencies of the modern state. This may be the reason why our English companies have done so much of late in the direction of disarming opposition. We hear a great deal, for example, of state pensions for the aged; but while the politicians and the philanthropists have been talking, more than one of our great companies has practically organized an adequate superannuation for every man in its employ. Again the state has imposed on lines having termini in London an obligation to run certain trains for workmen before eight in the morning or after six in the evening at fares averaging perhaps something like half a cent per mile. The obligatory mileage amounts to forty-seven miles per diem; but in 1883 the distance actually being run at these fares was 763 miles, while in 1890 it had increased to no less than 1,807 miles. Again, under the pressure of public opinion, an immense deal has been done to diminish the risks of railway employment. Very large sums of money have been spent with this object, in, for instance, widening tunnels and bridges to afford safe room for trackmen, and installing electric light in switching yards. It may be said that the published returns show but scant results of this solicitude; to which the answer is obvious that, if the death rate has been even kept stationary—and in truth matters are better than this—in view of the greater density of traffic and the constantly higher pressure at which the work is done, this alone would imply very considerable improvement. In nothing has the pressure of public opinion produced a greater effect than in relation to the hours of railway labor. There are still too many cases of overwork and indefensibly long hours, especially on small and semi-bankrupt lines; but the evil is nothing in comparison to what it was a few years back and, in fact, always had been since the beginning of railways. Of overwork of engine men and brakemen, such as is recorded in the latest returns of the United States Labor Bureau, where men, if I mistake not, are reported as on duty frequently for more than twenty-four hours on end, it would be impossible, I am persuaded, to find any instances in this country. For all that, now that the sore is practically healed, it is more than likely that our new Parliament will apply a carefully concocted legislative plaster to it.

To pass to another subject. How do our railway companies treat their customers? And first, of passengers. Passengers traffic may be judged from three points of view—speed, accommodation, fares. Let us say a word about each. In speed, an Englishman must reluctantly acknowledge that the United States holds the record with the Empire State Express. What is more, you seem likely to continue to hold it; for your speeds are rapidly rising, while our management is growing faint-hearted—it might not be patriotic to add feeble-minded—and is talking not of improvements and accelerations but of reductions in speed and retrenchments of service. But it is still possible to hope that this retrograde movement will end in talk. Meanwhile, we can still record with satisfaction that of fast and very fast trains—of all but the very fastest—we have many more than has the United States. Four years back Messrs. Farrer and Foxwell drew up a list of 672 trains running a total distance of 63,000 miles per diem in Great Britain at a speed of not less than forty miles an hour including stops. It is quite certain that no such figures could be produced in America. As to accommodation, there has been a good deal of loose talk by partisans on both sides. An impartial summary would, perhaps, run something like this. English third-class carriages on the best lines are more comfortable for a long journey than American ordinary cars. The absence of lavatory accommodation is an evil which on long-distance express trains is rapidly righting itself, partly by the extravagant system of attaching a lavatory to each compartment, partly by building what are known as corridor carriages with lavatories at either end. In fact, signs are not wanting that for long-distance express service corridor carriages will develop into corridor trains. American drawing-room cars are far from popular here. England is an island, and the average Englishman takes after his country, and likes to be as far as possible insulated from his neighbors. He is told his compartment is "lonesome and stuffy." He replies that solitude is what he wants, and that he obviates the stuffiness by letting down the window and sitting in a draft. It may be bad taste; but there is the fact. Dining-cars, however, are very popular, and their use is steadily extending. Sleeping-cars, also, have taken firm hold; once more, however, not open from end to end like your Pullman, but divided into sections, in each of which there is often only one passenger, and very rarely indeed more than two. As for fares, your statistics set down the average rate paid as something over two cents. The best estimate that can be made for this country would put the average at about 1.80 cents. As I have said, I believe our third-class carriages—comparing like with like, the Pennsylvania with the Northwestern or the New York and New Haven with the Lancashire and Yorkshire—are fully as comfortable as the ordinary American cars. It is, therefore, quite fair to compare our average charge for what we call third-class accommodation with your average charge, tho' it be for what you call first-class. It should, in fairness, be added, that our extra charge for the use of first-class carriages, which may be said to correspond to your drawing-room cars, is very much higher than with you. Our excess rates from third to first, say between Philadelphia and New York, would be nearly two dollars in many instances, as against half a dollar actually charged on the "Congressional Limited." But then with us it is practically always possible to travel third-class on every train—so that our fare from Philadelphia to New York would be $1.80 instead of $2.50—and for long distances, at least, nineteen people out of twenty do in fact so travel. Those who pay the difference can mostly well afford to do so.

It is difficult enough to compare the passenger traffic of the two countries. To compare the goods traffic is practically impossible. Half a dozen years back Professor Hadley wrote as follows:

"Any attempt at comparison of freight charges would be long, technical and unsatisfactory. On high-class freight it is altogether impossible, because the English rates for such goods include collection and delivery. No one can tell how much we should allow for cartage, or whether we should take American freight rates or express rates as our standard of comparison. An extremely rough estimate, not making allowance for any of the disadvantages to which

ENGLISH AND AMERICAN RAILWAYS. 145

English railroads are subject, would indicate that their charges per ton mile on all traffic average from 50 to 75 per cent higher than ours."

Where Professor Hadley confesses himself beaten, it would be rash for any other man to look for success. But this much perhaps may be said. On paper your average rate is less than one cent; our average is probably—there are no precise figures in existence—about 2½ cents, but your average haul being 127 miles, and ours certainly not more than a fifth of this distance, evidently our terminal expenses work out to more than five times as much per mile as yours. Then a large proportion of our rates include cartage and delivery; and cartage even of rough goods, in New York, costs I find, anywhere from one to two dollars per ton—a pretty heavy addition to the railway rates. Further, and the point is of primary importance, our goods traffic is essentially retail, worked in small lots at high speed and very frequent intervals, yours is essentially wholesale, worked in full train loads, at such speeds and at such intervals as the railway companies find most economical to themselves. If I may use again a metaphor which I have used before, a man pays one dollar for his dinner on condition of taking his meal with the rest and eating what his hotel provides at the ordinary hours; but it will cost him ten dollars if he goes to Delmonico and orders each dish to be cooked and served separately at his own time.

A point of more general interest is, I think, the question of railway competition. There are those who say that competition has practically ceased in England, because competing companies always enter identical rates in their rate books, and, what is more, exact those rates without discount or rebate. Certain it is that rate cutting has been practically put an end to by an understanding between the companies, which, like international law, has no sanction behind it except the agreement of the high contracting parties. Two years back there was a rate war, the first for twenty years; but it was confined to two small coal lines in Wales and it never brought the rate below something like .9 of a cent per mile, which to American readers would probably seem a stiffish rate for coal even in the most peaceful times. Over a considerable part of England the traffic is pooled; in some cases, as for instance at Hastings and Tunbridge Wells between the Southeastern and the Brighton Companies, or at Ramsgate and Dover between the Southeastern and the London, Chatham and Dover, by special statutory enactment. There are, however, numerous other pools, as, for instance, between the Brighton and Southwestern Companies for traffic to Portsmouth and the Isle of Wight; between the Great Western and the Northwestern for traffic to Wales and Ireland; between the Northwestern and the Lancashire and Yorkshire for traffic in the Liverpool and Manchester district, which are merely matters of private agreement, entirely unknown to the public at large. Some of these pools are subject to revision every ten years. Others are believed to be agreements in perpetuity; but in this latter case they are perhaps more of the nature of partititions of territory than traffic pools. There is only one agreement with which I am acquainted, that, namely, between the Southeastern and the Brighton Company in relation to the Eastbourne traffic, under which one company pays another a percentage of its receipts as an inducement to that other to refrain altogether from competition. The amount paid under this agreement is at present about £24,000 per annum. In this case, except so far as potential competition has a tendency to prevent the existing service (which is by the Brighton Company) falling below a certain minimum standard of excellence, the public appears to gain nothing, as the alternative service is thereby excluded. Such an arrangement is accordingly by no means popular, and as little is said about it by the companies concerned as possible.

But to pools properly so-called there does not seem to be any popular objection. Indeed, within the last year the two great Scotch companies, the North British and the Caledonian, have agreed to a twenty-five years' pool of their traffic; and tho' there was a good deal of opposition in Glasgow when it was first announced, within the last few weeks the Glasgow traders have confessed that they were mistaken and that none of the ills which they have anticipated have arisen. It may be, of course, that they congratulate themselves prematurely. But the fact is, the public see what looks like competition going on all around them. As traders they see the canvassers of the different companies coming to them, hat in hand, and begging for traffic, promising a later departure, more careful handling, and more prompt delivery; it may be, more generous settlement of claims. As passengers, they see the companies vying with one another in improvements in accommodation, in frequency of service, or in increased speed, as well as in a score of details which make up the comfort of passenger travel. Accordingly, when the theorist comes along with his assurance that competition is extinct, and that pools have done the mischief, they are apt to shrug their shoulders and take not much notice.

As for the financial success of English railways, this alone need be said: We have got in the British Isles 20,000 miles of line, which have cost us £900,000,000, or, say £45,000 per mile. For something more than twice the money, the United States has got more than eight times the length of track. Of course, to compare an average mile of your line with an average mile of ours would be almost as absurd as to reckon a mile of corduroy road in a Maine forest as the equivalent of a mile of Broadway. But for all that, it is evident that to pay 4 per cent interest on £45,000—and 4 per cent is what our roads do pay on an average of the total capital—a mile of line in this country had need, even at our high rate, to carry a good deal of traffic. And so, in fact, it does; for while your lines only earn some $6,000 per mile, ours earn, well over $20,000. Of this sum moreover, operating expenses only absorb some 54 per cent as against over 66 per cent with you. Within the last year or two, however, owing to various causes, of which enhanced cost of material, Board of Trade safety requirements, and higher wages and shorter hours of employes are the the chief, working expenses have increased out of all proportion to the increase of receipts. So far, our railway companies have not seen their way to any corresponding economies in methods of working, such as those which have so justly made American railway management a pattern for the civilized world. An Englishman, however, with faith in the future of his country cannot but believe that, once English railway officials have realized that the increase in expenses has come to stay, they will rise to the occasion, and consider the possibility of reforms other than the somewhat elementary ones of increasing charges and simultaneously retrenching facilities. Otherwise the outlook both for the English public and for English shareholders is but a poor one.

London, England.

HIGH SPEED RAILROAD TRAVEL.

By *Mr. Theodore Voorhees,*

General Superintendent, New York Central and Hudson River Railroad.

Time is money. The man of today learns this lesson early and keeps it ever before him. He gets the utmost out of every hour. This is carried to such an extent that it has become the ruling characteristic of our people. We must have go; energy, push; we must live at express speed, under constant high pressure, or we are not satisfied.

In no way is this feeling more plainly shown than in the steady demand for high speed in railroad travel. Trains that a few years ago were regarded as models of fast service are now voted slow, and are shunned by those who have to take long journeys. The distances to be overcome in this country are very great. Our business men think nothing of them. Time is getting to be more and more valuable. The telegraph and more recently the telephone have brought the most distant points almost within speaking distance one with another; so that there is a constant effort being made to reduce the time occupied in transit from city to city.

Only about ten years ago the usual time occupied in a journey between New York and Chicago was thirty-six hours. The trains stopped at regular intervals for meals, and the public was reasonably satisfied with the service. Soon some roads began running a train in either direction that only obliged the traveler to be one night in a sleeping car. Next was introduced the dining-car service; and now we have trains running regularly over the distance inside of twenty-five hours, or twenty-four hours apparent time.

Still the public is impatient for faster service, and projects are now on foot looking forward to a further considerable reduction in this time. It is confidently expected that during the season of the World's Fair, in 1893, it will be possible for a traveler to leave New York in the afternoon, after the day's business is completed, and be at Chicago the following morning in season for the opening of business hours.

Nor is this demand for high speed confined to long-distance

Reprinted by permission from The Independent of October 6, 1892.

travel. There is a constant pressure brought to bear on the railroad manager to increase the speed of trains, and so decrease the time between suburban points and different cities. The commuter measures his distance not by miles but by minutes; and if an established train, for any reason, has its time lengthened three or four minutes, there is an immediate protest and a demand that the time be restored or cut short.

There is constantly put before the railroad manager of America the example of what is being accomplished in England; and it must be confessed that until very recently the comparison has been considerably to the disadvantage of the American railroad. There are several reasons that can be advanced to account for this. The ideal railroad would be perfectly straight and level; with a roadbed and track heavy, substantial and thoroughly drained; with no grade crossings or openings to invite trespassers; with bridges whose floors should be as solid as the roadbed itself; and with stations so planned that no passenger could ever set foot upon the track. English railroads from the beginning have had this ideal in view, and the construction has been of a far more permanent and substantial character than has been possible in the case of railroads built in this country. The English law has been most severe in its requirements as to construction before any road has been permitted to be operated. American railroads, on the other hand, have been too often merely thrown upon the ground, so that some sort of operation might be made possible with the least outlay of capital, and the actual work of construction left to the future as the earnings of the line might provide the necessary funds. The result is, that with comparatively few exceptions, our railroads today compare unfavorably with those of England in respect to solidity of roadbed. In England, also, there is almost an entire freedom from grade crossings, and the roadbeds are so thoroughly fenced and policed that there is little or no danger of accidents occurring by reason of trespassers on the track. It is only within a few years past that there has been any attempt at all in this country to produce a similar condition. Grade crossings are the rule, and instead of being abolished, are being constantly added to in all parts of the country. Public opinion has not yet reached that point with us that the abolition of grade crossings is looked upon with favor by those whose personal interests may be affected. So far from our railroads being thoroughly fenced or policed, on the contrary they are in many cases openly used as a highway between adjacent places where the public highway may not be quite so convenient in point of distance. Public authorities pay little or no attention to this, nor will they assist in any effort that may be made on the part of railroad managers to put a stop to the evil. The result is, that all manner of persons are constantly walking on railroad tracks, and casualties are frequent. In some few cases efforts have been made in this country to absolutely prevent persons from walking on or across railroad tracks. One would suppose that this effort on the part of the railroad companies would meet with the approval, at least, of those persons whose safety was the object. On the contrary, every effort of this nature on the part of railroad managers is met with strong opposition and public protest from those persons for whose safety the fences, etc., are designed. Underground passages or overhead bridges, constructed to enable the public to avoid the necessity of walking on the track, are absolutely unused, and passengers insist on risking their lives to save half a minute rather than step a few feet above or below the rails and walk in safety.

An examination of the schedules published by the railroads of England and Scotland shows a large number of daily trains whose speed exceeds forty miles an hour, and very many where a speed of over fifty miles per hour is attained. Between Liverpool and Manchester, on one road there are seventeen express trains in each direction running at a rate faster than forty miles per hour, while several cover the distance, thirty-four miles, in forty minutes. Between London and Grantham on the Great Northern Railway there are upward of twenty express trains daily in each direction. The fastest use but one hundred and seventeen minutes for the one hundred and five miles. Between London and Leicester, ninety-nine miles, via the Midland, the express service gives thirteen trains each way daily, the fastest of which takes but one hour and fifty-five minutes for the trip, while on the same line the express train time between London and Liverpool, two hundred and twenty miles is five hours. Between Edinburgh and Carlisle, on the Caledonian Railway, a fraction over one hundred miles is traversed daily in exactly two hours by the fastest train, while several other trains make the time at better than forty miles per hour. This list might be lengthened indefinitely, but enough has been given to show that the express service in all parts of England and Scotland at a rate of forty miles per hour is common, while trains at the rate of fifty miles per hour, or even more, are by no means infrequent. The most noticeable thing about this train service to an American railroad man is the appearance of the locomotives and the weight of the trains. The majority of express trains in Great Britain are drawn by locomotives having but a single pair of large driving wheels. These are frequently seven feet in diameter, some are seven feet six inches, and occasionally one sees an engine with driving wheels having a diameter of eight feet. These large wheels cover a considerable distance at each revolution and so attain excellent results with comparatively low piston speed. But this is at the expense of power; so we are not surprised to find that the trains drawn by these engines are very light, and carry but a small number of passengers. The average weight of the trains mentioned above is one hundred and thirty-five tons. This would be about equivalent to a train in this country consisting of a baggage car and four ordinary passenger cars, or to a train of three Pullman sleeping cars.

There are some places in this country where our service will compare favorably with the best English practice. Between New York and Philadelphia, eighty-nine miles, by the Philadelphia and Reading route, there are twelve trains each way daily that make the run inside of two hours. One does the distance in one hundred and eight minutes. By the Pennsylvania Railroad equal time is made between the same places. Between Baltimore and Washington, via the Baltimore & Ohio Railroad, there are sixteen trains each way daily that pass over the forty miles inside of an hour, and several that make the run in forty-five minutes. On the Pennsylvania Railroad, with slightly greater distance from station to station, there are an equal number of trains making equally as good time.

The time of all the express trains between New York and Boston by the several different routes has been until quite recently six hours and thirty minutes. This has been reduced during this past season, on one or two trains in either direction, to five hours and forty minutes. This is about forty-one miles per hour for the distance. This is the regular rate of speed of the "Limited" trains running between New York and Chicago, both on the Pennsylvania Railroad and the New York Central & Hudson River Railroad. In comparing this service with that of the English roads mentioned above, the weight of the train load in this country should be kept in mind. The average weight of one of our limited trains, exclusive of the locomotive and tender, is upward of two hundred tons; while very many trains weighing over four hundred tons are met with in this country whose speed equals that given above.

On the New York Central & Hudson River Railroad between Syracuse and Rochester, eighty-one miles, there are a number of daily trains that make the run in either direction inside of two hours, and one that covers the distance, including one stop, in eighty-seven minutes. This last is the Empire State Express, that runs from New York to Buffalo, four hundred and forty miles in eight hours and forty minutes. Allowing for stops, this is at the rate of fifty-two miles an hour. Taking into account the distance, this is the fastest regular train scheduled by any railroad in the world. It weighs one hundred and thirty tons, makes the scheduled time with regularity, and can take on an additional passenger car or Wagner car and still make time with ease.

The tendency of the present time in this country is undoubtedly toward higher speed in all classes of train service. The public demands it and is willing to pay for it. The railroads must provide it.

The railroads in all directions are working towards this end. Very large expenditures are being made today in improving the alignment and permanent way of our railroads. New and heavier rails are being laid, bridges are being re-enforced and renewed in anticipation of heavier locomotives, improved power brakes are being introduced, and highly complicated and expensive signaling apparatus is being built with a view to insuring the safety of our trains. In a word, everything is being done to promote the safe and rapid movement of passengers. But no expenditures of the railroad companies alone, no matter how great, will result in the perfect railroad on which the highest speed may be attained. The co-operation of the communities through which the railroad passes and of the general public must be secured to achieve the best possible results.

Existing grade crossings must be abolished, not simply guarded by a watchman and a flimsy gate, and the opening of new crossings in the future rendered impossible by law. The writer recently traveled on a regular passenger train twenty-five miles in twenty-five minutes. About midway in this distance a town was passed through which there was one frequently used grade crossing. The engineer "slowed down" to a rate of forty miles an hour going over this crossing. The preceding miles had been passed over in from fifty-three to fifty-seven seconds each. It took four miles before the train recovered the speed it had been making prior to the "slow down," and a full minute was lost by reason of it; or, in other words, at least one mile was added to the length of that trip by reason of that grade crossing. The case of a passenger train discharging passengers at a station on the opposite side of the main track is still worse. In this case an approaching train is obliged for safety to come to a full stop. To a train scheduled at high speed such a stop means a delay of five minutes, or equivalent to five miles added to the length of the trip.

Imperfect as our roads still are as compared with the English, such is the skill and ingenuity of our locomotive builders that we are today able to equal the best achievements of English railroads in point of speed. Let public opinion once be aroused to the importance of the matter, so that the authorities will co-operate with the railroads in abolishing grade crossings and properly protecting stations and platforms, and we will have in this country railroads whose performances in respect to speed and safety shall be models for the whole world. Then we will no longer regard sixty miles an hour as phenomenal, for one hundred miles in an hour will be no more unusual than sixty miles are now. Then the New Yorker will leave home after breakfast, go to Boston or Washington, transact his business, and return home in time to dine with the same ease and comfort as the similar trip is made today to Albany and back.

New York-City.

THE RELATIONS BETWEEN CANADIAN AND AMERICAN RAILWAYS.

By Mr. A. C. Raymond.

Of Detroit, Mich.

When I was very courteously invited to read a paper before this convention there was no hint given me of the special field I was expected to glean, hence the few sheaves I may chance to bring you will doubtless be gathered somewhat at haphazard, and from the general surface of the relations between American and Canadian railways. The present discussion of this subject arises naturally and logically from the enactment of the interstate commerce act, without which the present aspect of the situation could not have existed. The plausible pretext is, that as American railways are now, at least *prima facie*, regulated in their operations by law, their Canadian competitors for American traffic should submit to the same regulations This is the favorite statement of those opposed to Canadian lines, and outwardly appears without a flaw, but beneath its fair seeming surface lurk numerous fallacies which need to be pointed out.

A brief retrospect of the condition of things which led up to the enactment of the Interstate Commerce act may not here be out of place. No single factor in our national progress during the last half century has been so potent, as the development of our system of transportation. Millions of acres of our fertile domain are today pouring their vast perennial treasures into the laps of our seaboard cities, from a distance of one thousand and two thousand miles, with greater ease and at a larger remuneration to the producer, than if those lands had been situated within two hundred miles of the same cities less than a century ago. Early in the fourth decade of this century a newspaper in Albany, N. Y., announced as the crowning result of our transportation system, that certain articles of merchandise could be transported between that city and Cincinnati at the unparalled and unheard of low rate of $2.40 per 100 lbs. Today our railroads carry the same merchandise between the same cities for one-tenth of that price per 100

Address delivered before the Traffic Convention held at Sault Ste. Marie, Mich., August 28, 1889.

lbs., and in one-fourth the time. For trading purposes with the seaboard, the city of Cincinnati, and all interior sections of our country at an equivalent distance, are more than ten times as valuable as they were fifty short years ago.

That rate of $2.40 per 100 pounds between Cincinnati and Albany was indeed a marvel of cheapness, when we recall that less than ten years previously the famous Conestoga wagon system in Pennsylvania was furnishing cheap transportation between Philadelphia and Pittsburg at $2.87½ per 100 pounds, and a six days' journey. These statements sound like ancient history to the present generation, and yet thousands of men touching elbows with us today can readily recall the pack saddle, the freight wagon, and the stage coach eras. In those days, as in these, transportation managers deplored competition, denounced interference with their systems, and resisted all attempts to initiate newer, better and cheaper ones. Projectors of the early railroads met little sympathy, but plenty of derision from the advocates of other systems, until a reluctant confession was finally wrung from them, that railroads might within certain limited areas become of some value in moving merchandise, but the passenger traffic would never depart from the safety, comfort and speed of the stage coach and the canal boat. The possibilities in the development of railroad traffic were first perceived on anything approaching a broad basis about the year 1850. In 1853 the famous New York Central system began to crystalize, the Erie Railroad was completed to Dunkirk, and the foundation of the Pennsylvania system was laid by a completion of a line from Philadelphia to Pittsburg, and the Grand Trunk system had its American beginnings by leasing a line from Portland, running northwesterly through Maine and New Hampshire. Massachusetts awoke to the interests of Boston by fostering the Boston and Albany R. R., and pushing other feeders into Vermont and New Hampshire. Up to this time the jealousy between the seaboard states was severe and oft-times bitter, in the efforts to hold traffic for their respective seaport cities. It was next to impossible to obtain a charter for a railroad to cross the territory of one state, if it diverted traffic to the seaport of a rival state. However, as I have stated, in the beginning of the fifth decade a broader national conception of railroad transportation was born.

Early rates were naturally based upon those which prevailed under the ruder and far more expensive systems, and profits were enormous. One short line between Utica and Schenectady, in New York, during fourteen years reimbursed its shareholders for its entire cost, besides paying annual dividends of 18½ per cent. Railroad building now progressed at a rapid rate, and the bases of great fortunes were speedily laid. Towns, cities, states, and finally the United States assumed enormous financial burdens for the development of railroads.

The wealth and power of the railway interests speedily developed the inevitable arrogance, favoritism and corruption, which tainted the state legislatures, the courts, and even the halls of Congress. The fair and equitable and common law right of the public to equal and impartial treatment by the corporate servants of its own creation, was scouted and denied; state jurisdiction over traffic which crossed its border was denied, and the Supreme Court of the United States sustained, in the famous Wabash case, this contention. The effect of this decision was to intensify the reckless indifference of the great railroad corporations to their obligations to the public. The fortunes of men and localities were subject to the capricious or malicious purposes of railway managers. Railway wrecking had become a fine art, construction companies a short cut to millionairedom, while cut rates, secret rebates, live stock eveners, pooling combinations, the shameless dishonesty of railway dealings among themselves as well as with the public, were current events. Uncle Sam's puny railroad baby had, in a few short years, become a lusty giant, who threatened to dominate the entire household. The remainder of Uncle Sam's family demurred to the situation, and are now attempting to somewhat restrain and regulate the giant by the Interstate Commerce Law.

When bluff and honest Senator Reagan, of Texas, introduced the first interstate measure in the House, in 1878 and 1879, he was met with contemptuous ridicule by the railroads, and quiet incredulity by the people. His dogged and unyielding determination, however, culminated in the appointment of a joint committee, which evolved the present law.

Railroad opposition was severe and unremitting during the time the bill was under consideration, and Senator Cullom was repeatedly told, as the chief objection to it, that he could not frame his bill so as to bring Canadian competitive lines within its provisions. Senator Cullom gave patient heed to this objection, and I believe I violate no confidence when I state, that he visited the city of New York, obtained the services of eminent and sagacious counsel, and so framed the first section of the act as to bring rigidly within the scope of the law all competitive interstate and international traffic of the Canadian roads. No American railroad attorney has yet been able to point out a flaw in this feature of the first section of the act, and no witness, before the Senate committee during its recent tour, has even attempted to do so. Yet we are daily told by reckless newspapers, and it is steadily reechoed by equally reckless and ignorant persons, that Canadian railroads are not subject to the interstate law. Let me read this section of the act:

"*Be it enacted by the Senate and House of Representatives of the United States of America, in Congress assembled:* That the provisions of this act shall apply to any common carrier or carriers engaged in the transportati · of passengers or property, wholly by railroad or partly by railroad and partly by water when both are used under a common control, management or arrangement, for a continuous carriage or shipment from one state or territory of the United States or the District of Columbia, to any other state or territory of the United States or the District of Columbia, *or from any place in the United States to an adjacent foreign country, or from any place in the United States through a foreign country,* to any other place in the United States, and also to the transportation in like manner of property shipped *from any place in the United States to a foreign country, and carried from such place to a port of transshipment, or shipped from a foreign country to any place in the United States,* and carried to such place from a point of entry, either in the United States *or an adjacent foreign country.* Provided, however, that the provisions of this act shall not apply to the transportation of passengers or property, or to the receiving, delivering, storage or handling of property wholly within one state, *and not shipped to or from a foreign country,* from or to any state or territory as aforesaid."

Every subsequent section of the law is subject to and controlled by this first section, which describes and brings within every provision of the entire law, as it was designed to do, every possible kind of American traffic in which a Canadian road can engage. What folly, then, for respectable railroad counsel, leading newspapers and other prejudiced parties, to claim that Canadian railroads are exempt from the provisions of the law. In a recent case brought before the Interstate Commerce Commission, this point was raised under circumstances which, if ever, would justify the claim of exemption. The Grand Trunk road was carrying coal at a local rate from Buffalo to local points in Canada and allowed a rebate from the published tariff rates to Canadian buyers; no American road participated in the traffic, neither was the traffic competitive with any American railroad. No American shipper of or dealer in coal was prejudiced or affected in any way by the rebate, except favorably, by making a larger demand for American coal. The only American territory crossed by the traffic, was included between the Grand Trunk freight station in Buffalo and the center of the International Bridge crossing the Niagara river. Nevertheless, the commission held that even this traffic was subject to the act, and that the rebates were unlawful. The Grand Trunk gracefully acquiesced in this ruling, and at once withdrew all rebates. This decision settles once for all, that every provision of the act is to be strictly construed against Canadian roads. It does not, however, and will not, prevent competitive American interests, through their organs and their agents, from serenely and unceasingly reiterating the unfounded assertion of exemption.

Some one may ask what is the secret spring and moving cause of the present agitation for additional restrictive legislation against Canadian lines. It certainly has not been asked for by the masses of the people, the great body of producers and consumers, for they are well aware of the invaluable regulative influence of the Canadian lines in establishing reasonable rates of freight. If the manager of a great American railway system like the Vanderbilt or Pennsylvania, desired to cripple or destroy a powerful Canadian competitor, and by false and misleading statements and claims, could induce Congress to assist in the work, the measures which set on foot the present agitation, might perhaps be adopted.

Such a movement may be legitimate and proper from the standpoint of a railroad struggle for business, and as between American and Canadian railroads or other institutions from the political point of view, my patriotism would compel me to unhesitatingly support the American. When, however, as in the present case, political relations are merely a mask to hide a great wrong upon the people, by restricting or prohibiting desirable competition, that same patriotism forces me to the defense of the people, even through the means of alien agencies. The competitive struggle between American and Canadian railroads is not a new one. It has raged with exceeding bitterness for many years, and to the enormous advantage of the people. It had its beginnings in New England under the following circumstances, which were related to me only two months ago in the city of Boston, by one of the most prominent manufacturers of boots and shoes in New England:

In the days when the avenue for Boston trade with the West was confined to what is now the Boston and Albany R. R., freight rates were so high that Boston was in imminent danger of losing her boot and shoe trade. Certain lines of goods were charged $1.50 per 100 pounds to Chicago. The merchants united in strong remonstrances to the railroad company, but to no avail. A certain railroad man suggested that perhaps the Grand Trunk of Canada could be induced to form a through line to Chicago in conjunction with certain connecting roads. The merchants sent him to Montreal. After several days of negotiations he returned with a proposition that, if the shoe trade would give its entire business to the Grand Trunk for one year, that corporation would carry it to Chicago for 50 cents per 100 pounds. Such an agreement was quickly drawn and signed, and the new line established. The Boston and Albany immediately lowered its rate from $1.50 to 30 cents per 100 pounds, but the shippers gave it no traffic, but manfully and honestly fulfilled their contract with the Grand Trunk. The merchants and manufacturers have never forgotten this act of the Grand Trunk, and every business man in Boston will fight to the bitter end every scheme to unfairly prejudice or injure it.

In 1875 the city of Chicago was suffering from a great diversion of trade to western and southwestern points, under the pooling system of the American trunk lines, then in vogue. This diversion assumed such proportions as to call for the appointment of a committee of her ablest merchants to investigate, and suggest a remedy. In 1876 the committee made its report, and suggested as the most feasible remedy that the Grand Trunk be urged to extend its system from Port Huron to Chicago. In 1880 this extension was completed, and from that hour to this, Chicago merchants have been practically a unit in asserting and insisting upon the necessity of the competition afforded by this road, as a check upon the American trunk lines. The bold and uncompromising position taken by them before the Senate committee a few weeks ago, astonished the committee, who were evidently unprepared for any such demonstration. No later than last Wednesday (August 21st) Judge Cooley himself is reported in a Chicago newspaper interview to have said: "The attitude of the Chicago Board of Trade in its defense of the Canadian low rates is a surprise to me, in view of the fact that these Canadian low rates are mainly instrumental in building up northwestern towns like Minneapolis, St. Paul and Duluth, to the detriment of Chicago." It is unquestionably true that the Canadian Pacific or Soo route is diverting, and will in an increasing ratio continue to divert a large amount of traffic of certain kinds from Chicago to the northwest, and Judge Cooley's surprise is all the more a tribute to the broad intelligence and sagacious judgment of the ablest and most energetic merchants of this country, which teach them to look below the surface of the matter and detect the far greater danger to their city's commercial supremacy which would follow the prohibition or serious crippling of Canadian competition. If the newspaper reports Judge Cooley correctly, I must in turn confess my surprise at some of his additional statements, in view of the important and quasi-judicial position he occupies. He says: "Canadian competition hurts the railways of this country, and anything tending to damage them must also affect Chicago, which is so largely made by them." "If," he says, "the railways of this country do not make shippers as low a rate as Canadian roads, I think it is because they cannot, and it will only make matters worse to encourage Canadian trade that will hurt them still more. American roads will make the best rate they can, and it is to Chicago's interest to meet them half way." Can it be that Judge Cooley has become oblivious to the fact that the American public is a larger consideration than American railways; that low rates for American traffic are more important to the enormous commercial and manufacturing interests of large areas of our country from New England to the Pacific slope, than that fat dividends should be earned by American railroads? If it is true, which I deny, that oui roads cannot give as low rates as their Canadian competitors, it is a humiliating and disgraceful confession, and calls for an immediate scaling down to an honest basis, of the two and one-half billions of watered and fictitious capital which H. W. Poor, the great railroad statistician says, is represented in American railway plant.

Can it be that Judge Cooley forgets that the people erected the great tribunal of which he is the head, for the express purpose of securing their rights against railway encroachment; that the prohibition of pooling and the long and short haul clause in the act were expressly designed to produce the most open and unrestricted competition and low rates, and secure their benefits to the public? The field of commercial enterprise is necessarily less familiar to Judge Cooley than to Chicago merchants. They know from experience and training, as he does not, that the commercial interests of their city do not depend upon the destruction of its northwestern rivals, but will thrive with their development.

This question assumes a still broader aspect when tested by the provisions of the Constitution of the United States. The 6th subdivision of section 9th, article 1, of that instrument, says: "No preference shall be given by any regulation of commerce or revenue to the ports of one state over those of another." The Interstate Commerce law is the first important legislation by Congress to regulate commerce between the states, and the mere suggestion that the port of Chicago should favor its amendment to the disadvantage of the port of Duluth, the port of Sault Ste. Marie, or any other port, in direct violation of the Constitution of the United States, sounds strangely enough from the head of the Interstate Commerce Commission. I would fain believe that the reporter misstated the remarks of our honored fellow citizen and judge.

It is urged that American railways have ample capacity for carrying all the American traffic, and the larger portion of this country never has had, and never will have occasion to use Canadian lines of transportation, which are consequently of little or no real value outside of certain areas along our northeastern, northern and norwestern borders. A proper apprehension of the basis on which through rates of freight are made in this country, will destroy this claim once for all.

A standard or unit freight rate is first established between Chicago and New York. All the stations which take through rates, which practically includes the whole of them, lying north of the Ohio and east of the Mississippi rivers, are divided into groups by imaginary lines drawn north and south. All the stations in each group take the same specified percentage of the Chicago or unit rate. The through or seaboard rates for all points along and east of the Missouri and west of the Mississippi rivers, are make by adding the local rate to Chicago, to the standard or unit rate from Chicago. When lake navigation is closed the competition of Canadian railways is the most potent factor in influencing the establishment by American railways of a reasonable standard or unit rate from Chicago. Thus it is that practically the entire through traffic of the country, whether actually passing over Canadian routes or not, receives an absolute and direct benefit from Canadian competition.

The agitation against Canadian railroads publicly began February 10th, 1888, when General J. H. Wilson, of Wilmington, Del., appeared before the Senate Committee on Interstate Commerce at Washington with a long tirade against these foreign corporations.

Gen. Wilson was a famous and successful cavalry officer in the war of the rebellion, and commanded the troops which captured Jeff. Davis and Senator Reagan, then Postmaster-General of the Confederacy. Gen. Wilson, after the war, became manager of a railroad in Indiana, and later the president of the New York and New England R. R., which, it is said, he handled with indifferent success. He then opened a broker's office in Wall street, which was closed by his financial failure. He next became the public champion of American railways as against Canadian, the financial outcome of which does not yet appear. March 16th, 1888, he repeated his attack upon Canadian railways before the House Committee on Commerce. The New York Sun then appeared as the newspaper organ of the agitation, printed Wilson's speeches in full, and has steadily pushed the fight from that date. The various merchants' organizations in Portland, Boston, Detroit, Chicago, Milwaukee, Minneapolis, St. Paul, Duluth and Peoria immediately adopted resolutions protesting against Wilson's scheme, which were hurried forward to their respective Senators and Representatives in Washington. Nevertheless, about the middle of April, Amos J. Cummins, member of Congress from Brooklyn, N. Y., and official correspondent of the New York Sun, introduced into the House of Representatives a set of resolutions calling for the prohibition of Canadian railroads from carrying American traffic. These resolutions were referred to the House Committee on Commerce, where they expired with the last session of Congress.

The subject next appeared in Congress in the guise of an amendment proposed by Senator Morgan, of Alabama, to the Senate tariff bill, to the effect of prohibiting the importation in bond through American ports, of merchandise designed for Canadian points. This was fortunately defeated by a majority of only one, on a strictly party vote. Congress next took notice of the subject by authorizing the Senate Committee on Commerce to make a tour of the country and investigate the relations of American and Canadian railways and waterways. This committee has visited New York, Boston, Detroit and Chicago, and will make a report to the next Congress. Every merchant or commercial representative who has appeared before this committee has entered his decided protest against any legislation tending to the prohibition or restriction of Canadian competition. The object of this convention is, I take it, to give added emphasis to these protests.

Eternal vigilance will doubtless be necessary if we shall retain these priceless competitive privileges.

There are seventy-six Senators and three hundred and twenty-five Representatives in Congress, exclusive of the four recently added states, comparatively few of whom are conversant with the details of this question, and the majority of whom represent constituencies remote from immediate contact with Canadian routes. With the deceptive cry of "protection to American railways against foreign rivals, built with foreign capital and subsidized by a foreign government," a powerful opposition to Canadian routes can easily be organized. The struggle has only begun, and before it is ended, the immense commercial interests dependent upon these routes, may need to make very vigorous efforts in their defense.

The Canadian Pacific railway, which is so closely allied with the hopes and prospects of this bustling, energetic city of Sault Ste. Marie, is the especial target of attack.

It is a great corporation, honestly built and efficiently and economically managed, by men who obtained their training in the service of the American railways, who combine Yankee push and and energy with English grit and solidarity. The enterprise has been conducted with the care and sagacity which would characterize a private business venture. No construction companies nor credit mobilers have been permitted to defraud its shareholders. It runs its own grain elevators, telegraph, express and sleeping car lines. It tenders to American producers and consumers, the resulting facilities of the most marvelous railroad undertaking of the age. The foreign capital invested in it is but a fraction of the foreign investments which help to swell the capital of American railways to the enormous total of upwards of nine billions of dollars.

The capital of some of the American railways is almost wholly owned abroad, notably that of the Illinois Central R. R., and there is no doubt but what the total amount of English, Dutch and German holdings in American railways would build several Canadian Pacific lines. The argument against this corporation on the basis of its foreign capital is utterly absurd and senseless. Equally senseless is the argument based on the subsidies from the Dominion Government. The actual amount of these is between ninety and one hundred millions, while the Union and Central Pacific lines will have received municipal and government subsidies by 1895, when its bonds are matured and paid, the enormous total of *more than four hundred and forty-seven millions of dollars.* These are official figures furnished by Mr. Patterson in his minority report, as a member of the Pacific railroad commission, rendered to Congress at its last session. As yet no one has had the hardihood to challenge the truth of these figures. From the proceeds and profits of this colossal deal, together with a heavy government subsidy, has since been constructed another transcontinental line, the Southern Pacific, the managers and owners of which rend the morning air with their shrieks and groans of poverty, as they point to their inability to compete with the dreadful, subsidized Canadian Pacific.

The comical aspect of the situation would provoke our laughter, did not a sense of our national disgrace flush our cheeks with shame.

The most reckless statements are made as to the amount of

subsidies paid over by the Dominion government; Mr. Joseph Nimmo, late statistician to the United States Treasury, placing the amount at from two hundred and fifteen to two hundred and twenty-five millions. Now, the gross federal debt of Canada at the close of 1887 was about two hundred and twenty-seven millions of dollars, all told, or but a little more than Mr. Nimmo's subsidy, while in 1881, the year in which the Canada Pacific was begun, the federal debt was upwards of one hundred and fifty-five millions. These figures tell their own story and characterize Mr. Nimmo's. Another bugbear is the annual subsidy of three hundred thousand dollars paid by the British and Canadian governments for the carriage of the mails from Halifax to Hong Kong. This is construed into a military menace of the United States. Much more then must the fact that the United States government pays more than twenty millions annually to American railways for the transportation of its mails, be construed as a military menace of Canada. The fact is that while subsidies are desirable as a means of swelling the profits of railroad projectors and builders, they are not depended upon as a measure of the ability of one road to compete with another. This is abundantly proven by the fact that three more transcontinental lines are already projected by American railway men, neither one of which asks or expects any material government aid. The argument is likewise untenable which is based on the advantage possessed by the Canadian roads under the long and short haul clause of the Interstate Commerce act, but time will not permit its consideration now.

Concealed behind all the specious arguments of the American railway interests, lies, in my opinion, a pre-concerted determination to have Congress legalize pooling, and leave the reasonableness of rates to the Interstate Commerce Commission to determine. Should this be accomplished, the regulative influence of Canadian lines in making rates reasonable, would cease to be of value, and except in certain localities like Detroit and Sault Ste Marie they would assume the position of poachers upon American traffic, while rendering no equivalent in return. Under such circumstances a demand for their expulsion from American territory would be much less easily met than now. The forces arrayed against us have unlimited command of resources, are powerful and subtle in their operations, and able to wage a long fight, which, if successful, means such enormous additions of revenue to the victors.

In 1866 the transportation, in bond, of American traffic across Canadian territory, was authorized by act of Congress. Based upon this act millions of dollars of American capital have been invested, not only in constructing connecting lines of railway, but in the countless industries and enterprises dependent upon them. This legislation ante-dates and is wholly independent of the fisheries question, which arises under the expiration of the Washington treaty, executed in 1871, and should not be confounded with it. For twenty-three years the government of the United States has maintained inviolate this privilege for the people, which it is now asked to yield to the already menacing predominance of American railways.

Happily public sentiment has not yet abdicted the reins of power in this country, and the people, if sufficiently informed and aroused, will still hold their own.

SOME CHARACTERISTICS OF THE AMERICAN RAILWAY SYSTEM.

Hon. Joseph Nimmo, Jr.

Excerpt from an argument delivered before the United States Senate Committee on Interstate Commerce.

The agreements and combinations whereby the American railroad system has become a great and beneficent possibility are the natural outcome of the harmonies existing between railroad management and the commercial, industrial, and social needs of the country, and it is clearly evident that those harmonies should be allowed to work out the beneficent results of self-government among the companies, the national government sanctioning and giving effect to the wholesome restraints and beneficent requirements of such self-government and punishing infractions thereof. This is evidently in harmony with the spirit of our institutions and with the general policy of the law, and it appears to be dictated alike by reason and the clear indications of experience. There is really no other practical line of policy which the country can now pursue. But there are certain disabilities and defects which characterize the American railroad system, certain lessons of experience which have an exceedingly important bearing upon the question of regulation. When all those intimate combinations for the direct transportation of the mails, of express goods, of passengers, and of freights had been formed, the managers of the different lines realized that to a very great extent, and in vitally important particulars, they had lost their independent character as rate makers, and had become essentially dependent parts of one great American railroad system. This was an unlooked for and in many cases an appalling result to the railroad managers. Some of the stronger companies attempted to resist this conclusion by such extension of their lines as would enable them to remain a law unto themselves, but in time they too were forced to acknowledge the compulsion of their interdependent relationships.

The combinations entered into among the railroad companies have had two results of the highest importance to the whole country. First, an enormously increased efficiency in the work of

Reprinted by permission from the Railway Review of July 19, 1892.

transportation, and, second, marvelous reductions in the cost of transportation. But beyond any power of resistance on the part of the companies, the control of rate making slipped from the hands of railroad managers and became subject to a great variety of competing forces of transportation and of trade. For several years the traffic interests of the railroads ran at loose ends. The oldest and ablest traffic managers became dazed by the complex conditions of an environment which had overshadowed them almost without their notice. Year by year they saw the difficulties of the situation gathering stronger above them. Rate agreements became mere idle talk, and rates went down, down, down. Many companies were forced into bankruptcy, and financial ruin stared many others in the face. The union of railroads had developed enormous possibilities to the commercial and industrial interests of the country, but it had stricken the companies with impotency. If no relief had been discovered the inevitable result would have been a general railroad bankruptcy, culminating in one great railroad corporation. Such a combination would, however, have transcended any possible beneficial exercise of administrative ability. The particular problem which confronted the companies was how to maintain just and, at the same time, fairly remunerative rates.

But the unavoidable and most mischievous consequence of this state of affairs was that absurd and ruinous discriminations arose and rates fluctuated violently. This obviously resulted from the fact that there was no balance wheel to the newly-formed Ameritan railroad system; no organization, and no administrative government competent to preserve order or to secure just and equitable methods of procedure. This state of affairs was in the highest degree prejudicial to the interests of commerce and of all industrial enterprise. Its effect upon trade was utterly demoralizing. The particular problem which challenged the attention of thoughtful men was, how to correct certain incidental evils attaching to the grandest and most beneficent system of transportation which the world had ever seen.

Evidently the difficulty was one to be solved mainly by railroad managers. At length some of the abler railroad managers, who comprehended the whole situation, saw clearly that the one thing needful was some sort of an agreement or plan in the nature of self-government whereby the various traffic combinations could be administered, and thus order be brought out of chaos. The plan which rapidly came into vogue was the federation of the railroads into associations upon the basis of agreements as to the share of the competitive traffic which should be awarded to each.

No other expedient had previously, or has since, been devised which has supplied a remedy for the evils of violently fluctuating rates and of rate cutting. These administrative combinations embraced the publicity of rates, timely notice of changes in rates, and agreement as to the division of traffic. Each one of these requirements was at once a restraint upon reckless and destructive rate wars and a means of maintaining the orderly conduct of the American railroad system. They had no other object in view, expressed or implied, and they met clearly expressed commercial demands.

The federations thus formed were merely voluntary associations, and yet they were productive of such excellent results that they were hailed as the correct solution of the whole problem of administrative reform. It was also seen that they were in perfect harmony with the American idea of regulating the commercial and industrial interests of the country by measures in the nature of self-government, and, therefore, that they constituted no departure from established methods of governmental procedure.

These agreements for self-government were entered into for the single purpose of meeting absolutely necessary administrative requirements. They were forced upon the companies by the logic of events, and they had been almost reluctantly submitted to by them as restraints upon their freedom to indulge in practices in the highest degree detrimental to the public interests. But in the face of these facts many sincere but deluded complainants against the very evils which such agreements were especially designed to overcome joined in a chorus of denunciation against them. This opposition appears to have arisen mainly from the fact that the mean and inappropriate name of "pooling" had been given to agreements as to a division of competitive traffic. The changes were also rung upon the word "combination," as though the American railroad system with all its beneficent results was not the natural evolution of intimate railroad combinations, approved and promoted by a statute never called in question, and as though the intelligence and spirit of the age did not everywhere, in labor, in commerce, in industry, and even in agriculture, demand the regulation of competition through combination as an essential condition of modern progress.

Thus an organized means of governing the American railroad system for the protection of the public interests was treated by certain misguided men as a measure opposed to the public interests.

When the "Bill to Regulate Commerce" was reported from the Senate Committee on Interstate Commerce, May 13, 1886, it contained a clear and earnest protest against interference with the measures of self-restraint which had been adopted by the railroad managers. In the splendid report submitted January 18, 1886, by Senator Cullom, it is stated that "the ostensible object of pooling is in harmony with the spirit of regulative legislation," and he further declared that if such "agreements between carriers should prove necessary to the success of a system of established and public rates, it would seem wiser to permit such agreements than by prohibiting them, to render the enforcement and maintenance of agreed rates impracticable."

Senator Platt of Connecticut, re-enforced these views in one of the ablest speeches ever delivered in Congress upon a commercial subject. He maintained that agreements as to a division of competitive traffic constitute wholesome restraints upon reckless and ruinous competition, that they prevent unjust discrimination in rates, and that their obvious tendency is to restore the orderly conduct of commerce.

The New York chamber of commerce, the Minneapolis board of trade, the Peoria board of trade, and other commercial bodies, declared in favor of allowing the railroads to enter into agreements as to the division of competitive traffic for the purpose of maintaining rates.

The Minneapolis board of trade, in its appeal to Congress, said boldly and truly: "The railroad pool honestly administered is the natural balance wheel of interstate commerce."

The leading men of the New York board of trade and transportation, an organization formed for the special purpose of correcting the evils affecting railroad transportation, had become convinced that the division of traffic had proved to be a beneficial expedient of self-government among the roads, and that it had suppressed the evils which at one time threatened to throw the commerce of the metropolis into confusion.

But in the face of all these opinions and of abundant evidence supporting them, the "anti-pooling section" was forced into the Senate bill, and with that absurd and suicidal provision it became law.

The natural result of the elimination of the essential principle of self-government from the associations formed by the companies for that purpose has been that against a solid rock of practical wisdom drawn from the hard lessons of experience the Interstate Commerce Commission has for the last five years, and is today, butting its head. The very difficulty anticipated has been realized; prohibition of agreements for the division of traffic has increased the difficulties of maintaining rates.

The present state of affairs would be infinitely worse were it not for the fact that in the face of enormous difficulties the companies have managed to maintain their administrative organizations for the orderly conduct of the American railroad system. Thus, to some extent, the mischief done by the law has been averted.

It would be an impeachment of the common sense of the gentlemen who have composed the Interstate Commerce Commission to assume that they have not clearly perceived the blunder which was made at the beginning in abolishing the principle of self-control from the regulation of our internal commerce over railroads. The commission has, however, seen fit to pursue a sort of prudential policy in regard to the whole matter. They have not committed themselves to the absurdity of defending this provision of the law, nor, on the other hand, have they exposed themselves to any dangers which might be involved in reporting against its provisions. Taking a middle course, they have simply stated what the law is, and have had recourse—although rather ineffectually—to the arsenal of remedies which it provides, viz: Fines and imprisonment. I believe that it is folly to expect that the error of eliminating the essential principle of self-government from the conduct of the American railroad system can possibly be cured by any such attempted administration by the Interstate Commerce Commission. The provision of the act to regulate commerce which compels this futile effort is evidently un-American in spirit as well as in form, and there is in the attendant circumstances of the case nothing whatever which can possibly justify such an abandonment of the fundamental principles of self-government cherished and proclaimed by the men who wrote the Declaration of Independence and who framed the Constitution of the United States.

In this connection I desire briefly to advert to certain of the controlling characteristics of our vast American railroad system.

1. There are now about 170,000 miles of railroad in the United States, the approximate value of which is not far from $10,000,-000,000. But the annual value of the products of the country transported by the railroads is undoubtedly over three times this amount, and more than thirty times the annual gross amount of railroad receipts from traffic. Every article transported has a direct influence upon rate making. ·

2. The evils and mischiefs which have engaged the attention of the commission are due mainly to two clearly apparent causes already mentioned: First, the fact that the combinations entered into by companies in order to form the American railroad system to a great extent destroyed the independent rate making power of the companies; and second, the fact that the act to regulate commerce forbade the companies from instituting adequate measures in the nature of self-government in order to restore the orderly conduct of the American railroad system.

3. There are influences more potential in the determination of rates than railroad combinations or agreements between railroad managers. I refer, first, to the indirect but all pervading regulative influence of the competition of soil with soil, of mine with mine, and of factory with factory throughout this vast and rapidly developing country of ours. Then there is another force more trenchant and more coercive as a regulative influence in rate-making than even the productive industries of the United States. I refer to the competition of commercial forces; the competition between commercial cities and between traders throughout this broad land. This sort of competition confronts the railroad manager at every initial point of trade. Several times during the last

fifteen years it has gained absolute mastery of the situation and the result has been in each case innumerable unjust discriminations and outrageous disorder, paralyzing to all the interests of productive enterprise, of transportation, and of trade.

The chief difficulty of the present day is not so much how to regulate the railroads as how to regulate the various regulative influences which determine rates. It is the excess and the unrestrained power of regulative influences which cause the most serious troubles.

THE DEVELOPMENT OF RAILWAY FREIGHT CLASSIFICATIONS.

By Mr. C. C. McCain,

Auditor, Interstate Commerce Commission.

From the inception of the business of transportion by rail, articles of an analogous character have been grouped for the purpose of imposing freight charges.

It was at the outset perceived that to provide each article with a distinct rate would, owing to their great variety and number, render any system of tariff-making burdensome and unwieldy. A more convenient and businesslike method was found in the grouping plan. Such an arrangement greatly facilitates the making of rate schedules, as it permits many articles to be rated together in a single paragraph by specifying the rate for the group or class. The forms of publication wherein all commodities are enumerated and classified are now widely known as Freight Classifications, and are employed by all railroads.

The freight traffic of the United States is conducted under two general classes of schedules, known as Commodity Tariffs and Class Tariffs. The former are applicable to such articles as grain, lumber, coal, live stock, oil, etc., transported between sections of the country where these articles have attained a commercial and shipping importance, which have made necessary specific rules for their transportation differing from those covering classified traffic, as well as a somewhat lower scale of rates than is applicable to the latter.

Class tariffs are arranged to show the rates of the respective classes provided by the freight classifications. These cover the great majority of articles carried by the railways; and altho' commodities similar to the ones above mentioned may be rated independently of the classification, they are amenable to many of its rules.

The absence in former years of the restraining influence of the law and of associations gave a stimulus to the energies of the soliciting departments of the railways and brought about the practice of keeping shippers well informed as to the current charges;

Reprinted by permission from The Independent of June 1, 1893.

DEVELOPMENT OF FREIGHT CLASSIFICATIONS. 171

this, together with the offering of special inducements to secure traffic, formed the principal occupation of the soliciting agencies. Another favorite way of attracting business was to remove articles from the classification and temporarily provide them with a lower commodity rate. At such times the schedules were practically abandoned and served the public no useful purpose. Shippers immediately fell into the habit of "shopping" for rates, and looked upon the published schedules as documents fraught with technicalities and especially designed for the guidance of agents and solicitors. Freight classifications were viewed in much the same light and regarded as simply prescribing certain shipping rules not essential to the ascertainment of freight charges.

In the last few years this condition has entirely changed; at this time relatively fewer articles are rated independently of the classification than ever before in the history of railroads. As now published the classifications are current guides to the shipping public, and are indispensably a part of the rate schedules. They are arranged in an enlarged and convenient form, wherein may be found all articles of commerce described in every probable form of shipment and classified in accordance with the various elements that enter into the determination of freight charges.

The necessities of an interchange of business between railways have resulted in co-operation and agreements, whereby associations have been given authority to make classifications for all its members. Under these arrangements the number of classifications have been gradually reduced until we find at this time the entire traffic of the country confined to three classifications.

It is a leading principle in the construction of Freight Classifications that the whole cost of the railway service shall be apportioned among all articles transported upon the basis of the relative value of the article, rather than upon the cost of carriage. Under this method the value of the article forms the most important element in determining what it shall be charged. There are also numerous other considerations which must not be overlooked when a classification is to be made. For example, some articles are bulky, others easily broken, and many involve special risks and are difficult to handle: the elements of competition, volume of business and direction of movement must each be considered, and quite as important is the analogy which must be preserved between articles of like character and value.

The above describes the general basis upon which classifications are constructed, and while to a large extent controlling, the classifications are in a great measure a series of compromises, the participants of which are not alone the railroads, but also shippers and representatives of business interests throughout the country, who are all the time afforded an opportunity to join with the railroads in the determination as to the proper classification of articles of shipment affecting their interests. To such importance has this feature of the transportation business grown that there have been established in different sections of the country officered bureaus accessible to the public, where claims for the adjustment of inequalities in the classification may be presented, or the introduction of new articles secured.

The commercial and transportation interests are regarded by the carriers as identical, and great care is taken in the assignment of articles to particular classes to avoid possible injury to any interest or section. These principles find recognition in each of the three leading classifications now governing the freight traffic of the United States, and although promulgated in varying forms, there is observed in each a constant tendency in the direction of uniformity.

There is probably no branch of the railway service in which the advancement noted has resulted so beneficially to the shipping public as that arising from the enlargement and expansion of Freight Classifications, and it is the purpose of this article to look into the extent of the changes which have taken place in the existing classifications, and to point out briefly what effect this development has had upon the freight charges to the public.

The three classifications referred to as now governing throughout the United States are, the "Official," the "Western," and the "Southern." The sections governed by each are as follows:

For the "Official": east of the Mississippi River and Chicago, and north of the Ohio and Potomac Rivers to the Atlantic Seaboard.

For the "Western": west of the Mississippi River and Chicago.

For the "Southern": south of the Potomac and Ohio Rivers, and east of the Mississippi River.

Prior to the date the Act to regulate commerce became effective —viz., April 4th, 1887—there were numerous classifications in the territories described. A distinction was made between competitive and local traffic, as well as the traffic moving in opposite directions, and the laws of various States made necessary to separate classification for business passing between points in such States. The rates under these were found in many instances to be at variance with the requirements of the new national law, and a very general revision of classification and rates became necessary. The territory described as covered by the "Official" will be recognized as the largest in point of tonnage and communities served. It has been stated that prior to April 1st, 1887, one hundred and thirty-one railroads within this territory had, to some extent, separate classifications. These grew up from local conditions, and were believed to be generally satisfactory to both the carriers and the public. In addition there were five associations of railroad companies, each having its own classification, applicable mainly to through traffic, and in many instances to local traffic.

DEVELOPMENT OF FREIGHT CLASSIFICATIONS.

Recognizing that the continuance of these separate classifications would have made it impossible to conform to either the letter or spirit of the act to regulate commerce, a consolidation was effected by the railroads, by which the classifications of the several associations, as well as the many local classifications, were brought together under what has since been known as the "Official." This classification, it is estimated, is now applied to over 50 per cent of the traffic of the United States. At about the same time the application of the "Western" was enlarged to absorb numerous local classifications west of the Mississippi river, and also throughout the South many local and state classifications were made to conform to the "Southern."

In 1886 the classification applicable to traffic from Atlantic seaboard cities to western competitive points provided for about 1,000 descriptions of articles. The division of these as between carload and less-than-carload quantities is strongly suggestive of the magnitude and character of the business at that time. For 85 per cent of the number of articles classified no distinction in rating was made between less-than-carload and carload quantities; both forms of shipment were rated alike, and only 15 per cent was given a lower rate when in carload amounts. While many articles provided with a classification for less-than-carload quantities only were often shipped by the carload, the failure on the part of the carriers to provide such commodities with a distinct carload rate may be taken as indicating to some extent the commercial necessities of that period.

The distribution among the several classes shows a preponderance of assignment to the higher classes, 70 per cent representing the proportion then in the first three classes, and 30 per cent in the remaining or lower classes. The latter figure, it will be noticed, is double the proportion given the carload rating, from which it might be understood that all of the carload classifications were charged the rates of the lower classes. This, however, was not the case, and many articles for which a carload provision was made were found in the higher classes. Few advantages are derived by shippers of carload quantities when no distinction is made in the rate charged on account of quantity.

The Consolidated, or new "Official" of April 1st, 1887, materially changed these conditions. Instead of 1,000 descriptions, 2,800 were now enumerated. Regarding the increase in the number of descriptions, it should be understood that this does not imply an addition of new commodities solely, but that it is due mainly to extending the application to cover the different forms of packages of articles which are found already classified in some form or other under the classifications now absorbed. Wherever these extensions have been made it has been noticed that a lower classification and consequently a lower rating has followed the one or more forms in which the articles affected are carried. New articles are continually being added, and the classifications are in other ways enlarged to provide a separate rating for each of the various forms in which articles may be offered for shipment.

Of the 2,800 descriptions 55 per cent covered less than carload shipments, and 45 per cent received lower rates when in carload quantities. An increase of 30 per cent is here shown in the number of descriptions of articles which received a carload rating.

Under the new classification of April 1st, 1887, we also find the distribution among the classes to show an increasing proportion in the lower classes with a corresponding decline in the higher classes. These are the results of the first "Official." This issue was largely experimental, and it was not anticipated that the commerce of so large an area could at once be made to conform to the new conditions resulting from the consolidation of the widely differing classifications formerly in use. A pronounced opposition was manifested by shippers to the new order of affairs, and the carriers were immediately in receipt of numerous protests and applications for changes, and a revision of the classification at once followed, resulting in the publication, in July 1887, of "Official" No. 2. Further revisions have been made necessary by the constantly changing conditions, and we have today the eleventh edition of this classification, dated January 2d, 1893. This is undoubtedly the most elaborate classification ever made, and it is difficult to contemplate what further development may be made in this direction. The present issue contains a most complete list of the articles of commerce, enumerated in every form of package, and by it shippers may readily ascertain the class under which articles are rated.

Five thousand six hundred and thirty-four descriptions are given in the present classification, or about double the number of the first issue. Of these, 2,100, or 38 per cent, are for shipments in quantities less than carloads for which no lower rating is given when in carloads; 3,105, or 55 per cent, are for shipments in less than carloads, and for which a *lower* rate is provided when in carloads; 408, or 7 per cent, are exclusively carload classifications.

All of these are distributed into six classes, 53 per cent of the total appearing in the first three, and 47 per cent in the lower classes. By these figures it is shown that the total number of items in the present classification exceed by 4,600 the number in the classifications applying from the seaboard in 1886, and also that the proportion classified as less than carloads with same rating for carloads has decreased from 85 per cent in the old to 38 per cent in the new, while the proportion classified at less than carloads with a *lower* rating when in carloads has increased from 15 per cent in the old to 62 per cent in the new. When an article is provided with a distinct carload classification the rate is invariable lower than when carried in less than carload quantities; therefore, when the number receiving a carload classification is increased such increase denotes reductions in the charges.

DEVELOPMENT OF FREIGHT CLASSIFICATIONS. 175

No adequate presentation of these results can be made without reference to the rates of the respective classes. The principal competitive rates under which the tariff is carried from the seaboard to western points have remained practically the same since 1886. The variation from classes higher than fourth class to lower classes of 14 per cent, therefore, indicates a lowering in the rates of the articles represented by this proportion. This figure, however, does not include the changes from first to second class, second to third, or from third to fourth, of which there have been many. The tendency downward is very fully presented in the following comparison:

```
                                        1886.                      1893.
Total number of descriptions.......1,000                          5,600.
    Proportion at 1st class 75c.    32 per ct. ⎫             22 per ct. ⎫
        "      " 2d   "   65c.    24  "   "   ⎬ 67 per ct.  12  "   "   ⎬ 53 per ct.
        "      " 3d   "   50c,    11  "   "   ⎭             19  "   "   ⎭
        "      " 4th  "   35c.    31 per ct. ⎫             19 per ct. ⎫
        "      " 5th  "   30c.     2  "   "   ⎬ 33 per ct.  23  "   "   ⎬ 47 per ct.
        "      " 6th  "   25c.     0  "   "   ⎭              5  "   "   ⎭
```
(Rates used are from New York to Chicago.)

More explicitly stated, in 1886, 67 per cent, or 670 of the 1,000 articles were charged 50 cents per hundred and higher; in 1893 the actual number is shown to be higher, although the proportion at the rates of the higher classes is very much less. The number in 1886 charged a rate of 35 cents per hundred and lower was only 330, or 33 per cent; in 1893 it is seen that this number is increased to 2,630, or 47 per cent. Another form of comparison shows the average rate of all descriptions in 1886 as 63 cents against 48 cents in 1893, or a reduction of 15 cents per hundred pounds.

The changes in the proportions of traffic carried in the various classes is also illustrative of the operation and effect of the changes in the classification. For the purpose of presenting the results in this connection the business from New York to Chicago may be taken as representative of the general movement from the East to the West. Previous to 1886 no considerable number of articles were permanently assigned to the fifth and sixth classes; these classes then embraced only a few commodities which had been given a special rate. At that time the fourth-class rate was on the basis of 35 cents per hundred pounds, and the greater portion of the lower-class traffic was carried in the fourth class. Since 1887 we find the tonnage proportion of the fourth class very greatly reduced, and a pronounced increase in the sixth class; the rate of the latter is now permanently 25 cents. Over 40 per cent of the total traffic is now carried at this rate, whereas prior to 1886 the proportion at the same rate was very much less.

It has also been stated that 47 per cent of the descriptions in the classification now applying westward from the seaboard is found in the fourth and lower classes. The tonnage of these classes from New York is 60 per cent of the total traffic, the greater portion of which now receives lower rates than in 1886.

No attempt is now made to present detailed comparisons of the reductions of the numerous other classifications absorbed by the "Official." The business from the seaboard to the West is almost entirely carried under that classification, and the results of the general comparison of the classifications covering this business are to a large degree representative of the decline which has taken place throughout the territory governed by the Official Classification since 1886. The fact should be emphasized that the changes in the rates here indicated are due solely to the lowering of the classification. This will be understood when it is recalled that the rates proper between the seaboard and the Mississippi River have not been materially changed.

The "Official" Classification is also now applied to the local traffic of most of the carriers east of the Mississippi River, and not only have important reductions been effected by placing commodities in lower classes than those to which they were formerly assigned, but the rates of the different classes of most of the roads in the territory described have been greatly reduced.

The section served by the "Western" Classification extends over a vast area of country west of the Mississippi River, and with the exception of certain Pacific Coast traffic, is now generally applied to all freight business throughout this section, and as at present arranged represents a consolidation of many local classifications formerly in use. The number of articles specifically provided for is not as great as found in the "Official," but it is noticed that the increase is nearly as large. Three thousand six hundred and fifty-eight descriptions appear in the present "Western." This is an increase of over two thousand since 1886. Fifty-five per cent of the whole number are now provided with separate and lower rates when in carloads, which is an increase of 15 per cent since 1886.

The tendency to lower classification is also observed in the distribution among the classes; the proportion in the higher classes is now much less than formerly, with corresponding addition to the lower classes.

These figures show quite forcibly to what extent the "Western" is expanding, and that with this expansion articles are rapidly finding places in the lower classes.

The "Southern" presents fewer changes of the character here described than either of the other classifications, yet the development in this respect is quite remarkable when the volume of business is taken into consideration. One thousand seven hundred and fifty-two descriptions are now given in the "Southern" Classification, and of these 18 per cent are provided with lower rates when in carload quantities than when shipped in less than carloads.

DEVELOPMENT OF FREIGHT CLASSIFICATIONS. 177

An exhaustive presentation of a subject as important as this is impossible in the space here allotted to its consideration. In very general terms only has the extent of the development been shown, yet sufficient is given clearly to present the benefits which the public have derived from the consolidations which reduced the number of classifications governing the freight traffic of this country to three, the subsequent enlargement of these to meet the demand of commercial development, and, what is most important, the lowering of freight charges resulting from each of these causes.

The freight traffic of the entire country will doubtless in the near future be conducted under one or a uniform classification. Pending the adoption of such a classification further progress in the line here indicated may be expected in each of the principal classifications now in use. It may also be reasonably expected that the charges for railway transportation will keep pace with the constant tendency to lower values and prices observed for the great majority of articles of commerce, and freight classifications will be largely the medium through which such results will be accomplished.

Washington, D. C.

THE INTERSTATE COMMERCE LAW.

Hon. Charles Francis Adams, Jr.

You have asked me, as the representative of one of the large railroad systems of the country, to express my views this evening on the subject of the interstate commerce act and its practical working, as seen through the experience of the last two years. Just now we hear, especially in financial and railroad circles, loud denunciation of this law. It is constantly referred to as the prolific source to which all the evils under which the railroad system is now suffering can be traced. For reasons which I shall presently state, I do not regard the interstate commerce act as in all respects a well-considered or a beneficent law. I am very sure that it has not produced the good results which were hoped from it; but yet I see no good reason for referring to it in the way so common of late.

· That the general railroad situation of the country is at present unsatisfactory is apparent. Stockholders are complaining; directors are bewildered; bankers are frightened. Yet that the interstate commerce act is in the main responsible for all these results, remains to be proved. In my opinion, the difficulty is far more deep-seated and radical. In plain words, it does not lie in any act of legislation, state or national; and it does lie in the covetousness, want of good faith, and low moral tone of those in whose hands the management of the railroad system now is;—in a word, in the absence among them of any high standard of commercial honor.

These are strong words, and yet, as the result of a personal experience stretching over twenty years, I make bold to say that they are not so strong as the occasion would justify. The railroad system of this country, especially of the region west of Chicago, is today managed on principles which—unless a change of heart occurs, and that soon—must inevitably lead to financial disaster of the most serious kind. There is among the lines composing that system an utter disregard of those fundamental ideas of truth, fair play and fair dealing, which lie at the foundation not only of the Christian faith, but of civilization itself. With them

---

Reprinted by permission from the Railway Review of December 29, 1888.

there is but one rule,—that, many years ago, put by Wordsworth into the mouth of Rob Roy:—

> "The simple rule, the good old plan,
> That he shall take who has the power,
> And he shall keep who can."

The state of things in this respect was bad enough before the passage of the interstate commerce act, but the operation of that act has gradually aggravated what was bad enough already. Since that act went into effect two years ago, there has been what might be called a craze for railroad construction. Great corporations, one after the other, have contracted the madness, and have built hundreds of miles of road, almost paralleling each other. In many cases they have actually paralleled each other across wide tracts of country in which no human being lived. This is true in Wisconsin, in Minnesota, in Nebraska, in Kansas. Only a day or two since, some citizens of the west called upon me, and wanted a branch of the Union Pacific built. I examined the map, and found that there was already a railroad between the two points named. They wanted us to build a parallel road a short distance from it. I suggested to them ironically that it would be better for us to build on the right of way of the other road, so as to make what would practically be one double-track road. To my surprise, they were so accustomed to railroad follies that the irony of the proposition did not suggest itself to them. They remarked, with all possible gravity, that this would be altogether the best way of doing the thing. They simply wanted a competing road, built by eastern capital, alongside of another road already built, also by eastern capital.

The construction of all these miles of railroad, for which hardly any immediate demand existed, made a readjustment of traffic necessary. That is, the moment the roads were finished, the problem passed out of the hands of the engineer into the hands of the freight agent, by whom traffic of some sort for the new roads had to be provided. The interstate commerce act was in operation. It was impossible to pool, and the long haul regulated the short haul. Then followed a depth of railroad morals among freight agents lower than had even previously existed,—and that is saying much. The dishonest methods of rate-cutting, the secret systems of rebates, the indirect and hidden payments made to influence the course of traffic, resorted to or devis.d during the last two years, I do not hesitate to say are unprecedented in the whole bad record of the past. In this respect, I endorse every word of indignant denunciation which Judge Cooley, of the Interstate Commerce Commission, is reported to have recently uttered. Names of members or employes of firms whose business it was desirable to secure, but to whom it was unlawful openly to allow a rebate, have been put upon the pay-rolls of companies at salaries equal to the estimated amount of what the rebate would have been; where the influence of a particular person was thought necessary to secure certain shipments, he has been advised that the company wished to consult him, but, in order that it might do so more conveniently he must live in a house in a certain quarter, —and the rent of that house has been paid by the company; where it was thought expedient to cut the rate on passenger tickets to a given point without affecting the rates to intermediate points under the interstate commerce act, tickets to that point have been placed by the hundreds in the hands of "scalpers," and they were allowed a commission equal to half the price of the ticket. This commission, the allowance of which the act did not specifically forbid, the "scalper" again shared with the purchasers of the tickets.

It will be asked why the penalties of the interstate commerce act are not enforced against those who thus directly and indirectly evade its provisions. The question may be asked of me,—Why do you not give information, and institute proceedings under the law? I merely say, in reply, that, apart from a prejudice against being an informer, while I am morally sure that these things are done, I cannot furnish legal proof of them. My information comes indirectly or at second hand; and, while I have no doubt myself of its accuracy, yet if I were brought to book as to time and place and circumstance, I could not give them. The thousand evasions of the interstate commerce act cannot be proved in court. Yet, among us railroad men, the fact that these things are done is notorious. It is all part and parcel of that sneak-thief and pickpocket method of doing business which has become a second nature in certain grades of the railroad service.

The community, and least of all the railroad community, should not, therefore, either be deceived or deceive themselves. It is this absence of good faith, this greed of acquisition, this turning over of business to subordinates to hack away at each other at the expense of the stockholders, which has brought the railroad system to its present low condition, and threatens to carry it still lower. To attribute it to the interstate commerce act is an utter mistake. If that act were totally repealed to-morrow, it would produce but a temporary and stock-jobbing relief. For a few days things might be apparently better; but they would be sure to drop heavily back again into their present bad estate, unless the knife of reform went deeper and cut at the root of the evils I have referred to. The railroad system must heal itself; no act of Congress, or repeal of any act of Congress, will greatly help it.

But in saying what I have said, I do not mean to imply that in my judgment the interstate commerce act is a harmless, much less a useful, piece of legislation. On the contrary, I am very sure that, as it stands, it is not. It has been in operation two years, and we now begin to feel its effect, and be able to forecast its results. And both its present effect and its future results are exactly those which its framers never contemplated, and from which, if they realized them as we do, they would recoil. The process of gravitation and consolidation, so far as the railroads are concerned, was going on fast enough before, but the interstate commerce act has given it a new impetus. It has done this through a process which is unmistakable to all who make a study of the subject. The practice known as pooling, which the interstate commerce act inhibits, was merely a method through which the weaker railroad corporations were kept alive. To prevent excessive and unequal competition, business was so divided that the less favored corporation had some share of traffic assigned to it. This practice the law put a stop to; and it further enacted that rates to competing points should not be less than rates to intermediate points.

These enactments struck at the very foundation of the business system under which the railroads in the country, and the country itself had been built up, and it took some time for them to produce their results. They have of late been doing so. Under the operation of the act, the smaller local railroads throughout the country are being ground out of existence. It is the long haul which brings in the profit. The smaller independent railroads cannot have the long haul, and can only be operated profitably in connection with the larger railroads. They are thus, one by one, becoming unrenumerative, and being forced, whether they like it or not, into the maws of the few great systems into which the railroads of the country are rapidly crystalizing.

So much for the practical working of a law inhibiting pooling. Next came the long and short haul clause. Just as the small, local railroads are crushed out of existence by the anti-pooling clause, so the local points of distribution and second-class centers throughout the country find themselves, because of the long and short haul clause, unable to compete with the great commercial centers. Traffic, under the provisions of the act, must invariably seek the railroad having the long haul to the most distant and largest center. The operation of the law in this respect is now beginning to make itself felt upon the smaller distributing points. They are deprived of their markets, for those who formerly bought of them can get the same goods on better terms from the larger and more distant centers. The old local system of distribution is broken up in favor of the centralized system. This fact is now making itself apparent to the manufacturers and jobbers of the smaller cities or towns as against Chicago, St. Louis, or Cincinnati;—but as sure as the law of gravitation applies to all places and works under all circumstances, this same long and short haul clause will next make itself felt against Chicago, St. Louis, and Cincinnati, and in favor of New York. In other words, contrary to every design of those who framed the act, its provisions have lent a new impetus to just those forces which it was intended to hold in check. Instead of building up the local road and the small distributing center, it is working the sure destruction of both. An artificial, but most powerful impetus has thus been given to the process of centralization. With the body politic, as with the human body, a mistaken remedy only aggravates the disease. The remedy in this case was a mistaken one, and the danger now is lest, seeing the disease aggravated, the physician should conclude that he had fallen into the vulgar error of not giving enough of his sure-cure remedy, and so proceed to double the dose. It is not another dose of the same treatment, but a wholly different treatment which is required.

Under these circumstances, it may perhaps be asked what my view of the future is, and what should now be done. While I do not care to set up as a prophet, the trend of events seem to me plain enough; nor do I believe that any act of Congress or of state legislatures can thwart or greatly change it. The railroads of this country are moving rapidly towards some great system of consolidation. I do not know when or how it will come about; nor is it necessary now to consider this. Neither do I believe it will prove an evil when it does come. Nevertheless, it is a matter of common notoriety that such a result is viewed with grave, popular apprehension. We have seen what the progress of the last twenty years has been in this respect. Crystallization has gone on during those years, so that, while then a railroad of 200 or 300 miles was considered large, one of 5,000 or 6,000 miles is now far from being the largest. As I have pointed out, the movement is today going forward more rapidly, much more rapidly, under the artificial impetus given to it by the interstate commerce act, than ever before. The next move will be in the direction of railroad systems of 20,000 miles each, under one common management. The interstate commerce act, acting on the tendency of natural forces, is at this moment rapidly driving us forward towards some grand railroad trust scheme. Even this, from my point of view, I cannot regard as a thing to be dreaded. I am very sure now, as I have been for the last twenty years, and as I long ago expressed myself, that a great consolidated corporation, or even trust, can be held to a far stricter responsibility to the law than numerous smaller and conflicting corporations. Under the existing system no one can be held to account. Evasion is always possible, and invariably it is "the other man" who is responsible for the wickedness. With one large corporation or trust, it would be otherwise. Both law and popular opinion could, and certainly would, be directed against it.

The course of events, so far as next week is concerned, seems to me, therefore, sufficiently apparent. Neither, I say once more, can I see anything in it which should cause public or private anxiety. The doubt in my mind exists as to what is going to happen between now and next week; what will take place tomorrow. Events are moving altogether too fast, even for our times.

I would, therefore, like to see the interstate commerce act amended as respects the pooling provision and the long and short haul clause, simply as a method of putting on the brakes. The time is not ripe for what is impending. They are talking of trusts and consolidations to be effected tomorrow, when it seems to me that in the natural order of events they would not take place until next week. An amendment of the interstate commerce act in the two respects I have indicated would, in my judgment, tend to delay this progress of events. It would not, it is true, touch those radical evils in the railroad organization—that absence of faith, that insatiable greed, that low sense of commercial honor—of which I have spoken. These can only be cured in one way. That one way is, by placing responsibility on individuals.

It is for this reason that I could not the other day but regret the signs of public disapproval with which a scheme for a railroad clearing house in the west was met. It was at once characterized in the papers as a vast "trust"—in these days everything is a "trust"—and denounced as a conspiracy. It was nothing of the sort. There was not a feature of what is known as a trust in the scheme—hardly a feature of a pool. On the contrary, a well-devised railroad clearing house scheme would prove in practice, whether so intended or not, in the direct line of the enforcement of the interstate commerce act in all its better features, and it has many such. That rates can in these days and this country be more than reasonable, I do believe. A reasonable system of railroad rates, publicly announced, equal to all and honestly maintained, is the commercial need of the day; and not less so for the communities of business men than for the railroads themselves. This was one of the results which it was hoped the interstate commerce act would bring about when, two years ago, it went into effect. In practice it has only aggravated the evils it was intended to remedy. In my belief, it cannot produce any other result until the railroads themselves co-operate with the act; and they cannot co-operate until they are brought together in one responsible organization to enforce its provisions. There must be some one somewhere to whom public opinion can look; and then, when the abuses to which I have referred are committed, the finger of public opinion will assuredly point to the responsible man.

For myself, and on behalf of the company of which I am the responsible head, I will say that to-day, and so long as it stands on the statute book, we would welcome the rigid and literal enforcement of every provision of the interstate commerce act. It is either a good law or a bad law. If it is a good law, it should be obligatory on all alike, the sneak-thief and the pickpocket as well as the law-abiding citizen; it should no longer be a cover under which the former ply their vocation undisturbed, to the extreme detriment of the latter. If it is not a good law, we believe in General Grant's aphorism, that the proper way to repeal a bad law is to execute it; and we would have every provision of this law rigidly enforced, to the end that it might produce its natural results with a view to amendment or repeal.

If, therefore, I were asked this evening for concrete propositions embodying the measures most likely to work an important and desirable reform in the railroad situation, I would say,—delay at least for a time, the present too rapid tendency towards crystallization or consolidation, by repealing the features of the interstate commerce act which are precipitating events in that direction. If the anti-pooling provisions of the act may not be wholly repealed, let them, at least, be so modified that contracts made among railroads, subject to the approval of the Interstate Commerce Commission, for the division of competitive traffic at reasonable rates, may be binding in law. Then, more and most of all, encourage and facilitate any movement among those interested which will tend to raise the standard of commercial morality in railroad circles; and be assured, nothing will tend more directly and immediately to that result than the organization of the railroads into some public and recognized clearing-house system through which the traffic management of the country can be taken out of the hands of irresponsible subordinates who now so vilely abuse it, and restored to those who should be responsible, in fact as well as in name, for the companies of which they are the heads.

This I hold to be the work of to-day. That the material and scientific development which is hurrying us forward towards greater centralization can be paralyzed or set at nought by act of Congress, I do not for an instant believe. But it is not wise to look too far into the future, for it is the unexpected which is apt to occur. The work of the present is clear, and it is enough; and the work of the present should, in my judgment, be to retard rather than to accelerate the tendencies to which I have referred on the one hand, and to create a higher standard of railroad honor through organization and individual responsibility on the other. The law and the influences now at work are doing neither the one nor the other.

DISCRIMINATION BY RAILWAYS.

By Hon. Martin A. Knapp,

Interstate Commerce Commissioner.

The relation of the railroads to the people is the most vital subject of public concern. The agencies by which the diversified products of industry are distributed over the vast areas of our country, and by which its immense population may travel, with surprising speed, comfort and safety, in every direction and from one end of the land to the other, are not only the greatest achievement of this generation but have the most potent bearing upon individual welfare. The more thoughtfully we study the problem of personal opportunity, the more deeply are we impressed with its increasing dependence upon just and equal charges for public transportation. Whatever, therefore, affects in any material degree the management, facilities or cost of using these necessary highways, must be of special consequence to every person.

The advent of railroads is so recent, their expansion has been so rapid and their stimulus to every form of enterprise so extraordinary, that in the contemplation of their surpassing benefits the evils of unjust rates and unequal treatment are frequently overlooked. The difficult conditions with which legislation has lately undertaken to deal were the necessary result of excessive construction and unregulated management in the two feverish decades which followed the Civil War. In many sections of the country this was a period of visionary schemes and rash speculation. The eager clamor of the people for the facilities of rail conveyance incited numerous projects which were doomed to financial failure. In the reckless haste to secure railroad transportation, an unwarranted premium was offered to those who would furnish it.

Enormous grants of public lands, donations of private property and endless obligations in the form of county, town and municipal bonds were freely and often inconsiderately given to aid the extension of railway lines into remote districts and undeveloped regions. The recently settled lands were heavily mortgaged, and the future discounted without reserve to gratify the passion for these public highways. They were built in many instances

---

Reprinted by permission from The Independent of June 1, 1893.

where little traffic existed and where a paying return could not reasonably be expected for many years. The energy thus exhibited was prodigious, but much of it was misdirected. The capital obtained for many of these ventures was secured upon conditions and coupled with exactions which prudence would have avoided, while lavish expenditure and dishonest management added to the evils of premature construction. The not uncommon result was a capitalization far exceeding the cost of the properties, and a system of railroads vastly greater in carrying capacity than the traffic furnished for transportation.

Not only were great trunk lines pushed through to the Pacific, but these were quickly supplemented with branches and feeders designed to secure a monopoly of the carrying trade in the territory claimed to be tributary to the original system. In their eagerness to take possession of districts relied upon for future business, the rival companies frequently overlapped each other, and duplicated roads in regions where adequate patronage could not be obtained for a single line. The fiercest competition for the limited traffic of this unsettled country was an inevitable outcome, while the necessity for sufficient earnings to meet fixed charges and operating expenses tempted resort to every device and allurement by which business could be secured. The same conditions existed, tho' in a lesser degree, in the more developed and productive portions of the United States. Railroad construction was everywhere stimulated by extravagant promises, and the popular demand taken advantage of by greedy capitalists and unscrupulous adventurers. At this juncture, also, the Canadian Pacific road was pushed across the continent, built by government aid and subsidized by government bounty, to increase the complication and multiply the opportunities for transportation abuses.

Moreover, it must be remembered, that this state of things was established before its evil consequences were perceived, and while false and mischievous views respecting the obligations of public carriers were widely entertained. Railway officials, as a rule, seemed to regard the interests which they controlled as their personal affairs, to be dealt with according to their own judgment or caprice. The agencies of transportation were treated as private property, subject to bargain and sale like any merchandise, and the prevailing sentiment among railroad managers was distinctly hostile to the idea of state or national regulation. Under these circumstances it is not surprising that favoritism was shown with little hesitation, and partiality practiced without much concealment; the granting of special rates and the payment of rebates were recognized features of railway management.

The devices by which discriminations were effected are too numerous for description, but most of them may be grouped in two or three classes. The first class embraces the various methods, more or less devious, by which one or more persons in a given locality obtained an advantage in rates over their competing neighbors. This is the most offensive if not the most dangerous phase of transportation abuses. Whether the preferential result is reached by open agreement, by secret rebate, by the allowance of commissions, by paying unfounded claims for damage or detention, or by some other process which secures lower freight charges to one shipper than to another, when both are in similar relations to the carrier, the practice in whatever guise is an unwarrantable injury to private rights and a gross violation of public duty. That one man should have an arbitrary advantage over his fellows, in respect of a common necessity, is repugnant to every notion of equality and offends the rudest conception of justice. Of what avail are industry, enterprise, integrity or any of the qualities which should lead to success, if the less capable and less honest competitor can control the market by bargaining with the railroads for reduced rates and special facilities? When this indispensable service is performed on varying and unequal terms, when secret concessions are made to one or more rivals in a given line of business, those from whom higher charges are exacted are placed at a a serious and often fatal disadvantage. In such a case the race is not to the swift nor the battle to the strong, but to the one whose freight rates are the lowest.

The effect of these discriminations is far more hurtful and dangerous than the injury to individuals which they directly occasion. The indirect consequences, none the less certain because often unobserved, extend to every related industry and even to the remotest occupations. It is impossible to measure the demoralizing results which follow an infringement of the common right to just and equal charges for public transportation. Practically the exercise of that right is not less necessary to the rewards of labor than the security of life or the protection of property. Its constant enjoyment is essential to success, its deprivation is a disaster. Prior to 1887, when the Act to Regulate Commerce was passed, the favoritism and partiality which characterized the management of railroads had grown to alarming proportions, and laid the foundations of numerous evils which have not yet wholly disappeared. The marked tendency of practices which common usage encouraged was to give favored shippers an advantage by which they secured a monopoly of the markets through the ruin or withdrawal of their competitors, These practices aided the formation and fortified the power of those vast combinations of capital which have excited such widespread apprehension. Whoever will read the report of the Special Committee of the United States Senate, commonly known as the Cullom Committee, will be astounded at the magnitude and extent of the abuses disclosed by their investigation. Those unfamiliar with the facts made public at that time can hardly believe the outrages which were proven to exist, and the manifold devices by which the most flagrant injustice was perpetrated. The obvious effect of preferential rates is to concentrate the commerce of the country in a few hands. The favored shipper, who is naturally the large shipper, is furnished with a weapon against which skill, energy and experience are alike unavailing. When the natural advantages of capital are augmented by arbitrary deductions from charges commonly imposed, the combination is powerful enough to force all rivals from the field. Production is controlled, wages fixed, prices fitted to the desired profit; monopoly reigns. If we could unearth the secrets of these modern "trusts," whose quick-gotten wealth dwarfs the riches of Solomon and whose impudent extortions put tyranny to shame, we should find the explanation of their menacing growth in the systematic and heartless methods by which they have evaded the common burdens of transportation. The reduced charges which they have obtained, sometimes by favoritism and oftener by force, are the unlawful means by which their colossal gains have been accumulated. Herein lies their chief power for evil. No man can acquire a hundred millions in less than a score of years without grossly defrauding his fellows by securing rates and facilities for public carriage of which others are deprived. That is the sleight of hand by which the marvel is produced, the key to the riddle which has amazed and alarmed the nation. Deprived of special and exclusive rates, an advantage far more odious and powerful than exemption from taxation, these trusts are shorn of their strength and divested of their supremacy. Indeed, it is not too much to say that no aggregation of capital, no monopoly in in the field of production, can be of serious or permanent danger if rigidly subjected to the rule of equality in all that pertains to public transportation.

The railroads are not wholly to blame for these discriminations. In some cases at least they have the excuse of apparent necessity. There are situations where competition is so sharp, where the traffic of some large shipper, or combination of shippers, is so needful to a particular road, that when reduced rates are demanded as the alternative of losing the business, the carrier can hardly refuse. Few traffic managers will submit to the diversion of important tonnage when a discount from schedule charges will retain it, for the maintenance of revenues is the price of their positions. This is the worst stage of evil. When the railroads as well as the people are in bondage to the trusts, the point of extreme danger has been reached. Then the grip of the moneyed monarchs is all-powerful and industrial freedom is at an end.

Widely different in character but equally far reaching in effect are discriminations between different localities. The equitable adjustment of transportation charges between rival communities is a many-sided and obstinate problem. In the Western sections of the country especially, where development is rapid and ambitious towns are springing up in every quarter, the varying and unequal rates from common sources of supply to points in the consuming territory which compete for its distributing trade, involve the prosperity of large numbers of people and give rise to the gravest contentions. Where the cost of an article is so much affected by the expense incurred in bringing it from the place of production, the relative rates applied to competing towns determine to a great extent the volume of their business and the measure of their growth. The power of the railroads in this direction is enormous. They can build up or destroy a commercial center almost at will. They can raise or reduce the prices of agricultural products, and so enhance or depress the salable value of wide areas of land. They can decree that one town shall be enriched by the impoverishment of its rival; that one community shall languish while another flourishes.

It stands to the credit of railway managers that this extraordinary power is not oftener abused. While discriminations of this kind are frequent and give rise to grievous complaints, they are rarely occasioned by arbitrary or vindictive action. In most instances the disparity finds plausible excuse, from the standpoint of the carrier at least, in the varying and dissimilar circumstances which surround the transportation. The justification most commonly alleged is the existence and controlling force of water competition. The rail lines must approximate the rates afforded by the cheaper mode of conveyance or be excluded from participation in the competitive traffic. Upon this asserted necessity is based the whole system of lower charges to distant terminals than are enforced at intermediate points, without the consequent anomaly of lesser rates for longer than for shorter hauls. In such cases the disadvantage to the interior town is always depressing and sometimes disastrous. Its trade is limited, its industries dwarfed, its development arrested. Whatever its location it remains suburban. The misfortune attending these discriminating practices, however compulsory they may seem, is the building up of great cities and the concentration of large numbers of people at a few central places, when a more general diffusion of business and of population would be a distinct social and economic advantage. This generation has seen, not without serious misgiving, the balance of political power transferred from the country to the town, and popular government thereby subjected to a severe and not wholly satisfactory test. In seeking the causes of this significant change we must not overlook the influence of these great railway systems, and the potent effect of unequal charges by which the cities have been constantly favored.

A third class of discriminations arises from the relative rates on kindred and competing articles of commerce. Generally speaking, there is always more or less competition in the consuming markets between raw materials and their manufactured products. If either of these rivals is unduly aided through the charges fixed by the public carrier, individuals and communities may receive incalculable injury. Upon the fair adjustment of rates between such commodities as wheat and flour, live animals and dressed meats, pig iron and hardware, and scores of others, the most important interests are in constant dependence. A slight increase, for instance, in the rates on flour, with a slight decrease in the rates on wheat, would transfer to Eastern points the great milling industries of the Northwest, and reduce the business in a city like Minneapolis to the limited demands of its local trade. So an inconsiderable variation in the relative charges on dressed meats and live animals might shift the location of every large slaughter house from one part of the country to another, with endless discomfort and loss beyond the reach of redress. These illustrations may be extreme, but they indicate the power for wrongdoing which the railroads possess through the manipulation of rates on related traffic. In view of their opportunities and the temptations to which they are exposed, it is creditable to their managers that the obligations of neutrality are so generally observed and that discriminations of this character so seldom occur.

It requires little consideration of the problem which these observations suggest to see the necessity for government regulation. Some authority there must be, superior to and independent of the railroads themselves, to supervise their management, restrain their exactions, and enforce their compliance with the rule of equality. The question whether such regulation shall be undertaken has passed the stage of discussion. Existing laws have accomplished much, and wise legislation will accomplish more. The limited extent to which the several states, for obvious reasons, can afford effectual relief, casts the principal burden upon the National Government. The Act to Regulate Commerce was the initial assertion by Congress of its constitutional power over the agencies of transportation. It was not framed to meet a temporary emergency nor in obedience to a transient and spasmodic sentiment; it was the the inauguration of a fixed and permanent policy. However crude and inadequate in some of its provisions, it is the legislative expression of a high and wholesome principle. It assumes that the railroads are engaged in a public service, and requires that service to be impartially performed. It declares that the large shipper is entitled to no advantage over his smaller rival either in rates or accommodations, and that the charges to both shall be measured by the same standard. It insists upon the right of every person to use the facilities which the carrier provides, on equal terms with all his fellows, and finds an invasion of that right in every deviation from rates commonly enforced. It makes favoritism an offense and unjust discrimination a crime.

To bring the business of public transportation into full conformity with this great principle, to enforce the beneficent rule of just rates and equal treatment, and to adjust this complex system of railroads to the enlarging needs of the people, is to bestow an inestimable benefit upon every pursuit and every person. It is at once the most difficult and most valuable service which the Government can perform.

DISCRIMINATIONS FROM THE USE OF PRIVATE CARS OF SHIPPERS.

Hon. Augustus Schoonmaker,

Ex-Member of the Interstate Commerce Commission.

One of the features of transportation at the present day demanding serious consideration is the extensive use of private cars owned by shippers. If the use of such cars concerned only carriers themselves it would be a private matter, to be dealt with between the managers of corporations acting as common carriers and the investors in the property, but the discriminations among shippers to which the practice leads make it a public matter of pronounced importance.

The use by carriers of private cars of shippers instead of their own equipment has developed in the last few years to very large proportions. Many thousands of them are now in use for the transportation of various kinds of traffic. The principal articles for which they are used are such staples as petroleum and cottonseed oils, turpentine, live stock, and dressed meats. These cars are mostly of improved styles, such as tank cars for oil and turpentine, live-stock cars adapted for feeding and watering stock on the train, and refrigerator cars arranged for the preservation of fresh meats; and they usually cost somewhat more than the cars owned and furnished by carriers themselves. In some instances, however, ordinary box cars similar to those furnished by carriers are supplied by shippers. Details with regard to the varieties and numbers of private cars used, owned, and furnished by shippers, their styles and cost, or even their advantages to the traffic carried in them, are not material to the present purpose, which is only to call attention to the public consequences of their use, in the form of discrimination between shippers who own such cars and those who use the carriers' own equipment.

The right of a railroad company to haul private cars of shippers

---

Reprinted from proceedings of the National Convention of Railroad Commissioners, held at Washington, D. C., March, 1891.

if it see fit to do so, is not now called in question; but a road is under no obligation to do so. It does so in the exercise of its own volition. The original conception, in the early period of railroads, that a railroad was only a common public highway upon which, as upon a turnpike, any one might place his vehicle and have it drawn by paying the toll, was long since justly discarded and has no existence in national regulation. Traces of it may, however, linger in some state statutes. Railroad companies are chartered for much more than the mere construction of their roadways. They are required and expected to equip and operate their roads, and their equipment must be suitable and sufficient for the business in which they engage. These are primary public duties, required as conditions of the franchise, and admit of no excuse for non-compliance.

They are intended to be, and are in fact, common carriers, and the relations and office of a common carrier are inconsistent with any meddling on the part of others with its property or its mode of carrying on its business. Subject only to the authority of government, its exclusive control of its tracks and vehicles of carriage is indispensable to its rights and duties, and this principle accords with sound public policy.

In contemplation of law, cars used by a railroad company in its ordinary business, however furnished, whether by itself or by private shippers, are, for transportation purposes, deemed its own, and the rules for the regulation of commerce, as well as the general rules of law respecting the responsibility of the company to the public for care and safety, apply alike whatever vehicles may be used or however acquired. If a railroad were under compulsion to haul private cars when offered, very serious questions might arise as to its responsibility for the safety of cars, or for accidents resulting from ill-adapted cars, defective safety appliances, or the like. The law therefore, here, as in England where great attention has been given to the subject, leaves railroads free to haul or not to haul private cars in their discretion, but brings the conduct of the company in its transportation business under the obligations and restraints of public regulation, without regard to the kind of cars used or the mode in which they may be procured.

The law for purposes of regulation recognizes only two classes to which its provisions apply. One consists of the carriers, whose function is to serve the public; the other is the whole public, whose right it is to be served; and the fundamental principle applicable to both is equality of service and charges under conditions that are substantially similar. The is no middle ground, nor an intermediate class to hold a dual relation as shippers and *quasi* partners of carriers, and so gain preferences over other shippers by sharing the earnings of the carriers as part of their profits as shippers. Shippers must stand on the same plane, and one shipper cannot secure to himself, by any pretext or device, a pecuniary advantage in transportation over other shippers. Every preference given by the acts of a carrier is under the ban of the law, and the methods by which it may be done are not material.

These observations lead to the particular point intended to be emphasized—the discriminations resulting from the use of cars of shippers. The method by which this is done is usually as follows:

A firm, or perhaps a combination, dealing in some article of commerce, not satisfied with the ordinary trade profits of its business common to others engaged in like business, desires to augment its profits by some auxiliary means in which its rivals may not be able to compete. It thereupon builds a large number of cars to be used exclusively for the carriage of its own traffic, unless, as is the case in some instances, some traffic can be carried on the return trips of the cars. The cars so built are usually of some improved style not furnished by the carrier itself. A contract is then made with railroad companies to haul these cars without charge therefor to the shipper, but the carrier to pay compensation for their use, in the form of mileage, usually three-quarters of a cent for every mile hauled both loaded and empty, though sometimes more. As the revenue from mileage depends on the number of miles hauled, it is part of these arrangements that the cars shall be hauled at high rates of speed and quick and frequent trips made. Sometimes some additional allowance is made for some terminal matter, such as yardage, actual or constructive, for live stock; and in all cases there is free storage of cars and terminal switching at the carriers' expense.

Investigations made by the Interstate Commerce Commission at different times have disclosed to some extent the very large sums received by shippers as mileage for the use of such cars. By an investigation made in 1889 it appeared that on a single line of road between Chicago and an interior eastern point—a distance of 470 miles—refrigerator cars owned by three shipping firms made in nine months, from August 1, 1888, to May 1, 1889, 7,428,-406 miles, and earned for mileage $72,945.97, being about $8,112 a month, or substantially at the rate of $100,000 a year.

By another investigation, made in 1890, it appeared that private stock cars to the number of 250 had been used upon a line made up of two connecting roads between Chicago and New York, beginning with 150 cars on September 1, 1888, increased 30 more a month later, 20 more another month later, and reaching the total of 250 in June, 1890; that the cars altogether had cost $156,500, and had earned for mileage in two years, from September 1, 1888, to September 1, 1890, $205,582.68; that the entire expense to be deducted during that period for car repairs and salaries for their management was $34,050.48, leaving net revenue to the amount of $171,532.20, being an excess of $15,032 above the whole cost of the cars. The cars were therefore paid for and a margin besides in two years, and thereafter, under the same arrangement and with a corresponding use of the cars, an income of upwards of $100,000 a year was assured on an investment fully repaid or in effect on no investment whatever.

It is obvious what advantages to a shipper furnishing cars such a revenue from their use affords him over a competitor shipping in cars belonging to the carriers. The latter pays the transportation charges in full. The former is reimbursed for a considerable part of these charges by the mileage received. If both sell in the same market and at the same price the shipper owning the cars makes a profit greatly in excess of the other, or, by reason of his combined business as car-owner and shipper, can undersell his competitor, command the market, and still make a profit, while the other must carry on his business at a loss or be driven out of the market.

By still other investigations at various times the gross discriminations that have characterized the transportation of petroleum oil in barrels and in tanks, in which payment for the use of tank cars has been a factor, have been developed. Thousands of such cars are owned by shippers and used exclusively for the carriage of their own oil. They are paid by the carriers for the mileage made by the cars, whether loaded or empty. The cars are practically part of the investment in their business, and the revenue received for their use, is, to an extent at least, a rebate from the rate, which gives the shippers owning the cars a corresponding advantage in the markets. Details need not be entered into. It is sufficient to say that the injurious consequences have been very generally felt and observed. Dealers who have been obliged to ship in barrels in the box cars furnished by carriers have met with disaster and been largely forced to relinquish the business, while the tank shippers owning their own cars have enormously prospered and rapidly absorbed the business of their less favored competitors, until one great combination has become an overshadowing monopoly, representing fabulous wealth with corresponding power and influence, able to command where other competitors must solicit—and too often solicit in vain—and accorded on the part of carriers an apparently eager subservience.

A full and careful statement showing the aggregate of private cars owned by shippers and of the moneys paid for their use, would exhibit results that would be startling both in their magnitude and character. A single railroad company, as shown by its official report for 1889, paid car mileage to sixty-five different companies and firms owning cars, of which fifty-four were shippers and the remaining eleven fast-freight organizations. The revenues of carriers are seriously impaired by the amount these payments add to the expenses of operation, and it is not uncommon when rates are abnormally low that after deduction of these payments not even the cost of carriage is left to the road, so that the traffic thus carried is sometimes detrimental to the carrier. The practice is therefore neither good transportation policy from the carriers' standpoint, nor, in a larger sense, good public policy, which, as its essential feature, requires the absence of every form of favoritism and preference on the part of government or the public agencies, and equal opportunities for enterprise and energy in the competitions of business, to the end that individual character—the state's chief security—may be developed and merit attain its just reward.

The railroads of the country are themselves responsible for the use of private cars of shippers upon their roads and for the abuses that have resulted from their use. The reluctance and even neglect of the roads to provide suitable and improved cars to meet the growing demands of commerce and carry certain kinds of traffic without injury to its usefulness and market value, at first impelled shippers themselves to do what the carriers should have done—to furnish cars suited to their business. The hauling of the shippers' cars then became a matter of competition among the roads, and they mistakenly adopted the plan of paying to shippers the same or even a greater mileage rate than the roads allow between themselves in the interchange of cars, where the allowances are reciprocal and for the most part substantially equalize each other. But in the case of shippers' cars there is no reciprocity. The money is paid directly to the shipper, and, to the extent that it exceeds current interest on the cost of the car and a fair allowance for depreciation, it is a direct loss to the carrier and a discrimination in favor of the shipper. Although three-quarters of a cent a mile is the usual mileage rate paid, the allowance is sometimes a cent a mile, or even a cent and a half a mile, and contracts have been entered into by carriers with shippers to pay such rates for a period of five years.

The point now aimed at is the discrimination to shippers. Under existing methods this has become an evil so general and of such proportions that it can no longer be disregarded, and a remedy is of urgent importance. Any plan involving the payment of mileage to shippers is evidently impracticable. No mileage basis can be fixed that will apply to different kinds of cars and that will effectually guard against discrimination. It doubtless is difficult to devise any plan that will be just and not liable to some abuse. In England, where many private cars are furnished by shippers, especially in the coal trade, a practice prevails of making an allowance to the car-owner for the tonnage carried, but obviously that method has defects and is open to abuse.

If a radical change, forbidding the use of private cars of shippers and requiring carriers to furnish all cars themselves, is impracticable, and if the practice of using cars of shippers and paying for their use is to continue, a feasible plan would seem to be that the payments in no case should exceed what the expense would be to the carrier if it owned the car—that is to say, the current interest on its cost and a just allowance for depreciation, and a right on the part of the carrier to use the cars for other shippers when their owners do not furnish loading—with the provision that all contracts for the use of such cars should be filed with the Interstate Commerce Commission and the reasonableness of the allowances be subject to its jurisdiction.

LONG VERSUS SHORT HAUL.

By Gen. E. P. Alexander.

Associate Editor of The Railroad Gazette.

The circuit court of the United States, for the northern district of Georgia, will soon render a decision upon a question of vital consequence to the transportation interests of the entire country— one which for twenty years has lain at the root of nearly all the agitation and legislation for the regulation of railroad traffic. The question involves the right of any railroad, or combination of railroads, to charge or accept a less rate of freight on articles carried over a greater distance than a charge for the same articles carried a shorter distance over the same line at the same time. No practice of railroads has ever excited such universal and indignant denunciation. It has been attributed to a purely gratuitous disposition to exercise and display a great power they are supposed to possess of building up or of pulling down commercial centers at their pleasure. To the ordinary man the argument seems irresistible, that if this servant of the public can afford to carry a carload of goods from A to Z, over the whole alphabet, for a certain sum, it is manifest extortion to charge a greater sum for a similar carload carried over but a part of the same route and stopped at some intermediate station, as Q, R or S. Against such extortion, the effects of which seemed capable of destroying or building up the manufacturing or commercial supremacy of whole communities, the strong arm of the law should be invoked. Congress undertook to investigate and legislate, and the committee rooms of House and Senate became battlefields, where ardent and able advocates of the popular view, and of commercial interests, which thought themselves unjustly oppressed, struggled with the representatives of railroad interests, who endeavored to explain that their so-called extortion and discrimination was but apparent and not real; that it was the result of circumstances beyond their control and the underlying principle upon which, the world over, railroad rates are necessarily adjusted. A brief *resume* of their arguments will be given below, but the outcome of the battles before the committee was peculiar, and has resulted in a sort

Reprinted by permission from The Independent of October 6, 1892.

of armed truce between headquarters, with guerrilla skirmishes on the outposts for five years. At last however, the leaders have joined issue in the United States courts, and the decision of the Supreme Court will doubtless be finally invoked.

Of course, in a matter of such importance and complication as the regulation of all interstate railroad traffic, there were many principles and practices discussed in the argument, and finally settled by the bill, which as a result, became law early in 1887; but we have only to do here with its dictum on the matter of "long *versus* short haul," as it came to be called for short. On this subject the prevailing sentiment in the House and Senate differed. The House generally favored an absolute prohibition, under all circumstances, of the practice of accepting less for the longer haul. The Senate generally believed that under certain circumstances the practice was proper and even necessary. So the Senate put in the bill the qualifying phrase that the practice should be unlawful only when the short haul freight was carried under "substantially similar circumstances and conditions" to those surrounding the long haul freight. If they were under "substantially similar circumstances," the charge made for the long should limit the charge on the short; if not, then the short haul charge must stand on its own bottom as to whether it was a reasonable charge for the service rendered.

Neither side could object to so fair-sounding a condition, even tho' it might be less definite than desirable in important prohibitive legislation; so the bill became a law, and the interpretation of the phrase was thrown upon the Interstate Commerce Commission.

Cases were speedily made before it, and now it becomes necessary to an understanding of the situation to explain the "circumstances and conditions" under which the railroads practiced and justified the apparently absurd habit of charging less for a greater service.

A full discussion of all the relations between railroad earnings, expenses and charges would be longer than the moral law; but as the moral law can be condensed into the Golden Rule, "Do as you would be done by," so the essential principles involved in all railroad rates and classifications can be stated in two very simple propositions.

The first is that railroad services must be sold rather by what they are worth than by what they cost. In fact, that is the general rule for all personal services the world over. To begin with, it would be as utterly impossible to divide out their varied expenses for management, wear and tear, accidents, and the innumerable varieties of traffic, and assign a cost to each one, as it would be for a doctor to estimate what it costs him to prescribe for each separate disease to which his patients are liable. Railroads the world over charge much more for carrying dry goods than for carrying bricks, ton for ton, tho' the difference in cost is imperceptible. If they did not the transportation of bricks would practically cease, and all traffic would be so reduced that, to live, the railroad might even have to raise the rates on dry goods.

But the principle is too simple and too universal in all business matters to need further illustration. Briefly, it may be expressed in the phrase that transportation must be charged for in proportion to the value of the service rendered.

The second proposition to be recognized in the consideration of all rate questions, can be most familiarly illustrated in the old proverb, that "carrying coals to Newcastle" is a profitless operation. Newcastle is supposed to be already abundantly supplied with coal as cheap as can be found anywhere else. If, therefore, a railroad starting five hundred miles away should carry coal toward Newcastle, as it came within the influence of the Newcastle market, the value of the service rendered would decrease the farther it was carried; for it would find cheaper coal already on the ground. Therefore the rates which the railroads could charge would decrease as the distance increased. For a certain distance the railroad, having its managing and accounting departments, its roadbed, crossties, etc., to keep up anyhow—and perhaps empty cars engaged in other traffic returning to Newcastle— might afford to carry more or less coal at rates far below its average rates, and still make a profit, while promoting traffic and competition for the public. But the business would finally reach a limit where even the extra fuel consumed in hauling a car full instead of empty would exceed in value the service rendered, and there the business would have to stop. It is clear, too, that the transportation of firewood to places near Newcastle would be under similar conditions to that of coal; for the price of the coal would regulate that of the firewood, which is an inferior substitute.

Now this perfectly illustrates the "circumstances and conditions" under which alone are railroads ever so generous and liberal-minded as to charge less for the longer haul. It is always where the place enjoying the lower rate for the longer haul has already a cheaper source of supply for the material to be transported, or of some substitute therefor. These conditions, they claim, are the most substantial which can affect comparative rates; and they justify and legalize the apparent discriminations, which are really the result of the Creator's distribution of different kinds of mineral and agricultural wealth, and of lands and seas, and rivers and mountains.

Under the law the first interpreter of the intent of the Senate amendment, as accepted by the House and made law, is the Interstate Commerce Commission. This body, in the first cases brought before it, seemed rather to stick in the bark of the question than to go to its heart, and decided individual cases upon their individual peculiarities.

For instance—to square some of the cases with our general illustration of carrying coal and firewood to places where they come in competition with coal from Newcastle—they decided that a railroad might be justified in accepting a lower rate for a longer haul on coal only, but not on firewood, and then only in case the competitive coal was brought from Newcastle by a water route. Within the limits of this article it is impossible to explain the peculiarities of different cases and the arguments of the commission, not always entirely harmonious, nor is it important to do so for an understanding of the issue now before the United States court. But, briefly, the general effect of their decisions in many cases was that competition resulting from the existence of water routes of transportation might legalize lesser rates on longer hauls, but that competition resulting from other causes—such as that from other railroad lines, or from competition of other markets or products—would not.

They therefore approved of some cases and disapproved of others; and for five years the arguments, pro and con, have been gone over, and the roads have complied more or less willingly and fully with the mandates of the commission. At last, however, a definite issue has been made.

The case is this: Buggies are manufactured largely in Cincinnati, and still more largely in Baltimore, New York and eastern cities; so that as Cincinnati buggies are carried into territory more cheaply reached from the east, this transportation—like that of coal toward Newcastle—becomes less and less valuable as it reaches places accessible to eastern cities by cheaper routes either of rail or water; and the railroads running from Cincinnati have always adjusted their rates accordingly. On the rail line, for instance, extending southeast from Cincinnati to Charleston, via Chattanooga, Atlanta and Augusta, the influence of eastern buggies was felt wherever a transportation line from the east came in. At Chattanooga it was of slight consequence, at Atlanta it was important, at Augusta it was of controlling force, and at Charleston it was overwhelming. The rates from Cincinnati increased gradually until after passing Atlanta far enough to be affected by eastern buggies coming up via Augusta. There the rate reached its maximum, about halfway between Atlanta and Augusta. Thence it decreased, and was the same at Augusta as at Atlanta, and at Charleston it was still lower. The case was made in a small town called Social Circle near the maximum point. The railroad commission, being appealed to, decided that it was illegal for the railroads to charge less for the longer hauls on buggies from Cincinnati to Augusta, or Charleston than to Social Circle. The railroads have refused to accept this ruling of the commission as the true intent of the law, and have appealed to the United States court to interpret it.

The point to be decided is, whether the words "substantially similar circumstances and conditions" refer to circumstances and conditions which affect the value of the service or transportation at the point of destination, and therefore limit the price which can be obtained for it; or whether they refer to some other circumstances, undefined and rather difficult to imagine, since all circumstances of time, place, direction and character of freight handled are elsewhere specifically referred to in the law.

There would seem to be no other "substantial" circumstances left save those affecting the value of the service rendered. These are all practically circumstances of competition—the competition of different routes, of different markets, or different products. It is the circumstance of competition which produces the effect according to its degree, whatever may be its source or character. It might be by other rail lines from the same or other sources of supply, by water or by balloon—the effect being the same in all cases.

This analysis of the underlying cause of the apparently gratuitous discrimination involved in the custom of charging less on certain longer hauls, indicates clearly, also, that the practice gives no arbitrary power, and has little effect in altering the commercial supremacy of different localities.

Newcastle does not derive her supremacy in coal from the fact that railroads give lesser rates on longer hauls of coal toward it, but from her natural advantages of location. Railroads are simply compelled to recognize these advantages, and adjust their rates accordingly; being forced, in the sharp struggle for existence, to accept half loaves when they cannot get whole. But free and unrestricted liberty to enter into this competition distributes its advantages to all adjoining places in proportion to their distances, thus promoting general prosperity.

The court, however, cannot make the law, and can only interpret it. Should their interpretation be adverse to the railroads the railroad transportation of this country will be put under conditions which do not exist in any other; for in Canada, England and on the continent of Europe, railroads are freely allowed to meet competition. The effect of strictly enforcing such a law here would be to attach a severe penalty to it, one which would inevitably largely restrict and curtail it.

This might indeed be to the railroads rather a blessing than a calamity, were a strict enforcement possible; but the effort would only produce confusion, and result in a repeal of the law; for any restriction so opposed to the spirit of the age cannot long prevail.

A very simple illustration will make clear the essential features of nearly every case in the United States where competition of routes leads to lower charges upon the longer hauls.

Imagine four cities, N, E, S and W, at the north, east, south and west points of any closed figure, as a circle. Then let an eastern railroad run from N through E and S to W, and a western from

N through W and S to E. There are then two overlapping routes from N to each of the two other cities, an eastern and a western. To S they are practically of equal length, but to E the eastern is much the shorter, and to W the western. Let 90 be a reasonable average rate from N to E or W, and 180 the same to S; or one for each degree of the circle traversed.

Now, if no restriction is placed on competition, the eastern route will not only compete with the western at S, but clear around to W; and while it could not hope with its longer distance to do a very large share of the business, yet it might get some remunerative employment for idle cars and engines in a dull season. But it could not charge more than 90 for the service, perhaps not even quite so much, for its service would be much slower than that of the western route, let us say 87. Similarly, too, will the western route compete for freight from N to E through S at 87.

Now let it be declared illegal to charge more for the shorter haul than for the longer, and what will be the result?

As a penalty for engaging in the competitive business to E and W each road must reduce its rates at S from 180 to 90 or 87, as well as all other rates at intermediate stations which exceed 87. Neither road could afford to give up a large business at average rates for a smaller business over a longer line and at a reduced rate; so it would simply withdraw from the long haul business, and would enjoy a monopoly of what it had the short haul on. As before stated, this might be a blessing rather than a calamity, so far as the railroads alone are concerned; but it is absurd to suppose that this country will permanently put any such penalty upon railroad competition.

It may be objected that no two single roads overlap each other, as in the figure suggested above. But by their innumerable connections working with them as through lines, nearly all competing lines do overlap and intersect and interlace in even a far more complicated manner.

So in conclusion it may be stated briefly that every case of competition of routes has its essential principles perfectly illustrated in the figure suggested above, and every case of competition of products and of markets has its principles perfectly illustrated in the old proverb that it is labor lost to carry coals to Newcastle. And the single underlying principle of the whole business and of all railroad rates is that they must be principally based on the value of the service and not on its cost. And when the value of any longer haul is less than that of a shorter from the competition either of routes, of markets or of products, then the essential conditions and circumstances are different, and the lesser rate for the longer haul is not only justifiable but necessary.

Savannah, Ga.

THE TREATMENT OF RAILROAD EMPLOYES.

By Mr. B. B. Adams, Jr.,

Associate Editor of The Railroad Gazette.

It may be assumed that the Editor of THE INDEPENDENT, in assigning to me the above-mentioned topic, phrased as it is, was actuated, more or less, by the feeling that railroad corporations do not always treat every employe as well as he deserves. Such a feeling exists, and it is widespread. There is often good foundation for it, as every railroad manager knows; but I am bound to say, in passing, that one of the most mischievous features of the matter is the false notion concerning railroad men's troubles that is propagated by the daily newspapers. Impelled apparently by the motive, perhaps laudable, to give large space in the reading columns to affairs which interest the most numerous class of readers—that is, the "workingmen"—the editors print ten times as much of the gossip and small talk of enginemen and brakemen as the subject deserves; and the reader, even when he discerns the true "thinness" of the alleged news, is unconsciously affected by its reiteration day after day. He magnifies the railroader's woes in spite of himself.

On our main question, What do the corporations give their men for the work performed, and how do the officers behave in giving it? no general statement can be made, for different corporations follow different theories. The "treatment" of workmen always includes wages *and* other things. This is particularly true in the railroad service. Free rides when off duty, and free rides for his family, are important elements in nearly every railroad man's treatment, whether he expressly acknowledges the fact or not. On a freight train the pay is generally by the trip, and the number of trips a week or the skill, or lack of skill, with which the trainmaster makes the hours favorable may often be as important as would be a five per cent change in wages. Railroads often overlook or lightly punish blunders involving large money losses which, in other employments, the workman would have to settle for. And these elements, which can be measured in money, are often less important than methods of discipline, which cannot be

---

Reprinted by permission from The Independent of October 6, 1892.

thus measured. A foreman who will not grant a furlough without seeming to convey an invitation to hand in your resignation, or a superintendent who shows by his manner that he will find an excuse for discharging you if you appeal to the president from a decision of his, may make life such a burden that it is better to leave the road. A president who promises to consider an application for higher pay, but who takes six months in which to prepare his answer, may do more harm than another man would by an actual reduction of wages.

Why do people ever think that railroad men are ill-treated? Well, they see that many station men have hard work, that telegraph operators have to work long hours, that trainmen are often killed or injured, that many in all these classes seem to be less intelligent and well-to-do than their occupations would lead one to expect them to be; and every now and then some trainmen or laborers strike. Wherein is the employer to blame?

The greatest fault of the corporations is that they do not properly train their men, but leave them to train themselves. The responsibilities of a locomotive runner, a brakeman or a telegraph operator are serious and important; and if the companies made it a rule to fill these places only with men who thoroughly appreciated those responsibilities they would raise the grade of intelligence, would incidentally be forced to pay higher wages, and would silence many complaints. A man trying to fill a larger place than he is competent for has a natural tendency to a state of dissatisfaction, for he has not comprehended his surroundings.

Railroad managers are noted for their shortsighted policies. In the worst cases they will let the track get into a dangerous state of disrepair, so that the published profits can be made large enough to favor the speculations of the directors in Wall street. The officers know that a settling time will surely come; that the track must be repaired some time; but they shut their eyes to the future. This shortsightedness affects all departments and has a marked influence in many otherwise good companies. A just demand for more pay or easier work is staved off, in the hope that next year it will be easier to meet it.

Railroads do not deal frankly with their men. A railroad corporation is a public concern and, its affairs being matters of public discussion, the employes, who are, *of course*, always wanting better pay, have a right to be told just why the company is too poor to comply with their wishes. In 1890 the Erie road, in answering a loud complaint from certain employes, issued to them a most carefully prepared pamphlet setting forth just why the wages could not be increased, and the employes were sensible enough to accept the argument. Such a statement, in substance, should be made every year or half year and every dissatisfied employe should not only receive it but be made to grasp its meaning. The earnings, expenses, rise or fall of rates and prospects for the future could and should be stated so that a schoolboy could understand them. It would not be easy at first, but perseverence would accomplish good results. But this, if done honestly, involves a degree of publicity that many directors shrink from. They do not want to expose the real state of their finances even to the stockholders, much less to the employes.

When, from the accumulated grievances of years, or the evil influence of new employes who are natural "agitators," a strike actually impends, the most conspicuous fault of the railroad company is narrow-mindedness. The directors do not seem to realize that their possession of superior wealth and intelligence places the employes at a disadvantage, and the rights of the company are maintained as strenuously as if the contest were with an equal. It is true that the employes *might* select an advocate as wise and shrewd as the railroad president, but generally they do not; and their fatuity must be taken into consideration by the employer if he would merit the approval of public opinion. I am not speaking now of raising or reducing wages, but of the manner of conducting negotiations. An employe has no right to send a brotherhood chief to argue with the superintendent; but he most certainly has a right to send an individual advocate, and superintendents have often made the mistake of refusing an audience to a man on this distinction when they would have made money had they ignored it; and with proper tact they need not have sacrificed any principle. The two greatest railroad strikes of the last five years, that on the Chicago, Burlington & Quincy in 1888 and that on the New York Central & Hudson River in 1890, are held by competent judges to have been precipitated by a lack of suavity in the vice-presidents who treated with the complainers. These strikes cost two or three million dollars each. The shortsightedness of directors, referred to above, keeps the salaries of officers too low, so that this same lack of tact is found among the division superintendents who conduct the every-day dealings with the men. A succession of small irritations aggravates the final one.

All these things are common enough to justify the existence, among many fair-minded people, of the feeling that railroad "labor" is often unfairly dealt with; but let us look for a moment at the other side of the shield. On many railroads the service is conducted so smoothly that the public seldom hears of any trouble. On all roads the disturbances are among the freight conductors and brakemen almost exclusively. This class includes the so-called "switchmen." The station agents and many other classes never strike, tho' their pay is smaller, in proportion to the skill demanded, than that of train men. The passenger train men generally do not join the freight men.*

---

* If there is any class which the companies do misuse without excuse it is the shopmen. These, located in country towns, remote from the large cities where other work in their line is obtainable, sometimes have their pay suddenly reduced in winter in order that the expenses may be kept down to some arbitrary limit, when the company, having plenty of repair work on hand, ought to keep them at work at regular pay, even at a slight financial sacrifice.

TREATMENT OF RAILROAD EMPLOYES.

The Pennsylvania road rarely has a strike. It has an insurance department through which the company grants the employes actual gratuities of $100,000 or $200,000 a year, besides affording incidental benefits. The Baltimore & Ohio has a similar department, older than the Pennsylvania's. The Chicago, Burlington & Quincy and the Philadelphia & Reading have started these departments. The Boston & Albany and other roads, employing 5,000 to 10,000 men each, have had no strike of any consequence in many years. A number of prominent companies pay premiums to the foremen of track repairs. The Fall Brook Railroad pays premiums to the freight conductors.

The narrow-mindedness of railroad officers is largely owing to their uncertain tenure of office. Strictly speaking, they are inexperienced. From the comparative newness of the country or the rushing times we are living in, the directors do not succeed in getting first-class officers and in *keeping them.* Superintendents assume an air of infallibility and yet make false moves and have to retreat, weakening the respect of their men. A railroad superintendent does not fit his place until he has held it a year or two. These conditions are partly due to the old trouble that directors do not direct. A railroad president, general manager or superintendent, if he does all required of him, generally does two or three men's work. Small corporations have been consolidated into large ones, so that the manager has to deal with his men at long range. The consolidating process has gone on so rapidly, owing partly to unfair legislation, that methods of discipline have not been properly adjusted to the new conditions. At present employes of small roads are often treated better than those of large ones.

Managers are loth to be frank with their men, because the men employ such rank demagogues or such young novices as spokesmen. Ten thousand good men will quickly acquiesce in the action of one hundred of their unreflecting fellows in empowering a half-dozen agitators to make impudent threats to the officers. The ten thousand may not actually join in a strike, but, feeling that they have little to lose, will tacitly encourage the most reckless agitators. Both the reckless and those not reckless make demands much larger than they expect to enforce, which is always dangerous for any one not skilled in sophistical arts. When an overbearing officer has to explain a strike, he always proves that the employes were more unreasonable than himself.

Railroads which keep wages down so as to keep profits up are generally sincere. If profits are not satisfactory stockholders will sell their stock, the price of it will fall, the company cannot borrow money, expensive improvements of the road are postponed, and the public suffers for the lack of them; and any lawful means to prevent this is deemed not only right but praiseworthy. To pay men better wages *and* keep up improvements, the road must have a good income. It must get the money before it can spend it. But good earnings at once prompt the legislator to demand a reduction of rates and fares *before* the road is improved. The training of the men, which the companies neglect, is bound up in the question of wages. They get as good men as they feel able to pay for.

As intimated at the outset, a general statement is hard to make, and dangerous; but, broadly speaking, we may say that those companies which do have trouble with their men are more to blame than the men are. The defense of the companies, which I have just outlined, does not quite meet the arraignment. As long as some companies get along without trouble the burden of proof is on those which do have trouble to show why they do not avoid it. Those companies which spend more money for wages, and which employ superintendents who know how to treat subordinates just right (this also implies increased expenditure), are satisfied with the financial results of their policy. The vital difference between these and the shortsighted companies is that the latter *will not wait long enough* for their profits. Improvements in service do not return a profit until they have been in use some time. Unjust restrictions imposed by the state should be regarded by a corporation as a misfortune, to be borne as best it can be. What justification is there for shifting the burden to the shoulders of the employes? The capitalist, who sees nothing but his capital and the immediate returns upon it, will dispute me here. When Iowa reduced wages by law, the boast was made on behalf of the companies, that employes' wages would be reduced in that state. In some cases the threat was doubtless carried out, in effect, if not visibly; but the companies were morally bound to show the justice of their act, for they, and not the employes, took the risk of adverse legislation.

Sir George Findlay, General Manager of the London & Northwestern, a fair-minded man of great experience, has lately said:

"The true preventive of strikes is to be found in *the cultivation of a good understanding between the men and their employers*, and in the establishment of sick, accident and benefit funds fostered and assisted by the directors, so as to show that the employers take as great an interest in their moral and material welfare as a private employer would do in the case of valued servants."

The dozen words that I have italicized contain the gist of the matter; and that is the only hopeful remedy for the defects I have enumerated. A "good understanding" would lead employes to put up with the inevitable, and employers to redress grievances in their incipiency. Arbitration is of no value in dealings between a corporation and its employes, because the employes can give no bond that they will abide by the decision of the arbitrators. The irresponsible character of the brotherhoods is the reason that railroads cannot make binding agreements with them on any point.

There are indications that the brotherhoods, whose rashness has been the cause of the worst railroad strikes, are growing wiser. Conservative leaders seem to be in more favor than they were a few years ago. Sweeney, whose weakness was so conspicuous at Buffalo, is probably not a fair sample of the brotherhood leader today. Mr. Arthur, leader of the locomotive engineers, probably the wisest trade-union leader in this country, has set an example which the others seem to be emulating. The railroad managers are also improving. Conciliatory tactics are growing in favor. Several roads have recently raised the wages of telegraph operators at the request or demand of their brotherhood. One of the chief dangers now seems to be that requests for additional pay will be granted without proper reflection, simply to avoid or postpone a conflict. Advances in pay ought to be made discriminatingly, by the superintendent or other officer who is familiar with the men and their respective abilities. To give more pay without getting better service is an expedient of doubtful value.

New York City.

THE BROTHERHOOD OF ENGINEERS AND ITS RELATION TO THE RAILROADS.

By Mr. Nat Sawyer.

Locomotive Engineer on the New York Central and Hudson River Railroad.

The Grand International Brotherhood of Locomotive Engineers was instituted at Detroit, Mich., August 17th, 1863, its name at that time being "The Brotherhood of the Footboard." (The "footboard" is the platform upon which the engineer and fireman of a locomotive stand.) The Order was reorganized at Indianapolis, Ind., August 17, 1864, as the Brotherhood of Locomotive Engineers. There are about 30,000 members of the Order.

No person can become a member of the Brotherhood unless he is a white man, is twenty-one years of age, can read and write, is a man of good moral character, of temperate habits, is a locomotive engineer in good standing, and in active service as such when proposed. He must also have had at least one year's experience as an engineer. Each division of the Order is to be the judge of what constitutes one year's experience.

One peculiar and stringent rule of the Brotherhood is that none of its members are allowed to join any other labor organization under penalty of expulsion. If a proposed member does belong to any other labor organization, he may be balloted for; but, if elected, he cannot be initiated until satisfactory evidence is shown that he has withdrawn from such organization. No candidate can be initiated while there is a strike on the road on which he is employed.

The influence or sympathy of the Brotherhood, as a body, is not allowed to be enlisted or used in favor of any political or religious organization whatever, and political or religious discussions are not permitted at any of the meetings.

If a brother has conducted himself in a manner unbecoming a man, and which may be calculated to bring disgrace upon the Brotherhood, or is guilty of drunkenness, or keeping a saloon where intoxicating liquors are sold, or is engaged in the traffic of intoxicating liquors, or joins a secret detective organization, a committee is appointed to examine the charges, and, if they are found

---

Reprinted by permission from The Independent of June 1, 1893.

true, he is expelled. He is also subject to the same penalty if he neglects his duty, or injures the property of his employer, or endangers the lives of persons willfully, while under the influence of liquor, or otherwise.

During the last month, for instance, according to the official record, members were expelled from the order for the following causes: non-payment of dues and assessments, intoxication, unbecoming conduct, violating obligations, keeping saloon, deserting family, "dead beat," defrauding Division, defrauding a Brother, etc.

Each member is provided with a traveling card, by which his identity can be established in other Divisions than his own; but he is not allowed to use it for commercial purposes, under penalty of expulsion.

In case of the death of a Brother in good standing a committee is appointed to inquire into the pecuniary condition of the family of the deceased. Should the committee report that they are in want of assistance, it is made the duty of every member of the Division to see that they are assisted by all honorable means; that the children, if there be any, are not allowed to suffer or be neglected, and the members extend over them their protection and care so long as they may stand in need of it. The widow is assisted in every way which may be deemed proper. It is made the duty of each member of the Division to use every effort, consistent with the rules of propriety, to prevent her from coming to destitution or disgrace; they must treat her with respect and consideration so long as she may prove herself worthy.

It is not generally known that the Brotherhood has a special funeral service of its own, which takes place at the grave. It may be interesting to reproduce the opening remarks, read by the chaplain or chief engineer :

"Again are we assembled, in accordance with an established custom of the Brotherhood of Locomotive Engineers, to pay the last sad tribute of respect and esteem to the memory of our Brother, who, when in health and strength, deemed it not only a duty but a privilege to contribute whatever he possessed of influence, of talent or of strength to the elevation of the character and standing of the profession to which he had devoted the best years of his life, and who always remembered that while his first obligation was to God and those whom, in His infinite mercy, had been made dependent upon him, a no less binding obligation made it his duty to seek to elevate and purify the organization of which he was an honored member,"

The closing prayer in the services is as follows:

"Our Father who art in Heaven, hallowed be Thy name; Thy kingdom come, Thy will be done on earth as it is in Heaven; give us this day our daily bread, and forgive us our debts as we forgive our debtors; lead us not into temptation, but deliver us from evil,

"And we further ask Thee to let Thy special blessing rest upon the relatives of our deceased Brother; comfort them, we pray Thee, in this hour of affliction; may they not mourn as those without hope.

" May the blessing of Heaven rest upon us, and the cement of brotherly

love unite us together while here on earth, so that when we are called by death's relentless hand, we may be found worthy to be admitted into Thy Kingdom above. Amen.
Response.—So mote it be."

A strong feature of the Brotherhood is an insurance system. Policies are issued for $1,500, $3,000 and $4,000. The loss of a leg, an arm, or a total loss of sight entitles the holder of the policy to the full amount of his insurance. There is also a widows' and orphans' fund, the donations for which at the last convention amounted to $16,000. There is also in the Brotherhood a regularly organized lodge of ladies who render valuable assistance in case of sickness or distress in the families of deceased members.

The *Journal of the Brotherhood of Locomotive Engineers*, published at Cleveland, Ohio, is the official organ of the Brotherhood. It is a magazine of about one hundred pages of the standard size, and is issued monthly. It contains a list of the general and local officers of the Brotherhood, scientific articles in regard to locomotives, railway law, correspondence on engineering and labor matters of current interest, a story, poems and sketches for the benefit of the lady readers, and personal items about members of the order who are expelled, suspended, reinstated or have withdrawn from membership.

In regard to the policy of the order, I believe there is a general desire on the part of engineers to foster a spirit of good feeling toward the railroad companies; in fact, it is to their interest so to do. Of course there are radicals in every organization, men who are never satisfied with any course of action, but the conservatives far outnumber the radicals and dictate the policy that is to be pursued. P. M. Arthur, the Grand Chief of the Brotherhood, is a conservative man, so is Mr. Sargent, of the Firemen's Brotherhood. Personally, I have always been a conservative, and I think the conservative element will always prevail in the Brotherhood. We believe that, as a rule, the railroad companies treat us fairly, especially the large trunk lines; but the smaller roads are sometimes open to criticism.

The Brotherhood of Locomotive Engineers has less trouble than any other labor organization with its employers. One reason is because any agreement the men make with the company they carry out to the letter. Our organization can be depended upon to live up to its promises. The railroad companies have found this out, and the consequence is that, generally speaking, it has fostered a spirit of good feeling between the organization and the companies.

And I believe that the railroad companies look at the question of their relation to their employes in the same way; that they really want to foster good feeling, and desire to pay the men fair living wages. This is especially the case on the New York Central. The men on this road have no better friends than the three principal executive officers, H. Walter Webb, the third vice president; John M. Toucey, the general manager; and William Buchanan, the superintendent of power and rolling stock. The famous strike on the New York Central in 1890 was not won by the railroad as such; it was won on the personality of these officers I have named. The engineers desired to show their gratitude for the many acts of kindness they had received from them in the past, and they stood by the company.

The subjects in dispute between a railroad company and the Brotherhood generally refer to long hours on duty and under payment for overtime. We will say that twelve hours constitute a day's work. For any work over that time the engineer wants thirty-five cents an hour. This demand is conceded on large roads like the New York Central, but some of the smaller roads refuse to pay the extra charge.

Generally, throughout the country, the regular hours of labor are calculated to be ten hours; but for two hours overtime (making twelve hours in all), the men will receive thirty-five cents an hour if they are laid off at a terminal point; *i. e.*, if they are not able to get back to the starting point with their train.

After a man is promoted to run an engine he receives, during the first year, $2.50 a day, and a pro rata mileage of 2½ cents a mile. The second year he receives $3 a day, with a pro rata of three cents, over one hundred miles. The third year he is paid $3.50 a day and a pro rata of 3½ cents for all over one hundred miles.

On a road where there is a good freight business the men will make about $125 a month on that kind of traffic. The engineers running passenger trains will average about $140 a month. But the engineer who runs the fast express train to Chicago will receive no more than the one who runs a slow train. As a matter of fact, the engineer who runs the Chicago express has the easiest job, because he is bound to have a clear road on which to run his train.

A strike is ordered on a railroad in this way: There has been a disagreement between some engineers and the company. We will say that the local committee of the Brotherhood of the Hudson River Division, another on the Middle Division, and another on the Western Division have failed in their efforts to bring about an agreement. They then notify the General Committee of the Brotherhood, which is called together and which consults with the highest official of the road. If, after a conference, they fail to come to an understanding, the Grand Chief of the Brotherhood is sent for. His first question is "Have you exhausted all your efforts?" If the answer is "No," he telegraphs back that he will not come; the committee must continue in the work. If they have exhausted all their efforts he comes. If, then, he gives the men permission to strike they can strike, and the Brotherhood supports the strike. But if he does not give them permission and they strike, they not only have no assistance from the Brotherhood, but are liable to be expelled for the action they have taken. But I will say here that, as a rule if, in the case of a disagreement between a railroad company and the men, the men go the right way to work they can nearly always obtain their demands. I was chairman of the local committee on the New York Central for a good many years. I have often seen the demands of the men granted when they have been presented in the proper way.

I am asked to express my opinion in regard to the Toledo and Ann Arbor strike in the west, out of which has grown an important legal question, which is to be adjudicated upon by the United States Supreme Court. People have seen so much in the newspapers about the legal proceedings growing out of the trouble that they are apt to lose sight of the original cause of disagreement. As usual it was about the question of wages. The men on the freight trains were paid from $3 to $3.60 per one hundred miles, fourteen hours constituting a day's work. The $3.60 pay was for what are called large compound, no-deck, consolidated mogul engines, and the men asked for this class, $3.70. In the passenger service the men were paid $2.45 per 100 miles. They were willing to meet their officials in this whole schedule for three cents a mile on passenger and $3.50 per 100 miles on freight. No first-class railroad in Michigan pays less than $3.50 for freight and passenger service. The engineers would have waived the point for extra compensation for the large no-deck moguls, if they had been met in the spirit of fairness, and would have cheerfully accepted an honorable compromise rather than struck; but the General Manager would not listen to a compromise or make the slightest concessions, nor would he modify an order recently issued that overtime would not be paid engineers and firemen until after twenty-one hours continuous service. The general treatment of the men had been very bad. Obnoxious bulletins were constantly being issued. One of these required the men to coal their engines after the trip was made, and no excuse was taken even tho' they had been on duty the twenty-one hours demanded by the company.

A boycott grew out of this trouble with the Ann Arbor railroad. This boycott was passed by the Brotherhood, I think, in 1888. It provided that wherever there was a strike on a road the men would refuse to haul the freight cars of a connecting road, when the cars of the road with which they had trouble were attached to the trains of said road. It is allowable to haul passenger trains but *not* freight trains. I think that rule is wrong, and I believe Mr. Arthur is of the same opinion. I do not think that the boycott should ever have been introduced in this country. It has no business here, and it is a wrong method. It has been said that Mr. Arthur has made the remark: "Take away the privilege of the boycott from organized labor and its fight against capital will be futile." I do not think Mr. Arthur made that remark, and I base my judgment on the fact that I not only know him very well, but I have been officially associated with him in the Brotherhood for many years. In the Ann Arbor case, if the officers of the road had treated the men in a fair spirit there would have been no trouble.

My opinion is that the men can gain more by arbitration than by the use of the stringent measures some of the more radical members of the order are inclined to adopt. The decision of Judge Ricks in the Ann Arbor case is what I expected it would be. I have told our members that some day they would come in contact with the Interstate Commerce Law. The final decision of the United States Supreme Court will determine the rights of labor organizations as they are affected by this law. Of course many of our men do not like the decision of Judge Ricks, because they believe it prevents them from enforcing their demand. The whole trouble is about the boycott. I do not think that belongs to this country; it belongs, if anywhere, on the other side of the Atlantic. I do not believe in transplanting the isms of European workingmen, anarchists, etc., into this country. I think we can take care of the interests of our workingmen without borrowing methods from the other side.

In the great Missouri Pacific strike in 1886, Grand Chief Engineer Arthur, of our Brotherhood, was denounced by Martin Irons, the leader of the movement, because the Brotherhood would not sanction what he had done. Irons endeavored to intimidate the men into joining the Knights of Labor, and so help the Knights in their strike. But Mr. Arthur went to St. Louis and told the men that they must obey the laws, which meant, substantially, that they should mind their own business and let other people's alone.

Irons then claimed that the Brotherhood did not sanction the stand Arthur had taken. Soon after this time our organization held a union meeting at Scranton. I have been a member of the executive committee for a good many years, and have always been an admirer of the Grand Chief. On that occasion I offered the following resolution, which was adopted unanimously, was published in our official journal, and by newspapers generally throughout the country:

"*Resolved*, That we, as the representatives of the Brotherhood of Locomotive Engineers, assembled in union meeting in the city of Scranton, Penn., Sunday, September 6th, 1886, do at this time express to our Grand Chief Engineer, P. M. Arthur, our strong and decided approval of his actions in the recent labor troubles in the Northwest and Southwest, and we say to him: 'Continue in the fight as you have in the past, as every act of yours has given entire satisfaction to every loyal member of this Brotherhood, regardless of the statements of the labor demagogs to the contrary—viz., that your action did not meet the approval of the Brotherhood. The entire Brotherhood, we say, is adhering to the agreements with your several companies. Carry out the compact to the letter, and if the agreement is broken let it not be said you were the first to break it.

"'Do your duty, regardless of the intimidations and threats of any organizations in existence, and remembering our motto, *We amalgamate with none.*'"

When it is asked, How will the men enforce their demands in the future? it must be remembered that the large railroad companies have never yet said, absolutely, that they would not make any concessions to the men. As I have already said, if men go about it in the right way to secure their demands, if they have the right kind of leaders to handle the matter each time, they cannot help but gain something.

It is asked, "What will the Brotherhood do in case the decision of Judge Ricks is sustained?" The public may rest assured that the Brotherhood will stand by the laws of the land and obey them to the letter. It must be understood that they are not going to incite a conflict between their organization and the United States Government. At a meeting of our order, held at Schenectady a few days ago, Mr. Arthur said: "This Brotherhood will obey any law of this country."

New York City.

THE NECESSITY FOR RAILWAY COMPACTS UNDER GOVERNMENTAL REGULATION.

By Mr. James Peabody.

Editor of The Railway Review.

The student of railway problems finds himself at the outset confronted by a labyrinth of vast proportions through which no well-defined highways have been marked out, but only here and there obscure and devious paths leading no one knows whither. Not that attempts at exploration have been lacking, for investigation has been busy in all directions, and concerning the particular topic under consideration—that of traffic compacts—much has been said and not a little written. The public addresses on this topic have been mainly denunciatory and of no permanent value. The essayists have less uniformly opposed the idea; but their productions when once read have, as a rule, and in many cases fortunately, been laid aside without serious consideration. The discussion has, however, been of value. It has attracted public attention and thus prepared the way for a more intelligent consideration of whatever in this line may be proposed for legislative or other public action. The subject matter of these various arguments for and against traffic compacts, known in Europe as joint purse arrangements and in America commonly called pools, must be largely repetitious, but its presentation may be so varied as to create new impressions or correct old ones. It is not, therefore, in the hope of contributing anything essentially new that, in response to the invitation of *The Independent*, I venture to discuss the question; but if I shall be able to suggest some thought for which any reason shall serve to promote investigation, my purpose will have been served.

It is axiomatic that business which is common to two or more persons must permit of division; otherwise it is not common. The division may be effected by agreement or strife, consent or competition; but it must be equally apparent to all candid minds that competition, unregulated, becomes self-destructive, involving in its progress toward self-destruction large waste. This is true not only of the carrying business, which because of its quasi-public nature occupies a unique position, but it applies as well to other

---

Reprinted by permission from The Independent of June 1, 1893.

NECESSITY FOR RAILWAY COMPACTS. 217

business. The procedure of insurance companies in the conduct of their affairs furnishes an illustration which, by reason of the public interest involved, is somewhat analogous to that of railways. It is a matter of common knowledge that the rates charged for fire insurance premiums are, in all cities, fixed by agreement and enforced by rigid provisions, extending so far as to require the discharge of agents found cutting the rates and the termination of all relations with companies that fail to conform to the agreed scale. Such compact, altho' preventing strife does not eliminate competition, but operates to divide the business measurably in accord with the facilities and advantages offered by the various companies, supplemented by the energy and ability of their representatives. It is conceded by the public that in this business strife is as fraught with danger to themselves as to the insurance companies, because it is apparent that the value of the indemnity offered is predicated upon the ability of the companies to obtain rates sufficiently high to be profitable, and the public know that without some combination that will prevent excessive competition and secure a proportionate division of earnings, the rate of premium would soon be forced down to an unremunerative basis, and the protection upon which they depend would be a minus quantity. From this illustration it will be perceived that in this and other lines of business compacts having for their object the maintenance of systematic distributive methods are simply a means looking to the preservation of competitive forces.

It is the almost universal practice in connection with railway operations, when referring to towns served by two or more railroads, to designate them as common or competitive points, the words being used interchangeably; but it will be noticed that as descriptive of the character of traffic subject to distribution the word "common" instead of "competitive" is employed; and in order better to understand the point involved in the choice of the words it may be well to define them. According to the Century Dictionary "common" means—of or pertaining to all; being a general possession or right; and "competitive"—the act of seeking or endeavoring to gain what another is endeavoring to gain at the same time. Webster defines "common" as belonging to, or relating equally or similarly to more than one; shared by all members of a class; and "competition" as strife for one and the same object. It will be seen, therefore, that the one admits the rights of others and presupposes equity; while the other denies the rights of any and, if justified, proclaims that might makes right.

Railroads are the creatures of the state. So far as they serve a public function they exist not because of any inherent right, but by permission. With this fact in mind and heeding the distinction between the words "common" and "competitive" it will be apprehended that, by use of the word "common" as descriptive of traffic at junction points it is suggested that all carriers, who because of chartered rights and privileges have constructed railroads to such points, are thereby entitled to such a proportion of the common traffic as their presence, together with their facilities, legitimately commands. Not what they can get by means of strife, for that might result in a monopoly of the business by a single carrier, but a division of that which is common to all, in order that the rights of each may be preserved.

It is well understood that the purpose underlying the act to regulate commerce is the prevention of discrimination as between both shippers and localities. In the framing of the law the common practice of carriers in favoring one shipper or one locality over another was sought to be prevented, but it was not perceived that discrimination, as fatal in its results to the shipper or the locality could be effected through the independent action of different lines acting within the law, as was possible by the action of an individual line in the absence, or the direct violation of the law. Suppose, for illustration, that A has a grain elevator on the line of one road at X, and B has an elevator located on another road at the same point. These elevators have a common source of supply. Naturally either elevator cannot ship by any other road than the one on which it is located. Now although both roads may comply with the law so far as their individual lines are concerned, the making by one road of a less rate for a similar service than is made by the other is a discrimination as between shippers as surely as if both elevators were located on the same line, and the different rates made by the same road. So also in regard to localities. The State of Iowa is crossed from east to west by five different railways running on approximately parallel lines a few miles apart. The areas of territory lying between these several lines are dependent upon them for transportation facilities, and if the rates made by one road are less than those made by the parallel lines at corresponding stations, discriminations as between localities as surely results as if different rates were made by either one of the roads from contiguous stations on its own line. From these simple illustrations it will be perceived that traffic compacts whereby equality of charges for like services between coincident points, or between shippers by different lines at common points may be sesured, are not only in harmony with, but absolutely essential to the perfect operation of the law; if indeed the statement is not warranted that in no other way can its successful operation be hoped for outside of a general consolidation of all lines and the destruction of the American railway system as at present organized.

The law very properly assumes a position in respect to carriers' rates very different from that of other business, in that it stipulates that charges shall be reasonable, going so far as, in some instances, to determine the maximum limit of reasonableness. But stability in connection with traffic charges is perhaps more import-

NECESSITY FOR RAILWAY COMPACTS.

ant than reasonableness. In these days of sharp competition and narrow margins a slight difference in railroad charges is often sufficient to determine the question of profit or loss; and the same necessity that exists for the prevention of discrimination for contemporaneous service as between shippers, is operative in a large degree with respect of time. It is not of vital importance to the tradesman whether the rate on his merchandise from New York to Chicago is a dollar or fifty cents, provided his competitor in business pays the same rate; but it is essential to him to know when he goes to New York to lay in his stock of goods for an ensuing season, that this competitor, who follows him a little later, will not be able to obtain any less rate of freight on his purchases.

As between this question of low rates and stable rates there has always been a difference of opinion, arising chiefly from a misapprehension of the relation they bear to traffic. The scale or amount of charges is chiefly important to the consumer, while stability or uniformity in rates is mainly of interest to the dealer; but the control of the one is no more important than the regulation of the other.

But in addition to equal, reasonable and stable service the people of this country are of right demanding that the convenience and efficiency of railway service shall be maintained in a constantly increasing ratio. The response to this demand creates a paradox in that it is conducive to both economy and waste; that is to say, the supply of transportation facilities adequate for the propet handling of traffic in time of pressure is much in excess of thar required for the aggregate traffic of the year, provided it could be equally distributed over that period. It will be naturally understood that to comply with this very proper demand for extra equipment, railroads must charge a sufficient margin above expenses and interest charges (to say nothing of dividends) to provide for the required outlay; but it should also be understood that if a railroad can, by the reduction of a rate on special shipments secure traffic which otherwise would go to another line, any rate above actual movement expenses is a source of profit, altho' if all of its rates were correspondingly low bankruptcy would be inevitable. It therefore follows that if aggregate tariff charges on the entire traffic of the country is, as required by law, adjusted on a reasonable basis, there is no room for rate reductions; and that if reductions are made the people as a whole suffer because thereby railroads are precluded from earning a sufficient amount to supply needed facilities. This is a fact not generally apprehended by either railway men or the public, because of the common failure to understand that the railways of this country are practically parts of one great system instead of being, as is popularly supposed, made up of individual lines, each having the right to act independently of the others. For the prevention of this waste of strife as well as contributing to equality of service, that form of traffic compacts called a pool agreement promises to afford the desired relief by removing from carriers the possibility of profiting either individually or collectively by such means.

The word "pool," as applied to compacts by which the equitable distribution among carriers of common traffic is sought to be effected, is both inapt and inaccurate, especially as there is attaching to it a disreputable flavor growing out of its intimate association with gambling operations. This is unfortunate, for notwithstanding that in the contribution and distribution of traffic of its earnings the conditions inherent in gambling pools are directly opposed to those operative in the railway pool, the term conveys an erroneous idea. To the majority of persons it implies something excessively wrong; something to be vigorously opposed and if possible effectually prohibited. This general impression is further strengthened by the all too-common belief that because railway compacts are advocated by railway managers they are necessarily detrimental to public welfare. Without pausing here to indicate wherein this idea is fallacious, or to show why and how the interests of the carriers and the people are, and in the nature of things must be identical, it is sufficient to say that altho' neither wholly good nor altogether bad, railway pools are demonstrably the best ascertained method of fostering the mutual concerns of the carriers and their patrons, and therefore should be made legally operative; but also because they readily lend themselves to the possible abuse of the same interests they should be subject to supervision and regulation.

Pooling as applied to the carrying business expresses an effort on the part of carriers to distribute common business in an intelligent and economical way instead of allowing it to seek, through the medium of rate wars, those channels which will pay the most for it. At first railway officials sometimes employed the pool to accomplish that which is so generally charged against the practice —viz: the exaction of the highest possible rates. It soon became apparent, however, that other forces than the agreement of railway men controlled transportation charges, and the idea was modified through various stages until at the time the act to regulate commerce became effective it had come to include the fundamental principles of the act—to wit: the removal of discrimination as between shippers, and the maintenance of equal rates for similar and contemporaneous service. This is a very different thing from the making of rates, the one involving compliance with the principles of justice and equity and the other arrogating the right to consult individual interests to the exclusion of others. As already stated, the original object of a pool agreement was the maintenance of railway earnings on the basis of "charging all the traffic would bear." This has been wholly abandoned, and in lieu thereof has been substituted the theory of maintaining equality on the basis of charging what the traffic ought to bear. It is now generally admitted that traffic compacts should provide for the maintenance of such rates as will, first, put all parties subject thereto on a basis of absolute equality with respect to each other, and second, to make them, all things considered, as favorably situated with regard to markets as are their competitors in the same lines of business outside of pooled territory.

It is unfortunate that among railways the idea prevailed that pooling compacts would not be accorded a standing in court, and that in consequence no appeal was made to that tribunal for the enforcement of such contracts anterior to the passage of the act to regulate commerce. Since that time, however, such contracts have been carried into the courts and are fully sustained both as to their binding force as between the contracting parties, and as to their being in full accord with public policy.

To recapitulate,

First. The public may properly demand from carriers equality of treatment on the basis of reasonable rates, and the carrier may with equal right demand protection against the dishonesty of his fellow carrier who violates his compact for the benefit of the shipper who unjustly profits thereby.

Second. Railroads are the creatures of the state and, as subject to the requirements of continuous and indiscriminate service, are entitled to share in the carrying business. Therefore, the traffic accessible to two or more lines should not be regarded as " competitive " in the sense that it is to be sold to the highest bidder, but as " common " in the sense that each line is entitled to a fair proportion of it at the legally published rate.

Third. Traffic or pooling compacts which provide for the equitable division of common traffic are the only yet discovered means whereby the interests of all parties may be conserved.

Fourth. Inasmuch as unrestricted pooling and unrestricted strife are alike capable of being used for harm, government should assume the regulation and enforcement of such compacts, to the end that they may not be allowed to work an injustice to the people on the one hand or to the railways on the other.

Chicago, Ill.

THE APPORTIONMENT OF TRAFFIC AMONG COMPETING RAILROADS.

By Hon. Joseph Nimmo, Jr.

The chapter on Railroad Federations and the Apportionment of Competitive Traffic, herewith republished from my official report on the Internal Commerce of the United States for the year 1885, constitutes a part of the results of an investigation of the commercial interests of the country and of writing reports upon that subject during the period from 1875 to 1885. In the course of that investigation I carefully considered every objection to "pooling," so called, of which I could conceive or which was brought to my attention by other students of the subject. I also challenged every prominent advocate of the expedient to a proof of all that he claimed for it. Finally, as the result of such inquiries, relating not only to the commercial and economic aspects of the question, but also to its merits from the point of view of public policy, I was forced to the conclusion that agreements as to the division of competitive traffic for the specific purpose of maintaining agreements as to rates between competing lines were in the nature of self-restraint; also that they had served the purpose of correcting certain flagrant evils in the conduct of transportation by rail. These conclusions were reached two years before the passage of the Act to Regulate Commerce. As an officer of the Government, I did not at that time feel entirely justified in recommending the legalization of the apportionment of competitive traffic, preferring to await the developments of experience. A somewhat careful observation of the course of events during the last eight years has, however, not only verified the conclusions which I reached in the year 1885, but has forced upon me the conviction that agreements as to the division of traffic among competing lines lie at the very foundation of order in the conduct of the internal commerce of the country, and that such agreements are, besides, essential to the successful administration of the Act to Regulate Commerce.

There appear to be but two fundamental questions to be considered by any person who sincerely desires to reach a right conclusion upon this important matter, viewing it solely in the light of the public interests. Those questions are:

First. Are combinations for the purpose of restraining the full

---
Reprinted by permission from pamphlet published by Author.

force of competitive struggles in commercial and industrial pursuits in any case justifiable upon considerations of public policy? *Second.* Should agreements as to the pooling or division of traffic for the maintenance of rates among competing railroads be regarded as in the nature of just and beneficent combinations?

It is too late in the day to spend much time in debating the first of these questions. The evolution of the commercial and industrial enterprises of the age constitutes its full and complete answer. Our country is to-day, on all sides, confronted by combinations for good and combinations for evil; by combinations which protect competition and promote progress, and by combinations which stifle competition and arrest progress. The very intensity of human activity in commerce, in industrial pursuits, and in transportation have compelled certain restraints through combination, the necessity for which and the beneficent character of which have been clearly proved by the lessons of experience. Combination is the most pronounced symptom of our civilization. By it the largest results in science, in art, in trade, in education, and in religion are being evoked. Combination shields capital and draws it out into active employment, and it also protects labor against itself and against capital.

Besides all this, the jurisprudence of Great Britain and of the United States clearly sustain restraints upon destructive competition. This is no new doctrine of the law. In the case of Mitchell *v.* Reynolds, decided about the year 1711, and reported in "Smith's Leading Cases," the policy of the law of England at that time is stated as follows:

"The present doctrine is that while contracts in total restraint of trade are void, yet if the restraints imposed be partial, reasonable, and founded on good consideration, they are valid and will be enforced."

I believe there is nothing in English or in American jurisprudence which conflicts with that doctrine.

I turn, therefore, to the second of the test questions above propounded, viz: *Should agreements as to the pooling or division of traffic for the maintenance of rates among competing railroads be regarded as in the nature of just and beneficent combinations?* My answer to this question is in part embraced in the extract from my report on Internal Commerce for the year 1885, which these statements preface.

The reasons there adduced in favor of the legitimacy of agreements in regard to the division of traffic for the purpose of maintaining rates are based upon the following considerations: first, the physical infirmity of the railroad which prevents it from ever becoming a free highway of commerce; and, second, the fact that the evolution of the American Railroad System, with all its dependent relationships, compelled the adoption of administrative methods which lacked the conservative influence of that caution which attaches to ownership and to personal responsibility for results.

But there is a third and much more cogent reason why agreements as to the share of competitive traffic should be legalized. It is a reason which emerges from the overshadowing fact that the evolution of the American Railroad System has begotten a competition of commercial forces vastly more potential than any power which the railroads of the country can exercise, either singly or through any possible form of combination. The railroad managers of the country foresaw the loss of independence and of power which was involved in the formation of the American Railroad System, and they opposed every step toward that loss of power until opposition was seen to be useless. The tendency toward a substantial union of American railroads was irresistible. The economies of transportation and the needs of the commercial and industrial development of the country tended strongly in that direction. Connected tracks, a common guage, union depots, through rates, the classification of commodities, rate agreements, prorating, through tickets, related time schedules, the unimpeded passage of freight, passenger, express, and postal cars, and of locomotives over the tracks of different companies, and to a considerable extent the employment of operatives on the lines of different companies—all these co-operative arrangements came about in spite of every effort to preserve the autonomy of different railroads as independent factors in the great work of internal commerce. This wonderful economic and commercial evolution was fully recognized and legalized in the act of June 15, 1866. That act, the most important concerning the internal commerce of the United States which has ever been enacted by Congress, reads as follows:

AN ACT to Facilitate Commercial, Postal, and Military Communication among the States.

Whereas, the Constitution of the United States confers upon Congress, in express terms, the power to regulate commerce among the several States, to establish post roads, and to raise and support armies; therefore,

Be it enacted by the Senate and House of Representives of the United States in Congress assembled, That every railroad company in the United States whose road is operated by steam, its successors and assigns, be, and is hereby, authorized to carry upon and over its road, boats, bridges, and ferries all passengers, troops, Government supplies, mails, freight, and property on their way from any State to another State, and to receive compensation therefor and to connect with roads of other States, so as to form continuous lines for the transportation of the same to the place of destination. * * *

SECTION 2. *And be it further enacted*, That Congress may at any time alter, amend, or repeal this act.

This act of Congress constitutes essentially THE CHARTER OF THE AMERICAN RAILROAD SYSTEM.

Furthermore, all that is involved in this vast system of transportation in the nature of co-operation is sustained and, with respect to freight traffic, made obligatory upon the companies by the provisions of section 7 of the Act to Regulate Commerce. This section reads as follows:

That it shall be unlawful for any common carrier subject to the provisions of this act to enter into any combination, contract, or agreement, expressed or

APPORTIONMENT OF TRAFFIC. 225

implied, to prevent, by change of time schedule, carriage in different cars, or by other means or devices, the carriage of freight from being continuous from the place of shipment to the place of destination; and no break of bulk, stoppage, or interruption made by such carrier shall prevent the carriage of freights from being and being treated as one continuous carriage from the place of shipment to the place of destination, unless such break, stoppage, or interruption was made in good faith for some necessary purpose, and without any intent to avoid or unnecessarily interrupt such continuous carriage, or to evade any of the provisions of this act.

The physical, commercial, and financial union of railroad interests has proceeded to that point at which the entire American Railroad System must be regarded as "many members but one body."

This wonderful railroad system constitutes the most gigantic combination of material interests that the world ever saw—a combination essentially in the public interest, formed not by the volition of those who control its constituent elements, but by an overshadowing compulsion of circumstance which forced those elements into union.

The most important result secured by the formation of the American Railroad System was that it presented an opportunity for the free and untrammeled competition of commercial and industrial forces.

Thus it has come about that the commercial and industrial interests of the country, which many times exceed the interests of transportation, in point of capital invested, have secured a complete mastery over the latter. The unforeseen and most portentous outcome of this wonderful commercial development is the fact that men engaged in commercial pursuits and in productive industries, seeing the advantages which this condition of affairs opened up to them, have united in trusts and in combinations of various sorts, some of which are in restraint of the freedom of trade and of industry, and unmistakably and flagrantly in the nature of monopolies.

Thus trusts and monopolistic combinations not only interfere with the inalienable right of all men to live and labor in an open field and in a pure atmosphere, in the prosecution of commercial enterprise, but they also demoralize and oppress the transportation interests of the country. These trusts sometimes combine so as to throw their shipments upon one road or another in such manner as to baffle railroad managers and to produce outrageously unjust discriminations. The value of the commodities carried by rail each year is at least three times the value of the entire railroad property of the country, and thirty times the annual gross earnings of all the railroads of the country. This clearly exhibits the enormous preponderance of the forces of trade over those of transportation, and it also suggests the ease with which trusts and combinations of trusts are able to thwart the railroads in their efforts to protect themselves, or to observe the requirements of the Act to Regulate Commerce.

15

The evil of allowing large shippers to dominate the internal commerce of the country, and of permitting the railroads to become parties to such unjust discriminations, was first brought to my attention by Mr. Albert Fink in the year 1876, and is presented on page 40 of the Appendix to the First Annual Report on the Internal Commerce of the United States, submitted June 30, 1877.

Just here it appears proper to invite attention to certain radical differences between trusts and monopolies in trade and industry, and agreements between railroad companies as to the apportionment of competitive traffic for the purpose of maintaining rates:

1. The commercial and industrial trust is formed between a select few, who keep all the rest of the competitors out of the combination; they then proceed to break down all the outsiders; whereas a railroad traffic apportionment must of necessity embrace all of the competitors in its provisions, and, besides, it preserves the weaker lines from destruction.

2. Again, each member of a commercial or industrial trust steadfastly seeks to retain his place inside of the organization, while each member of a railroad "pool" or apportionment of traffic is desirous of escaping from its restraints; the tendency, in the absence of legal sanction of the agreements entered into, causing such associations to be unstable, and in many cases leading to their dissolution.

These are distinctive traits of radically different sorts of combinations—the one in the nature of monopoly and in restraint of wholesome competition, and the other in the nature of restraint of monopoly and protective of wholesome competition.

At the present time agreements as to the apportionment of competitive traffic constitute the only known antidote to the baneful influences which are exerted over transportation affairs by commercial trusts, and large shippers.

In passing, I would remark that in my opinion there is no subject which at this time so loudly calls for earnest and thorough investigation at the hands of state legislatures and of Congress as do the evils arising from the assaults of illegitimate trusts and other pernicious combinations upon commerce, upon industrial enterprise, and upon the conduct of the transportation business of the country. The sole end and aim of such assaults, in so far as relates to the railroads, is to produce discriminations in rates, which shall be for the benefit of the parties to such iniquitous combinations. The act of July 2, 1890, "to protect trade and commerce against unlawful restraints and monopolies" is especially directed against such trusts as are here referred to, but there is need of amendments which shall enable the courts and the general public more readily to distinguish between combinations and practices which are legitimate and beneficial toward the public interest, and such as are illegitimate and baneful in their purposes and tendencies.

Thus I have attempted to show that in the evolution of the American Railroad System unforeseen and apparently overwhelming difficulties have arisen, which difficulties are in some measure traceable to infirmities of administration, but mainly to the assaults of commercial and industrial trusts upon the transportation interests of the country.

The result of this untoward course of events has been that the rate-making power has gradually slipped from the hands of railway managers, to whom it is nominally delegated, and that it has been remitted to the more potential shippers. It needs no word of explanation to prove that this is at once demoralizing to trade, to industrial enterprise and to transportation. Manifestly, also, it is the very inspiration of commercial disorder. At last, for self-protection and to maintain the orderly conduct of commerce, the railroad companies were forced to enter into agreements as to the maintenance of rates. That I believe to be unimpeachable history. The experience of railroad managers has also proved to them that such agreements, essential to self-preservation and to the preservation of commercial order, can be maintained *only upon the basis of precedent agreements as to the share of the competitive traffic or of the receipts therefrom which shall be awarded to each competitor.* That I believe, also, expresses the logic of events. I have been forced to my studies of the internal commerce of the United States to accept these conclusions as fundamental law of railroad transportation, and to maintain that their practical recognition is vital to the existence and beneficent administration of the American Railroad System.

The first of the conclusions just enunciated, viz., the necessity of agreements as to what competitive rates shall be, and as to the maintenance of such rates, now commands general public approval. This fact is clearly expressed in the sixth section of the Act to Regulate Commerce, which section requires ten days' notice of advances in rates and three days' notice of reductions in rates.

The second of the conclusions above noted, viz., that agreements as to the share of competitive traffic which shall be awarded to each competitor are essential to the observance of the law touching the maintenance of rates, is, to my mind, simply a corollary to the first proposition as to the necessity of agreements in regard to the maintenance of rates, and I entertain little doubt that this view of the case will ere long be generally accepted. I do not express this opinion as the dictum of any philosophy other than the philosophy of practical experience in the conduct of the railroad transportation interests of the country, under enormous difficulties, which in an imperfect manner I have attempted to sketch.

In this connection it is with great pleasure that I advert to the exceedingly able and exhaustive report submitted to the Senate, January 16, 1886, by the Honorable Shelby M. Cullom, Senator of the United States, in his capacity as chairman of the Senate Committee on Interstate Commerce. The language there employed (page 201) by Senator Cullom is as follows:

"It" (*i. e.*, the various forms of restraint upon competition, as described) "would not destroy the benefits of legitimate competition, but it would place a wholesome restraint upon reckless competition, and in that way lessen unjust discrimination, which is developed in its most objectionable forms under the nourishing influence of unrestricted competition. For these reasons the committee does not deem it prudent to recommend the prohibition of pooling."

In his speech in the Senate January 6, 1887, in opposition to the fifth section of the Act to Regulate Commerce, Senator Platt, of Connecticut, adopted my nine general conclusions upon pooling associations as his conclusion in regard to the whole matter. If I were to rewrite those theses today I would make no change in them other than to make them more emphatic, and to add that the lessons of experience have proved beyond all doubt that agreements as to the apportionment of competitive traffic are so manifestly in the nature of self-restraint, and so essential to the orderly conduct of the American Railroad System, as to demand their legalization under no other constraints than those imposed by the common law relative to unreasonable rates and unjust discriminations, which provisions of the common law are adopted into, and made a fundamental part of, the "Act to Regulate Commerce."

And now I desire to invite attention to the exact conclusions at which I arrived in the year 1885:

1. Agreements as to the apportionment of traffic between competing railroads, for the purpose of maintaining rates, are beneficial toward the public interests, and ought to be legalized.

2. The question as to whether any particular agreement in regard to the apportionment of railroad traffic is justifiable, upon the ground of maintaining rates, or of securing any other laudable object, is one which might well be left to the determination of a national railroad commission.

These conclusions were reached two years before the Act to Regulate Commerce became a law, and when, in the language of a distinguished jurist, I viewed this whole subject "with a mind illuminated by the sense of official responsibility." Now, viewing it I trust with as sincere a regard for the public interests, I have no hesitancy in saying that my confidence in the intelligent judgment and patriotic impulse of the gentlemen who constitute the Interstate Commerce Commision leads me to the belief that it would be well to confide to that body the responsibility of determining whether any particular agreement as to the division of competitive traffic is or is not characterized by the conditions above mentioned as constituting the essential requisites of legality.

POPULAR AND LEGAL VIEW OF TRAFFIC POOLING.

By Hon. Thos. M. Cooley.

Perhaps nothing in respect to the relations between the railroad companies and the public attracts more attention at the present time than the arrangements to which the name of pooling is popularly given. In railroad circles these arrangements are looked upon as necessary to prevent all railroad property becoming absolutely worthless to the stockholders, as a very large part of it is now; and those managers who are hoping to earn dividends are therefore laboring earnestly to make these arrangements effectual. On the other hand, an impression is largely prevalent that pooling contracts are contrivances whereby inequality and excess in rates can be maintained, and a monopoly injurious to the public interest established; and they are by many persons condemned as being unquestionably wrong if not absolutely illegal. As the relations between the public and the railroads are so necessary, so constant and so extensive as to make harmony between them in all that relates to railroad service of very high importance, it seems desirable to give some attention to these arrangements—their nature, their purpose and their legality—and to bring together some considerations bearing upon these points respectively, with a view to giving in brief space the means of forming some opinion in respect to them. Space will not admit of this being done with any completeness, but perhaps the salient points may be presented. What is said will refer especially to pooling in freight traffic, but in principle it will apply to passenger traffic also.

WHAT THEY ARE.

The pooling arrangements between railroads in this country have not all been on the same plan, but it is probably not important now to take notice of any attempts in that direction which have been made and then abandoned. The suggestion of pooling, though likely, perhaps, to occur anywhere, comes to us from England, where pooling contracts in the railroad business and others

---

Reprinted by permission from The Railway Review of January 8, 1887.

of a semi-public nature have been held not to be illegal, both when they were made on the basis of an equal division of profits (¹) and where the basis was a division of business between the contracting parties. (₂). In this country the method of pooling seems to be for the several contracting parties to create some common authority upon which will be conferred the power to establish and change rates for the transportation of property within a certain territory or over a certain line, and also to apportion the business between them. The apportionment will be made upon a consideration of what the companies severally would be likely to obtain under the operation of free competition, and it will be changed from time to time if found to be relatively unjust. The feature of arbitration upon controversies arising between the contracting parties will also be prominent in the arrangement. The contract will be made for a definite term of years, with liberty to dissatisfied parties to withdraw upon reasonable notice, and it will be likely to provide that a commission acting for all shall give direction to shipments when this shall be necessary to give each road its allotted share. But as shippers will have a legal right to have their property transported by a line of their own selection, it may well happen that some roads will carry more and some less than their proportion, and provision will therefore be necessary for a periodical adjustment of balances, and for the payment of moneys from one to another as may be needful, upon such allowance for the business done above the allotted share as shall be fixed upon as just. Perhaps clauses will be inserted in the contract which will have for their purpose to make it for the interest of shippers to send forward their property according to the directions of the commission, but compulsory power in this direction must practically be very limited.

THEIR PURPOSE.

The avowed purpose in pooling is to avoid ruinous competition between the several roads represented, and the unjust discrimination between shippers which is found invariably to attend such competition. The desirability of the last mentioned object is agreed to on all hands. The existence of unjust discriminations is one of the chief complaints made by the public against railroad management, and one of the reasons always assigned for interference by law. It may therefore be taken as agreed that, so far as pooling arrangements have the correction of this evil in view, the purpose is commendable.

But the primary object unquestionably is self-protection against ruinous competition; and it is not to be expected that as to this the public opinion of the country will be prepared to give spontaneous approval. A pooling arrangement is a combination; and

---

(1) Hare vs. Railway Co., 2 Johnson & Hemming's Reports, 80.
(2) Collins vs. Locke, 4 Appeal Cases, 674.

all combinations in a business which so intimately concerns the public look like attempts to establish a monopoly, and may sometimes result in establishing one. To monopoly the public is instinctively hostile, because it takes from them the power of dealing on equal terms with those who control it. Besides, a combination that has for its object to check competition, seems to stand in hostility to the industrial maxim that "competition is the life of trade," a maxim which from time immemorial has been greatly prevalent, and is commonly supposed to be one admitting of no question and of universal application. The advantages of unrestricted competition are apparent to the public in industrial life all about us, and while in some kinds of business this is sharp, yet selfishness is generally sufficiently active and sufficiently intelligent to prevent its becoming ruinous. It does not detract from the worth or soundness of the maxim that under the operation of unrestricted competition individual disasters must occur; for when this happens it is very likely to be found either that the parties did not understand the business they were engaged in, or managed badly, or lacked the necessary capital, or in some other particulars were inadequately equipped. Against ruin from these causes protection is impossible. The maxim referred to is so commonly accepted that courts have made it a basis for important judgments; and it is not to be wondered at, therefore, that the question should be made whether it is competent to erect barriers to free competition in a business so important to the public as that which is carried on by the railroads.

The answer made on behalf of the railroad companies is that the business and the necessary preparation for carrying it on make their case so peculiar that competition necessarily affects them in a way different to that in which it affects others; so different that it may be destructive to them where to others it would only be stimulating and wholesome. Some of the reasons which will be assigned for this will be recognized by every one as possessing force. In most kinds of business, competition easily and naturally regulates the extent to which a business shall be carried on; persons engage in it only when they think they see a reasonable opening for profit; they push the business with men and money when the promise of success is such as to warrant it, and when it is not, operations are reduced; some perhaps, go out of the business, and capital seeks other investments. The merchant, when competition becomes too severe for him, may turn farmer or manufacturer; the manufacturer may change his line of production or temporarily reduce it; and these changes it is generally possible to make without serious loss Very seldom the whole plant for one business will be useless for any other. The general results of competition will therefore be such that, while the whole public will have the benefit of low prices, a general equilibrium of demand and supply will be maintained without bringing disaster to individuals.

Much of this is as different as possible in the railroad world. The investment for the purpose of a railroad is permanent, and is available to a single purpose only. If it can not be made available for the transportation of persons and property it is a wasted investment; as much so as if it had been cast into the sea. But when the construction of railroads is entirely unrestricted, there is always a tendency to build more than are needed, and more than can be made profitable. The reasons for this are numerous. Railroads are a great local convenience; every village wants one or more; and it is easy for plausible men, who see individual profit in their construction, to convince the local community that a road which will accommodate their local needs must be profitable. If the law permits a levy of municipal taxes in aid of the local scheme, it will not be difficult to obtain a popular vote in its favor; if taxation for the purpose is not allowed, the popular credulity will be appealed to with assurance of great increase in property from the building of a road which will give easy access to market; and men will give freely in the expectation that in one way or another they will receive large returns. Roads have thus in many cases been constructed at general expense in which a capitalist for the purpose of investment would put nothing, But roads are also built under an expectation, on the part of those who originate and push them, that in some way the originators will be enabled to make them available for their individual benefit, regardless of their real value; sometimes through holding the control and managing them; sometimes by forcing the owners of other roads to which they would be rivals to buy them. For these and other reasons roads are brought into existence for which there is no adequate demand, and whatever people have been induced to put in them is a dead loss. In some other countries the government endeavors to provide against such losses by refusing charters for roads which seem not to be called for by any public need, or which can only be profitable by rendering worthless some existing line; but the policy in this country has always been to leave railroad building practically unrestricted, and the best and most useful line, though it may fully accommodate the public need, is never secure against being ruined by the construction of a rival line which scheming and unscrupulous persons induce the credulous to furnish the capital for.

But such roads when constructed remain, and will be operated so long as the cost of operating can be paid from the earnings. They may pass from the hands of stockholders into those of bondholders, and though even then pay nothing upon the bonds, they will continue to be operated. This is the condition of very much of the railroad property of the country to-day; hundreds of millions of the capital invested in it is absolutely sunk, but the plant remains and the road will be operated, though those whose property it represents neither receive dividends upon their investment

LEGAL VIEW OF TRAFFIC POOLING. 233

nor have any reasonable prospect that they ever will. If then a company to which the bankrupt company is a rival shall not only endeavor to pay operating expenses and the interest on its indebtedness, but also to pay dividends to stockholders, it must do so in competition with one whose managers expect to pay no dividends, and no interest except as perhaps they may find it necessary to do so in order to retain control. Such a state of things can exist in no business from which a transfer of capital is possible; and the competition it creates instead of being "the life of trade," is as to this business destructive of the capital invested in it. It becomes a matter of necessity, then, that the competition which is so likely to be destructive should be restrained within the limits which will admit of reasonable and reliable prosperity; and some common arrangement between the roads seems to be the only means yet found by which this can be accomplished. The common arrangement agreed upon for the purpose is that of pooling; it has grown out of the necessities of the case; and, while it is necessary to the railroad companies, it is unjust to no one. This, briefly and imperfectly stated, is the railroad view of the necessity and propriety of pooling compacts.

It is proper to add to this statement that the want of harmony between the railroad companies which has its most noticable manifestations in wars of rates causes injury and inconvenience to the public in ways which railroad managers in public discussions are not likely to dwell upon or make prominent. In other kinds of business when competition is unrestricted dealers find it to their interest to study the convenience of the public, and to invite custom by being as accommodating as possible; and what they do in this regard is no wrong or injury or inconvenience to their rivals, but only incites them to be equally accommodating. But railroad companies cannot be accommodating to the full extent of the public needs unless they are accommodating to each other; for a very large proportion of those who have occasion to use their facilities, desire to pass, in person or with their property, from one road to another, and wish to do this without unnecessary cost of transfer or unnecessary delay. But hostile competition, while it may incite the roads to run a race in popularity, also leads them to make many arrangements which are inconsistent with the full accommodation to the public which might be and ought to be given. Rival lines have their station buildings on different sides of a town when they might with the same convenience to themselves and with greater convenience to the public be together; they have different station houses at crossings when one would answer for all; their time tables are so arranged as to cause inconvenience whenever a passenger leaves their line to pass upon another which is not working in harmony with them, and they establish soliciting agencies which are only made important by the rivalry. In all these things the several companies think they advance their individual interest in the competition; but in doing so they not only make the service they render to the public less valuable but also more expensive. Some of the evils of unrestricted competition have been generally recognized by those who have been most earnest in demanding congressional legislation, and it has been one feature of the bills introduced that restraints, more or less considerable, should be imposed.

It is also proper to add that, whether the railroad companies anticipate it or not, no pooling arrangement, unless the aid of the law can be had for its enforcement, can possibly put an end to competition between them. The arrangement may regulate competition but cannot stop it. The apportionment of business, as has been said, will be made on a calculation of what the respective roads would be likely to obtain under free competition; and every company, in view of the periodical readjustment of percentages, will be interested in showing that its facilities and its management naturally bring to it a larger proportion than it now receives; and the rivalry for public favor will go on as before, though it may be expected that some of the features of rivalry which, when it is hostile, are peculiarly injurious to the public, will be eliminated by the agreement to work in harmony. Moreover the several soliciting agents of the roads will have a personal interest in showing their value to their employers by presenting good results from their service in the employment; the permanent value of each road, as well as the market value of its stock, will depend largely on the shares awarded to it in the periodical readjustments; all the prejudices which concur in bringing about first secret and then public departures from common agreements will only be repressed by the pooling, not removed; and not only will competition continue notwithstanding the common agreement, but it will by force of the circumstances be so far active and efficient in keeping rates within bounds that one would hazard nothing in saying that, within the territory whose business is naturally affected by the competition of the trunk lines, the period when rates can be controlled by combinations and kept at figures limited only by the discretion or the greed of the managers, is gone forever.

THE LEGALITY OF RAILROAD POOLS.

But it is said that all contracts which have for their object to restrain competition are illegal at the common law, because they are in conflict with a general principle of public policy. The term illegal is somewhat ambiguous. A contract may be illegal in the sense that it is forbidden by a law which imposes some penalty for entering into, or it may be illegal, because, though not forbidden, it is considered to be of an injurious and demoralizing tendency, and therefore the law will not favor it, but will refuse to lend its aid in enforcement. If a contract is only illegal in this last sense, parties are at perfect liberty to enter into it if they please, but

LEGAL VIEW OF TRAFFIC POOLING.   235

performance of its conditions must be entirely voluntary. It is under this head that pooling contracts are supposed to come.

It is a familiar principle in the law that contracts in general restraint of trade are void. Therefore if a man contracts with his rival in business that for any agreed consideration he will no longer pursue his customary calling within the state in which he resides, the promise is one he may keep at pleasure or break with impunity. The reasons are that such a contract if enforced would deprive the public of the benefits of competition, and at the same time impose restraints going far beyond what would be needful for protection to the party bargaining for them. But it was always agreed that competition, in so far as it operated injuriously to individuals might with entire competency be limited by contract; and in a great variety of cases it has been held that a man may lawfully bargain to put an end to an injurious competition in his business in the locality where he carries it on, or that he may bargain to prevent the establishment in that locality of a competing business which he fears may be injurious. It is only when he exacts terms that go beyond giving him protection that the law holds his contract to be unreasonable, injurious to the public, and therefore illegal. The reader unfamiliar with the law reports will find many of the cases referred to in the note; and it will appear on an examination that in all of them the legality of bargaining to limit competition when it is kept within the bounds of reasonable protection, is either assumed or expressly affirmed. (1)

The principle upon which these cases are decided is that by which pooling arrangements, so far as concerns their legality, must stand or fall. If they are illegal it is because they establish unreasonable restraints upon competition in business; if they can be supported in law, it must be upon the ground that they only give to the parties concerned that reasonable protection against competition which is needful to their prosperity. Having this in mind it may be useful to refer to such judicial decisions as seem to bear most directly upon this peculiar class of contracts.

It has already been said that pooling arrangements have been sustained in Great Britian. One of the cases passed upon was a pooling arrangement between stevedores; another was between competing railroads, and in neither case was it deemed an objection that the effect of the contract was to limit competition, or that this was to be accomplished by a combination. In the railroad case (2) Vice Chancellor W. Page Wood said among other things: "It is a mistaken notion that the public is benefitted by

---

(1) The following cases are selected from the great number which recognize the principle, because the republication in the volumes here given is accompanied by valuable notes and references: Mitchell vs. Reynolds, Smith's Leading Cases, 508; Perkins vs. Lyman, 6 American Decisions, 158; Pierce vs. Fuller, 5 American Decisions, 102; Bowser vs. Bliss, 43 American Decisions, 93; Grundy vs. Edwards, 23 American Decisions, 409; Morgan vs. Perhamus, 38 American Reports, 607; Pike vs. Thomas, 7 American Decisions, 741; Drill Company vs. Morse, 4 American Reports, 513; Hoyt vs. Holly, 12 American Reports, 390; Hubbard vs. Miller, 15 American Reports, 153; Cook vs. Johnson, 36 American Reports, 64.
(2) Hare vs. Railway Co., 2 Johnson & Hemming's Reports, 80.

putting two railroad companies against each other until one is ruined; the result being at last to, raise the fares to the highest possible standard."

Before either of these cases was decided it had been held by the supreme court of New York [in 1847] that a contract between the proprietors of canal boats for fixing rates and for a division of net earnings was void, though the object was expressed to be "to establish and maintain fair and uniform rates of freight, and to equalize the business of forwarding on the Erie and Oswego canals among themselves, and to avoid all unnecessary expenses in doing the same." The argument of the court is brief, and is summed up in two short sentences: "The object of this combination was obviously to destroy competition between the several lines in the business engaged in. It was a conspiracy, between the individuals contracting, to prevent a free competition among themselves, in the business of transporting merchandise, property and passengers upon the public canals." "It is a familiar maxim that competition is the life of trade. It follows that whatever destroys or even relaxes competition in trade is injurious if not fatal to it." (1) Thus it will be seen that by giving a bad name to the arrangement and quoting the old maxim, the court was supposed to have sufficiently reasoned the case out, and the judgment followed as of course. A similar agreement was shortly afterwards condemned by the same court, in the case of Stanton against Allen, (2) as being designed to exempt the standard of freights, etc., "from the wholesome influence of rivalry and competition."

These cases have not passed entirely without criticism in this country. They were cited to the supreme court of Wisconsin not long after they were made, and were there dissented from in very vigorous terms. (3) Referring to the maxim that competition is the life of trade, Judge Howe, speaking for the court, said that it "is one of the least reliable of the host that may be picked up in every market place. It is in fact the shibboleth of mere gambling speculation; and is hardly entitled to take rank as an axiom in the jurisprudence of this country. I believe universal observation will attest that for the last quarter of a century competition in the trade has caused more individual distress, if not more public injury, than the want of competition. Indeed, by reducing prices below or raising them above values—as the nature of the trade prompted—competition has done more to monopolize trade, or to secure exclusive advantages in it, than has been done by contract. Rivalry in trade will destroy itself, and rival tradesmen, seeking to remove each other, rarely resort to contract, unless they find it the cheapest mode of putting an end to the strife. And it seems to me not a little remarkable that in the case of Stanton vs. Allen

---

(1) Hooker vs. Vandewater 4 Denio's Reports, 349.
(2) 5 Denio's Reports, 434.
(3) In Kellogg vs. Larkin 3 Chandler's Reports, 133.

it should have been urged against the agreement that its object was to exempt the standard of freights, etc., 'from the wholesome influence of rivalry and competition.' For it is very certain that because of that very purpose—because they did tend to protect the party against the influence of rivalry and competition—courts of law have upheld like agreements in partial restraint of trade, ever since the case of Mitchell vs. Reynolds." (1)

But there are several other American cases which, in their general reasoning, must be conceded to give some support to the cases decided in New York. Among these are the cases in which combinations between coal companies to control the production of coal and its price in the market have been held illegal. (2) An agreement between dealers in a certain line of goods not to put any upon the market for three months has also been held to be illegal. (3) So has a combination which had for its purpose to effect a corner in the wheat market. (4) So has a combination between parties furnishing recruits in time of war, whereby they agree not to furnish them for less than a fixed price. (5) So have agreements not to compete in bids for public contracts. (6) So have combinations to keep up the price of salt. (7) And combinations to put up or to put down the wages of laborers, whether entered into by laborers or by employers, must in general depend for their observance upon the good faith of those who make them. (8) It would be easy to show that many of these cases have no important bearing upon the question of the legality of railroad pools, but they are likely to be brought under consideration in any legal controversy on that subject, and the propriety of their being here referred to will thereafter be apparent.

In the light of the judicial decisions as they now stand in this country, it cannot safely be affirmed that the law will lend its aid to enforce the pooling contracts between railroads. It seems on the other hand more than probable that the courts will declare that such contracts are not sanctioned by the law. This is said irrespective of any opinion upon the question whether, as an original proposition, such ought to be the result. The early decisions in New York, which have given a certain tendency to subsequent judicial thought and action, were made with little or no investigation of the subject involved, and without any attempt whatever to

---

(1) This is the leading case on contracts in restraint of trade, and was decided in 1711 1 P. Williams' Reports, 181. 1 Smith's Leading Cases, 508.
(2) Morris Run Coal Co. vs. Barclay Coal Co., 68 Penn. State Reports, 173; Arnot vs. Coal Co., 68 New York Reports, 558.
(3) India Association vs. Kock, 14 Louisiana Reports, 168.
(4) Raymond vs. Leavitt, 46 Michigan Reports, 447.
(5) Marsh vs. Russell, 66 New York Reports, 288.
(6) Atcheson vs. Mallon, 43 New York Reports, 147. People vs. Stephens, 71 New York Reports, 527. Ray vs. Mackin, 100 Illinois Reports, 246. Swan vs. Chorpenning, 20 California Reports, 182.
(7) Salt Co. vs. Guthrie, 35 Ohio State Reports, 666.
(8) Journeymen Tailors' Case, 8 Modern Reports, 10; Commonwealth vs. Hunt, 4 Metcalf's Reports, 111; The Queen vs. Rowlands, 17 Queen's Bench Reports, 671; Hilton vs. Eckersley, 6 Ellis and Blackburn's Reports, 47.

show that the principle by which the legality of the arrangements to avoid injurious competition must be tested had been overlooked or disregarded in the contracts before the court. But they have stood without much question to the present day; in their conclusions they fall in with prevailing notions of what is public policy on the subject, there is, *a priori*, a strong presumption, legal as well as popular, that they are correct; and they are likely for all these reasons, whether sound or not, to stand as precedents which courts will expect to follow. If that shall be the result of any litigation, or if the companies themselves shall look upon such a result as possible, and therefore decline litigation, the companies entering into pools must rely for the enforcement of their contracts upon the honor of the corporate officers and agents, and upon the methods that may be devised for making it to the interest of the several contracting parties to observe their agreements.

SANCTIONS FOR POOLING CONTRACTS.

Penalties to be imposed by the association will be out of the question. They will not be paid voluntarily by parties who will not voluntarily observe their agreements, and they cannot be collected by law. No doubt it might be made part of the pooling arrangement that a fund should be provided by proportionate contributions, and that from the sum paid in by any member a penalty assessed against it should be paid; but it would be easy for such member, if dissatisfied, to enjoin the payment, or in case of its failure to take steps for that purpose, for any of its stockholders to do so. Penalties, therefore, cannot constitute a reliance.

The principal danger to be guarded against is the cutting of rates. In the unregulated and unreasoning strife between railroad companies this cutting is not only carried on to an extent that is ruinous to the companies themselves, but it becomes a disturbing factor in all commerce; and it is perfectly correct for the railroad companies to say, as they do when defending pooling, that unjust discriminations are a necessary result. The sort of competition which is "the life of trade" in a war of rates, incites every agent to make secretly and by every form of indirection such terms as will secure the business; it is inevitable that these shall be without uniformity, and that those who push hardest and bargain most—which will generally be the large shippers—will be most favored. Low rates, when they can be depended upon for any considerable time, increase the prices of grain and other market commodities in the hands of producers; but they affect prices little if at all when it is uncertain from day to day and from hour to hour what they are to be, and consequently such benefits as come from the hostile cutting of rates are reaped principally by speculators and other large shippers. It is doubtful if the shipping interest ever receives benefits equivalent to the losses which the railroad interest suffers in a war of rates, and the benefits to the general public will seldom equal the incidental injuries.

Nothing therefore can be plainer than the desirability that reasonable rates should be maintained with general uniformity, so that they may be calculated upon in the making of contracts and purchases, and so that small shippers as well as large, the man who merely sends his household goods as well as the speculator in grain and provisions, may have the benefit of them.

So far as the steadiness in rates tends to the benefit of the railroads, it is also particularly desirable for a reason not often mentioned. It is a great misfortune to the country that so many of its roads pay no dividends. Though worthless to the stockholders such roads have in the stock market a speculative value, and in the hands of speculating men the stocks become mere implements of gambling, and the roads are managed with a purpose alternately to put up and put down the quotations on the stock board, that the managers may make profit from the sales and purchases. It is beyond doubt that larger fortunes have been made in the manipulation of some worthless roads with a view to deceptive appearánces for stock jobbing purposes than would have been derived from dividends equal to the current rate of interest. This is an evil, not solely because of its fostering the prevailing tendency to demoralizing and ruinous speculation, but also for the further reason that it increases and strengthens among the people at large a widespread prejudice against railroad managers as men who contrive to accumulate great fortunes at the public cost. Under the influence of this prejudice it may well happen that the charges a railroad makes for transportation, though barely sufficient to cover all the items of expense, will be thought exorbitant by the community, who see the members of the managing board acquiring wealth through the ownership and management of the stock. Nor are the community to be blamed for this, for they have a right to assume that all the profits made by managers are derived from the earnings of the roads. Thus, non-paying roads not only foster speculative gambling, which is one of the most demoralizing of existing evils, but they also tend to excite in the community a feeling against railroad managers and railroad property, which gradually extends to embrace all forms of aggregate and especially of corporate wealth; and this feeling in any time of unusual excitement or distress is liable to break out into uncontrollable fury, and to seek gratification in destruction. All property owners, and all law-abiding and patriotic people, are therefore directly concerned in removing, so far as may be in their power, the causes which are likely to originate or to foster such dangerous tendencies.

But without the aid of the law to enforce pooling arrangements, it is not as yet apparent that any scheme can be devised whereby the cutting of rates can be effectually prevented. Entering into a pooling arrangement is an admission that unrestricted competition is destructive; but when the pooling agreement is departed from and one road begins to cut rates, the others, in self protection, must be suffered to cut also. This is not enforcing the pooling agreement; it is destroying it. Possibly if the combination were sufficiently extensive, a refractory road might be temporarily crippled, and thus brought to terms by the others refusing to exchange business with it; but their power in this regard is much restricted by the law prescribing the duties of common carriers. Besides a road boycotted by others because it is cutting under their rates will be likely to have the public sympathy as a road suffering persecution in the public interest; and this sympathy will give it valuable assistance. It may well happen, therefore, that an attempt at boycotting will prove a mortifying failure. It is certain that it could not be relied upon as a general remedy for the breach of a pooling agreement.

But these common arrangements, though unprotected by the law have, nevertheless, done very much to save railroad property from needless injury. They bring into existence a commission or other authority in which all the parties have confidence, which is charged with the duty to keep the peace between the roads, to hear mutual complaints, to investigate charges of the breach of their common agreements, to give redress, so far as advisory power can do so, and concentrate public opinion in railroad circles upon any member failing to observe its covenants and make it feel the public censure. It is natural to expect that the benefits will increase as the managers become accustomed within the agreed limits to submit to the direction and control of the common authority. But a pooling arrangement is only a treaty of peace; as a combination it has little coherence; and the passions of a single railroad manager, the failure of a single agent to keep faith, or the nervous eagerness to keep rolling stock employed when the offerings of property for transportation are light, may at any time break it down. No treaty is law except so long as the contracting parties can see that it is probably for their interest to observe it, and the suspected breach of good faith in a treaty is commonly sufficient to breed an actual breach.

THE FUTURE.

That the railroad problem, so far as it is involved in wars of rates between the roads, cannot as yet be solved is very manifest; the railroad companies have only made an effort in the way of solving it. Common agreements, if they had the encouragement and protection of the law, would very probably supply it; but for that purpose legislation would seem to be essential. But legislation would be mischievous rather than beneficial, unless it was conceived in the spirit of statesmen, and was made to express neither special favor for, nor special hostility to, the interest it would regulate. The railroad interest of this country represents an enormous aggregate of wealth, and an increasing aggregate of corporate poverty; and it has immense capabilities for good or evil to the people. It cannot possibly be for the interest of any country that so large a portion of the invested capital should be wasted or unremunerative, especially when in that condition its necessary tendency is to favor dishonest management and gambling speculation. On the other hand, it is for the interest of the country that the public shall receive, in as large a degree as shall be possible, the benefits which were calculated upon in providing by law for the building of the roads. Regulating legislation should, therefore, be conceived neither exclusively in the interest of railroads nor in the spirit of hostility to them. What the country needs is that they shall be made useful; not that they shall be crippled or bankrupted, or made stock-jobbing conveniences for their managers. And no doubt ·when the whole subject is carefully examined and wisely considered, it will be found that the true interests of the owners of railroad property may be made to harmonize perfectly with the true interests of the public, and that it will be as wise for the state to encourage and protect whatever in corporate arrangements is of beneficial tendency as it will to suppress what is mischievous.

THE INTERSTATE COMMERCE ACT—POOLING AND COMBINATIONS WHICH AFFECT ITS OPERATION.

By Hon. Thomas M. Cooley.

I believe I am expected to say something on the subject of Combinations and Concentrations of Interests with special reference to the business of transportation of persons and property by railroad. The occasion for saying anything may be attributed, I suppose, to the desire now being expressed in some quarters that the act to regulate commerce should be repealed, or at least be amended by striking out certain clauses which are supposed to bear heavily on the railroads.

I do not understand that the question of the repeal of the act is to be discussed at this time, and if it were, I do not know that I should care to speak upon it. I may say, however, that the act has a good purpose in view; It was intended to correct enormous abuses previously existing; but they cannot be corrected without cutting off some sources of improper income. These did not all accrue to the benefit of the railroads or of railroad men; other classes profited upon them also, and it is expecting altogether too much to suppose that they will acquiesce in the sources of their illegitimate profits being cut off without making an effort to retain them. The reform therefore which the law intends must embrace other classes besides those who are in railroad service, and it must be expected that others besides railroad men will for personal reasons desire to get rid of it.

The urgent call for a modification of the act which comes from railroad circles has sprung up recently. There were indeed some objections made to it immediately after its passage as well as before, but when it was given effect it was found quite to the surprise of some who had prophesied disaster to the railroads from it that the disasters did not follow. Indeed for six months or more after the act took effect it was generally conceded it helped the railroads instead of harming them. They gained in revenue from the anti-discriminating clauses more than they lost from the

---

Address delivered at a dinner given by the Boston Merchants' Association, January 8, 1889.

prohibition of the greater charge upon the shorter haul. Every one ought to have been gratified with this, because the gain to the roads was not at the expense of the general public; it was, on the other hand, to their advantage, because it was a gain resulting principally from taking away unfair advantages which before were benefitting favored persons at the expense of others upon whom the burden was proportionally increased.

I desire to call special attention to this fact; that the period during which the law operated most to the benefit of the railroads was precisely that during which its provisions were best observed. I think this to be an undeniable fact; and if it is a fact, it is deserving of more attention than up to this time it has received from the managers of railroads. It was also the period during which the law was complained of the least.

There are very vigorous complaints now. They relate mainly to the clause of the act which forbids the greater charge on the shorter haul on the same line in the same direction where the circumstances and conditions are similar, and that which makes pooling unlawful. The first-mentioned clause embodies a principle right in itself. In large sections of the country the roads have come into conformity with it and not suffered loss from doing so. In others it was not practicable to do so, at least immediately. But the difficulties are greatly increased by the excessive competition of the roads at leading points, and they will diminish as the managers come to better understanding among themselves. The provision does not establish an iron rule; it is meant to be sufficiently elastic to operate justly, and if the managers give their best efforts to come into conformity with it, they will be very likely to find, perhaps to their surprise, that they can do so without injury. What they lose in one way they will make up in others.

But the chief reason the railroad managers bring forward for an amendment of the law concerns the matter of pooling. The privilege of pooling is supposed by them to be of vital importance, and their opinions on the subject are entitled to respectful consideration.

I have referred to the fact that the law was best observed at the outset. But in a few months it began to be noticed that many persons in railroad service were giving more attention to contrivances for evading the spirit and intent of the law than they were to obeying it. Their ingenuity in this regard may almost be pronounced marvelous; the old mischiefs were reproduced under new guises just so far as plausible excuses could be invented for the purpose. One curious feature of the sort of railroad management that was indulged in was that the methods that were devised for evading the law instead of increasing the pecuniary returns from railway service almost invariably diminished them. A secret rebate made to a favored dealer does not increase the aggregate of railroad shipments, and is therefore a total loss to railroad revenues. When property is allowed to go forward under-billed, there is a like loss. If any member of the Association had been in Chicago a few weeks ago and had had occasion to look into one of the general railroad ticket offices he might have thought that all travel had ceased, for nobody seemed to be calling for tickets. In the "cut-rate" office across the way, however, he might have discovered a very different condition of things. It was the scalpers who were selling the tickets, and they were doing so on such terms as enabled them to grow rapidly rich while the roads were growing poor.

I know of no reason for supposing that the general travel of the country was increased through the assistance of this class of men, and so far as could be seen the commissions paid were altogether lost. Very likely some roads lost more than others through the improper diversion of revenue from their treasuries; possibly some of them may have been actual gainers by their illegitimate courses; but the probabilities are all against it.

Any misconduct of this sort on the part of one road is imitated at once. The general practice has been for each road to give rebate for rebate, make cut for cut, and in the end the account of profits and losses shows gains by no one. It is all loss, and all the roads share it.

These things are done in ways supposed not to be actually criminal under the law, but the whole business is very plainly opposed to the spirit of the law, and it is done with a purpose of evasion. The law intends that the rates for the transportation of persons and property shall be the same for all classes and shall be steadily maintained. It also intends that the railroad business of the country shall be done openly and with full publicity. This equal and just purpose of the law is defeated by contrivances that are clearly opposed to the intent of the law if not to its terms.

Now when parties are thus busy in contriving methods for rendering the law of no effect, and their evasions of its purpose are seen to have a direct tendency to diminish the corporate revenues, they are hardly the parties to put themselves upon the stand to prove that the law is injuring their roads. Besides, the evidence they bring forward is not to the point.

We can all see that the old practices which the law undertook to put an end to, but which are still persisted in, are harmful. What we need to be shown is that the fruits of obedience to the law would be equally injurious, or perhaps more so. These are precisely the proofs that are not brought forward.

The reply made to us when this is said is that the disregard of legal obligations comes from excessive competition. Formerly this was kept within bounds by the device of pooling, but pooling is now prohibited, and there are no means within the reach of the railroads to protect them against rate wars. These wars will break out inevitably, and when they do the roads will reach for traffic by every available means. If one gives rebates another will: if one puts its passenger tickets into the hands of outside parties its competitor is compelled to do the same. This is the plea.

Putting aside for the time being the question whether pooling ought or ought not to be allowed, I must insist that the argument now made for it is radically unsound and vicious, because it rests upon an assumption that violation of law by one is justification for violation by another. The sentiment in railroad circles on this subject is not only opposed to sound public morality, but it necessarily tends to the perpetuation of the very evils under which the roads are now suffering.

Every man ought to be a law-abiding citizen; railroad managers just as much as any other class of persons. Violation of a law which has a just purpose in view, and especially of any provision of the law that is unmistakably just and right in itself, ought to be odious. Any citizen knowing of the violation, instead of imitating it, ought to assist in bringing the offender to justice. If the violation particularly affects any one business, the persons engaged in that business ought to feel themselves under special obligation to see not only that the crime is punished, but that it is made disreputable. If a sentiment to any such effect exists in railroad circles it has not been made known outside of them. In saying this I wish distinctly to be understood that I do not join in any general indictment of railroad managers. I understand too well that a great many among them desire that the law shall be enforced, and would willingly obey it to the letter if they thought under the circumstances they could do so, but many even of these are affected by the old notions growing out of old and chronic abuses, and when a competitor breaks the law they do not hesitate to do the same thing in order to get even with him. The crime thus spreads from one to another until all are involved. Each one justifies his own conduct by the bad conduct of the one who preceded him in disobedience or is supposed to have done so. He would have us understand that he would not have done what he did if he had been a free agent, but what the other had done left him no choice but to follow the example. He was thus compelled to violate the law because another did, and he fails to recognize an obligation as a citizen either to institute prosecutions himself or to furnish the evidence on which the public authorities can prosecute.

Now I know nothing corresponding to this in other lines of business. If one merchant cheats his competitor by dishonest and criminal means the latter does not retort in kind, but hands the case over with the proofs to the public prosecutor. We never hear from one merchant that the criminal conduct of his competitor forces him into like conduct. The plea of a saloon keeper who should throw open his doors at forbidden hours because he found his rival had a back door open and was likely to draw away business, would be overruled as promptly by public sentiment as it would be by the courts.

Even where an alleged secret cut in rates is met in a perfectly legal manner, by an open reduction, the question often remains whether the alleged offense was not imaginary rather than real; and whether, if not, it would not have been possible to correct it by an appeal to the law instead of making a costly sacrifice of revenues by measures of retaliation.

We see in these facts the radical error on the part of many who are now saying that pooling is indispensable to railroad harmony and prosperity. The evidences they bring forward do not prove or tend to prove the fact. They only prove that they themselves have been culpable in failing to give the law the proper support: in failing to make the effort fairly required of them to render the law beneficial to themselves and to the public with that privilege denied. A duty to this effect rested upon them as citizens, but also specially and particularly because they were in the management of great properties charged with a public trust.

But putting this aside for the present, we need when one pleads for the privilege of pooling to be informed exactly what it is that he means by it. The term is used in very different senses nowadays. Does he mean the voluntary pooling as formerly practiced, and which existed without any legal basis; or does he mean pooling sanctioned by law with the power of enforcing the pooling contracts? Or does he perhaps mean something quite different from either, something in the nature of a trust? It is very important that we should have definite information on this subject before pooling, vaguely suggested, is either condemned or indorsed.

The old pooling was never so harmful as some persons supposed, and was probably condemned by law more because of what it was feared it would become, or might become, than because of what it was. But, on the other hand, it was never so beneficial to the roads as it is now customary to claim. The most that can be said in its favor is that it had a tendency to the steady maintenance of rates. It was a contrivance whereby it was made to the interest of roads not to push competition to excess, and not to engage in destructive rate wars. But in order to have pooling it was necessary, in the first place, to agree upon a basis; and this agreement was not always possible. And when the basis was agreed upon it had no stability; it had no legal support; it depended for its existence from day to day upon the continuous consent of parties. The result was that pooling agreements were constantly being broken up, and the most destructive rate wars in railroad history occurred before pooling was prohibited. The little practical value of the old device was often confessed by those who made greatest efforts to render it effectual. This fact is not to be ignored in the talk for restoring it.

For a very large proportion of railroad controversies voluntary pooling cannot possibly be a remedy, for the very obvious reason that they concern matters which have to be settled before there can be any pooling. They concern the substructure, so to speak. Take, for illustration, the difficulties that have existed in Trunk-Line territory during the last year. They concerned the basis: they related to controversies which had to be determined as a preliminary step to any pooling; so that, so far as we can see, the controversies would have run their course and been just as active and violent with the right to pool in existence as they were without it. And the peculiarity of railroad service is such that controversies of the sort are never really settled, for pooling itself only establishes a temporary truce in respect to them.

Let us see what pooling involves.

It is desired to establish it, we will say, in Trunk-Line territory. There are some strong lines there and some very weak ones; there are short lines and long; there are direct roads for the business between leading points, and there are roads twice as long which nevertheless demand a share of the business. There are local roads which have fair claim to nothing but local business, but which are nevertheless capable of being made links of long but circuitous lines, and of thus becoming disturbers of rates for the whole territory. The problem, when pooling is proposed, is how to satisfy all the parties; how to apportion the business so that all will be content and remain so. And at the outset it must be understood that there is not business enough to make them all profitable, and inevitably some must have precarious existence.

To expect to satisfy all under such circumstances is as vain as to expect to satisfy a miscellaneous collection of carniverous beasts by dividing among them a carcass which is insufficient to more than whet their appetite. Content with the division is out of the question. Each will take what is allotted to it if it sees no chance of getting more, but with such mental protests as will make it eager to embrace any circumstance which seems to give promise of a better division if the pool is broken up. And such circumstances are constantly presenting themselves. The pooling family is very seldom a happy family; it is seldom, if ever, bound together by friendly ties. Each considers his neighbor unfair and unjustly grasping, and chafes under the fact.

Thus all the elements of disorganization attend it from the start. Moreover, the most perfect pool is liable to be invaded by means of arrangements that may seem altogether unnatural and yet be very effective. The Canadian Pacific, notwithstanding its enormous length of line, showed itself quite capable of dictating terms to the American transcontinental roads in respect to business between San Francisco and the cities of the interior;

and a pool which should embrace all the lines of the Northwest might find its arrangements broken in upon by a line connecting Chicago and New York, but made in part by roads south of the Ohio and the Potomac. There is almost no limit to the possibility of forming such roundabout lines as may constitute disturbers and disorganizers of rates; and the ingenuity in forming them is sufficiently active to prevent pooling being more than an experimental device for keeping the peace, whose duration is dependent first on the good faith of the parties, and next upon the power of others to upset their arrangements.

Pooling with a legal sanction would have all the elements of weakness that attended the old pooling except one. When the pool as it used to be formed broke up, there was no enforcing such obligations as had been incurred while it existed; there was no compelling payment of balances. With a legalized pooling there might be the power to do this; but there would be the same difficulty in forming the pool, the same elements of disorganization would be involved, the same continuous good faith would be essential, and the same possibilities would exist of fatal intrusions from outside.

The difference between a trust and a pool is almost as great as that between a despot on the throne and the player who mimics him on the stage. I do not understand that I am expected to speak particularly of trusts. They are of course a feature of the times to which all thoughtful men must now be giving some attention, but at this time I do not care to dogmatize on the subject. A few things can, nevertheless, be said of trusts without danger of mistake. They are the things to be feared. They antagonize a leading and most valuable principle of industrial life in their attempt not to curb competition merely, but to put an end to it. The course of the leading trust of the country has been such as to emphasize the fear of them, and the benefits that have come from its cheapening of an article of commerce are insignificant when contrasted with the mischiefs that have followed the exhibitions in many forms of the merciless power of concentrated capital. And when we witness the utterly heartless manner in which trusts sometimes have closed manufactories and turned men willing to be industrious into the streets in order that they may increase profits already reasonably large, we cannot help asking ourselves the question whether the trust as we see it is not a public enemy; whether it is not teaching the laborer dangerous lessons; whether it is not helping to breed anarchy? One thing would seem manifest: there are some trusts whose members are estopped from complaining of organized laborers when by strikes or boycotts or any kindred means they seek to force compliance with their demands. They are estopped because their own methods have been of like nature, and having been employed with greater skill and power, have been generally more effective and mischievous.

Anything in the nature of a trust, that should bring the railroads of the country, or of any considerable section of the country under a single head, with irresistible power to divide business and make rates, would be more to be dreaded than any other trust ever formed or proposed. The reason is obvious: it would control more property, have more power of controlling and coercing the action of individuals and of the public authorities. It would besides, if formed now, in all probability fall to the control of that class of managers who in handling railroad property do not hesitate to subordinate LAW to corporate interests and rivalries. No prudent man would give assent to a railroad trust until he was first shown that very effective legal restraints had been put upon it.

If it were not taking time unwarrantably, something might be said about excessive railroad building as one of the reasons for enormous recent losses on railroad stocks. A gentleman of considerable experience remarked recently, "The most profitable business now is the building of worthless railroads; no matter how worthless if the bonds can be sold. The projectors put nothing in, and they determine for themselves how much they will take out for building." The proposal of a new railroad is very often a mere confidence operation. Many roads are built that instead of increasing the aggregate value of the railroad property of the country, diminish it very largely. The millions put into them are sunk, and perhaps as many millions more previously put into roads which the new roads make unprofitable.

I trust that what I have said sufficiently indicates the weakness of pooling as a specific for railroad evils. But this further must be said of it. It is not at all probable that pooling will be legalized before managers show *first*, a different attitude towards the law, and *second*, a better disposition to observe mutual engagements. It is right - at this point that the radical mistakes have been made. If the obligations entered into in forming railroad associations had been observed, pooling would have been of much less moment than is now contended. But the obligations in many cases seem only to have been assumed that they might be violated, and when men guilty of the violation ask for the legalization of pooling to enable them to obey the law the request does not have a winning sound; it repels votes instead of gaining them. Before further law is made at their request they should show a purpose to obey the law they now have. This is the way it is likely to strike a legislative body. The true method of railroad management is undoubtedly something in the nature of representative regulation under Government control, and to this pooling is not half so essential as is the creation of a sentiment in railroad circles that will not tolerate the disregard or open breach of mutual engagements.

Many recent rate wars have not had the slightest justification in either policy or in morals. The railroad companies had not long since an arrangement regarding the transportation of emigrants which was accomplishing for them the purposes of a pool. Suddenly it was broken up and a horde of harpies brought in to feed upon railroad revenues. An actual pool would have been of no service there. The evils of course did not end when the war did.

All these things go to show that something else needs reforming besides the law. It is poor reformatory work that the law can do in any line of business unless the moral forces in the same business come to its support. Of course effectual reform will necessarily reach beyond railroad circles. Large dealers who formerly prospered upon special favors must be content to forego them. The bribing of a railroad servant to underbill goods or in some other way to give an advantage to a shipper ought to be as disreputable as the hiring of a thief to steal a neighbor's goods.

In an address made by Charles Francis Adams in this city a few days since, that gentleman did not speak any too strongly on this general subject. And we all know that on railroad subjects he speaks from ample knowledge and experience.

I have spoken of the want of reformatory power in the law. One who investigates railroad disorders will be surprised to find how many of them, though plainly opposed to the spirit of the law, may still be practiced legally. Rate cutting in passenger service is very largely done by the use of tickets which the law expressly exempts from its provisions, and coupon tickets are so manipulated by one company as to cut the rates of another without the other being a participant otherwise than as it suffers from a fraud practiced upon it, The general manager of a long line of road who was careful as he thought to render cutting on his line impossible, was astonished recently by having a ticket broker to whom he was a stranger offer him a ticket over his own line at a cut rate. He at first pronounced the ticket a forgery; but it was not a forgery, nor was it a ticket which had been partly used; it was his part of a coupon ticket which had been put into the hands of the passenger agent of a distant road, and this agent had cut it off and passed it to the scalper as a means of cutting the local rate. One of the crying evils in railroad service now needing attention is the combination between the scalper and the unscrupulous general passenger agent. This will be broken up just as soon as there are applied in railroad matters the same general maxims of business prudence which are expected to control in other interests. If the combination in the same person of the two characters of railroad manager—in whatever official position—and of speculator in railroad stocks could be rendered impossible, we might hope to see the time when the question *What is right and wrong in railroad matters*, would be heard a good deal oftener than it is now, and the question *What can be done in evasion of the law without encountering its penalties*, a good deal more infrequently.

A PLEA FOR RAILWAY CONSOLIDATION.

By Mr. Collis P. Huntington.

President of the Southern Pacific Railroad Company.

The question has often been asked of railroad men; What is the remedy for rate wars and the demoralization that results from the rate-cutting incident to their business as at present conducted? I know of but one answer to this question, and that is consolidation or joint ownership; and as the solution of a purely business problem I began advocating this many years ago. The process of consolidation itself (which is simply the endeavor to secure the largest possible amount of tonnage and transport it with the least expenditure of money) is a logical outgrowth of circumstances, and, although the projectors of the earlier lines did not perhaps foresee the advantage, and even the necessity of it, yet it was not long before the natural tendency of railroad corporations towards unification of interests began to manifest itself.

There are men now living in the full activities of life who have travelled from Albany to Buffalo over the Albany and Schenectady, Schnectady and Utica, Utica and Syracuse, Syracuse and Auburn, Auburn and Rochester, and Rochester and Buffalo railroads, all of which were connected in a continuous line of track. But it was very soon discovered by the proprietors of these fragments of roads, so to speak, that they gave little return to their owners, while the result to the people who used them was unsatisfactory, as it was difficult to get through rates of freight, and, when obtained, to locate the responsibility for damage to property, or for detention in transit from the point of shipment to destination.

The disadvantages arising from this lack of unity have induced a continuous effort from that date to the present time, on the part of the builders of railroads, to devise ways by which the people could be better served and the owners more satisfactorily compensated for their risks and outlays of capital, until the ablest men have come to the conclusion that the most effective, and probably the only practical remedy for the many evils and demoralizations that now exist is joint ownership, as it would appear that only in that way can the minimum of cost of transportation, and, there-

---
Reprinted by special permission from The North American Review of September, 1891.
Copyrighted by Lloyd Brice, 1891.

fore, the maximum benefit to the public and to the roads, be secured; and this, too, to use the words of Lincoln, "not rending or wrecking anything," but, instead of this, creating harmony out of discord, order out of confusion, and largely increasing the value of the property of the stockholders of each road, each of whom thus becomes a stockholder in the whole property.

Thus came into existence the present New York Central and Hudson River Railroad, from which the general public has reaped enormous advantages, while the owners have been rewarded by an exchange of shares of little or no worth for stock in the new organization, of vastly increased value. This great corporation may be said to represent the genius of that giant of railway finance, Cornelius Vanderbilt, whose keen foresight, indomitable will, and tireless energy combined to produce this example of railway enterprise.

The same may be said of that vast network of roads controlled by the Pennsylvania Railroad Company, which has been slowly but steadily built up by purchase and consolidation, by the interweaving, as it were, of many short roads of little or no value into the completed fabric known as the Pennsylvania system. To the organizing force and intellect of Edgar Thompson, and, after him, of Colonel Thomas A. Scott, is due this unparalleled achievement in the history of railway-building. That the owners and managers of these and other large corporations of their kind have been able to continue the success that was guaranteed by the sagacious policy of their predecessors reflects no less credit on the earlier actors than it does upon their successors, who were quick to perceive the wisdom of the policy and mentally equipped to carry it out.

When both of the great systems alluded to were in the process of amalgamation they were severely criticised; but I think no one will at this time dispute the fact that both of the organizations, as at present constituted, serve, and are able to serve, the people better than it was possible for the fragmentary sections of which they were composed, to have done, and that they, moreover, give much better returns to those who have invested their capital in them. As Sidney Dillon has well said in the April number of *The Review*, "Combinations that do not combine, and monopolies whose constant tendency during a long series of years has been to bring producers and consumers into closer relations with each other and lessen the cost of living to both, deserve praise and support rather than censure and adverse legislation."

That this merging of several properties into single organizations is a natural process of improvement is shown, also, by the fact that it is all the time going on and never takes a step backward; and we have yet to learn of a single instance where it has been considered advisable, either by those financially interested or by the public, to disrupt a system thus consolidated and restore it to its original parts, or to make any part independent of the others. Nor has the writer ever known of a consolidation that has not brought a reduction of rates, except where there had previously been such a cutting of rates as would inevitably have landed the property into the hands of a receiver, with all its evil results to both the owners and the public, had not sagacious councils arrested the impending ruin.

It is not for the interest of the public that property wisely created and capable of so much good to the country should be used in such a way as to invite bankruptcy, for by such misman-. agement many needed improvements will not be created. There are a few individuals in every community, and probably always will be, who spend their lives in the effort to find some place where they can take up something without laying anything down, and to whom wasteful, and I might almost say wicked, competition among railroads is welcome, so long as it affects favorably their own individual pockets. From these people opposition to legitimate transactions that are based upon the principle of giving the greatest good to the greatest number, may always be expected; but I am satisfied that the mass of the intelligent people of the country look with disfavor upon the unhealthy strife between the railroads of this country, which has resulted not only in no permanent good to the patrons of the roads, but an irreparable harm to vested interests and the interruption of that process of development of the country's resources the advance of which, under a more enlightened policy, should be steady and rapid.

The time was when people were afraid of corporations and looked upon them with jealousy and distrust; but the history of the world's industry has, I think, taught the majority of the people that corporations are the means whereby the multitude can combine for mutual benefit and protection. In no other way can they compete with the vast capital that is concentrated in the hands of a few individuals; and, this being so, the time should, and I believe will, soon come when communities will call for the same treatment of corporate property that is accorded to individual possessions. Then railroad corporations will not be unjustly interfered with in the exercise of their rights, based upon the most obvious rules of business, by such legislation as culminated some years ago in the Interstate Commerce Act.

It should be possible for the railroads to move the product of the farm and the lean ores of the mine at a small profit over train expenses, and thus develop large and important interests, as well as accommodate a large number of men by giving them employment that cannot be obtained when the rates on freight are arbitrarily fixed by law so that these products of the farm and the mine cannot be moved to a market that will take them. The great expense of operating a road of light traffic, the construction of which has been somewhat costly, consists not in the actual expense of running the trains themselves,—which includes only the wear of the track and machinery, the consumption of fuel, oil, and waste, and the wages of the crew,—but in the fixed charges, in which are included the interest on the cost of property, the taxes on the same, and the maintenance of the different departments connected with its mangement.

Where the price of moving a ton of ore is compulsory, whether ore be rich or lean, the rich will be sent to market and the poor will remain at the dump, instead of being removed, and thus possibly opening a path to richer and more remunerative beds of ore; and in the case of forest products, the fine timber will be profitably taken out, without interfering with the profits of the lumberman, while the cheaper stuff will not be handled. Lean ores and cheap timber should be moved at a small profit over the actual train expenses, but this cannot be done under the present law. I believe the Interstate Commerce Act has caused the loss of millions of dollars to the producer, as it would seem evident that no manager of a railroad would fail to bring out over his line tonnage of this character, the marketing of which means so many dollars to the lumberman and the mine-owner, employment to many who must otherwise remain unemployed and the encouragement of worthy industries. These things are so apparent that they should be understood by all.

With many of the railroads of America, which run through large areas of arid country, the problem of existence is a hard one, and the only apparent solution is to secure something out of the bowels of the earth that will bear transportation; and upon the theory that there is something for man's use everywhere, it should be found here in the form of ores, possibly lean ores; but so long as they will pay something over train expenses, their transportation may provide much work for men and some remuneration to those who carry them.

The railroads known as the overland or Pacific railroads have lost much business because of their inability, on account of the Interstate Commerce Law, to compete with the Canadian Pacific, which is able, through the fostering care of a paternal government, unrestricted by legislation, to bid for business on better terms than its American rivals. The struggle between the different companies is not for the interest of a majority of the people who use the railroad, as the very large shippers at the great competing points reached by two or more roads get an immediate benefit from the reduction of rates, while the small dealers are injured in their business to a very considerable extent. Assume that a hundred men are dealing in some particular commodity. Ninety-nine of them may each have a car-load, or less, to ship, which is not enough to make it an object for them to go and "shop" among the different transportation companies for rates; and if they did, the tonnage is not enough to make it an inducement for the companies to cut the rate in their favor; but one man who has, as is sometimes the case, five hundred car-loads to ship is vitally interested, and he accordingly goes about among the various roads until he finally succeeds in obtaining the desired rebates. This not only takes money from the railroad itself, but does great harm to the small shippers, who are crowded out of the market or compelled to sell their product at less net profit than they are fairly entitled to. The shippers who live along the line away from these competing centres are compelled to pay more, as the sums lost at the competing points must be recouped to prevent the railroad company from going into bankruptcy, as very few of the small roads of the country are paying anything beyond their current and fixed expenses, leaving nothing for the holders of the shares.

What possible remedy is there for such a state of things except joint ownership? As a simple business proposition, it seems to me unanswerable, for, by its application, it can be readily seen that much of the expense of maintaining separate organizations and separate offices will be cut off, and a great multitude of agents and agencies will be dispensed with. On the one side of the people quite as much good will be the outcome. The complaint of charging more for a short than for a long haul, which comes from the shipper located between instead of at the important centers, will cease to be heard, because the pernicious system of giving rebates and commissions, or whatever they may be called, that cost the roads so much money and really do their patrons, as a whole, so much harm, will no longer be practised, the excuse or necessity therefor no longer existing.

While the uniting of small roads has been productive of great benefits to the owners and to the public who use them, yet I am satisfied that the best results may not be reached until substantially all the transportation business of this country is done by one company. The accomplishment of this would reduce the cost of transportation to the minimum which would admit of the lowest possible rates to shippers and passengers. There would be no longer any necessity of charging more for a short than for a long haul, except where water competition existed, as the crossing of railroads at various points would have no further effect upon the rate schedules.

The raising of rates at non-competing points is one of the things done by railroads which it is hard to explain to the satisfaction of those who buy transportation; but it will continue to be done as long as railroads are controlled by scattered interests, and neither agreements nor laws will entirely prevent it. If, on the contrary, all the railroads of the country were held in joint ownership, they would need much less rolling stock than is now required, as the staple crops of the country are moved at different seasons of the year, and cars and locomotives could be transferred from one section to another as needed, thus saving a large amount of capital which otherwise, for a considerable portion of the year, would be idle.

There is another feature of this question that is perhaps hardly taken into account in the public mind, because its bearing upon it appears, at first glance, to be remote; but we are dealing with a problem of the future, and the time is coming when its close relation to it will be appreciated. The existence of an undoubted security for institutions and for the great mass of conservative investors of limited means, who demand above all other qualifications a security that shall be safe, and who rely upon their investments for the incomes which are to support themselves and their families, is soon to become a necessity in America. Our government bonds are constantly being called in and cancelled, whilst the surplus capital of the country is continually increasing. Unless a stable and safe security for the multitude is forthcoming, it does not need the astuteness of a financier to comprehend the possible situation of the future when the investor who seeks an assured income from his savings will have to place his reliance upon the wisdom of his own selection among a list of many hundreds of railway stocks and bonds, subject to all the serious fluctuations that follow in the wake of selfish competition and inefficient management.

The writer has never regarded the existence of a large national debt as an evil in a prosperous and growing country like the United States, whose obligations do not affect the credit of the government and are not significant of any financial embarrassment; but our people have decided otherwise, perhaps not unwisely; nevertheless there must be a substitute for the people to invest their savings in—a security that shall possess the confidence of the entire public. What shall it be? It seems to the writer that nothing will be safer than shares or bonds of the united railroads of this country, and few, if any, other securities will be so easy to negotiate or raise money on. If this true, why should not a very large number of the people who use these roads invest their money in such an organization, and thus become, to a large extent, the owners and controllers of the railroads that they use?

Ours is a vast country, and no doubt produces more and a greater variety of food for man than any other nation on the earth. All are interested—those who produce and those who consume—in having the enormous tonnage of food gathered and distributed at the lowest possible cost. How to do it is the question that all want to see solved. It was once believed by many, and it may still be thought by a very few, that if the farmer had no machinery for reaping, sowing, and gathering his grain, many would get employment and thereby be helped, even if it cost something more to produce. Is there any one who would be benefited by having the transportation cost more than the least possible sum for which the product of the farm could be moved? If that be so, let us all look for that way. It cannot be done by little fragmentary companies, for they cannot practise the economies of wealth, as their poor road beds, crippled rolling stock, and lean management will testify. What is wanted is not more than two or three—and one would be better—great carrying companies, with their steel tracks and road bed as nearly perfect as they can be, with all their machinery of the best quality, with their capacious warehouses at intermediate points, and their almost unlimited terminal facilities. With the best talent in the country to manage and control such an organization, many millions could be saved to those who use the railroads of this country, and millions also to those who own them over what is now being received by the fragmentary, badly-equipped, and inefficiently-managed roads that, with but few exceptions, now exist.

Some fears have been expressed that the great transportation companies of this country would override the rights of the people; but surely there need be no apprehension of that, as certainly there is no danger. Any capitalist, or combination of such, would be weak—yes, worse than weak—to make the effort to stand between the people and their rights, and I am quite sure that few honest and intelligent citizens fear any such combination. To be sure, there are demagogues who cry "Monopoly!" and assert that the great corporations are about to override the liberties of the people; but solicitude for the people is not the real reason of their outcry. It is because they hope to climb up on the noise they make into high places, and into seats that they are not worthy of and have not the ability to fill.

The branch of the government in which all good people have faith—the sheet anchor, so to speak, of all we hold dear—the judicial department of the government, will stand between the rights of the many and the few, and—what is even more important, because the danger is greater—will see that the rights of the few are protected against the improvident, and hence impecunious, many. The rights of all should be and, I believe, will be protected. If not all, very soon none.

In the general trial of Warren Hastings, Edmund Burke addressing the House of Lords, is reported to have said: "It is well for you to remember, gentlemen, that if the time should ever come when British law does not protect the life, the liberty, and the property of the humblest Hindoo upon the banks of the Ganges, no nobleman will be safe on the banks of the Thames."

Justice Brewer, of the United States Supreme Court, lately delivered an important address that should be read by every American citizen; and amongst other things he said:

"Public attack upon private property appears conspicuously under the guise of regulation, where charges for the use are so reduced as to prevent a reasonable profit on the investment. The history of this question is interesting.

Certain occupations have long been considered of a quasi-public nature—among these, principally the business of carrying passengers and freight. Of the propriety of this classification no question can be made. Without inquiring into the various reasons therefor, a common carrier is described as a quasi-public servant. Private capital is invested, and the business is carried on by private persons and through private instrumentalities; yet it is a public service which they render, and by virtue thereof public and government control is warranted. The great common carriers of the country, the railroad companies, insisted that, by reason of the fact that they were built by private capital and owned by private corporations, they had the same right to fix the prices for transportation that any individual had to fix the price at which he was willing to sell his labor or his property. After a long and bitter struggle, the Supreme Court of the United States, in the celebrated 'Granger' cases, reported in 94 U. S., sustained the power of the public and affirmed legislative control.

"The scope of this decision, suggesting a far-reaching supervision over private occupations, brought vigorously up the question as to its extent. On this line the struggle was again renewed and carried to the Supreme Court, which in the recent case of Railway Company vs. Minnesota, 134 U. S., 418, decided that regulation did not mean destruction; and that under the guise of legislative control over tariffs, it was not possible for state or nation to destroy the investments of private capital in such enterprises; that the individual had rights as well as the public, and rights which the public could not take from him. The opinion written in that case by Justice Blatchford, sustained as it was by the court, will ever remain a strong and unconquerable fortress in the long struggle between individual rights and public greed."

What has been said in this article of those who deal in the products of the forest and mine applies to an even greater extent to the farmer and herdsman. Flexibility in the carrying rates is needed, and there are many reasons why this should be so; for the farmer often has poor crops, frequently the market therefor is too low, and the best interest of the transportation company lies in helping him over these lean places, as it gives him heart to enter the year that is to follow with courage to plant largely, in the hope that, when the harvest time comes again, he will have a larger output, with better prices, and thus be able to recover the loss of the previous season; while those who control the carrying companies and who, by their protective policy, have helped the farmer in the hour of his trouble and made him happy, would look back with satisfaction upon the wisdom of their own action, which has given them a continuing business, for nothing is much worse than having the cars and machinery of a railroad stand idle upon the tracks.

Again, a great drouth may occur in some sections of our vast country, and it becomes necessary under such circumstances to take out from such districts all the live stock or to carry food in. Should this not be done, on humanitarian grounds alone, for lower rates than may be charged in sections not so afflicted, and that, too, without much regard to the distance? And when such consideration on the part of the railroad company is really advantageous to itself in the long run, can there be any doubt of its wisdom? What the carrying companies want is a continuing business and a fair profit for each decade, and in this reasonable expectation they should have the right to help their patrons during the "off" years, in the common interest.

Now, all this cannot be regulated by legislation, however carefully such legislation may be devised, simply because no provision of law can anticipate the varying requirements of trade. It can only be done by working upon flexible lines, so to speak, letting prices go up and down as will best serve the interests of both contracting parties. Why should it be otherwise? The judicial branch of the government has decided that it has the power, under the Constitution, to say what is a fair income for railroad and other quasi-public institutions that do business for and with the public. Why should state legislatures endeavor to arbitrarily fix the rates, when no doubt the best interest of both shipper and carrier will be served by a graduation of those rates in accordance with the changing conditions of business? Of all property railroads should have the largest freedom, in order that they may be able to earn sufficient to pay a fair interest upon the capital invested, and to earn it in a way that shall most nearly conserve the interests of their patrons and themselves. When a fair return upon invested capital has been received, the people, through the courts, can prevent rates from going up, and thus restrict the earnings of a railroad to reasonable figures.

Transportation companies can sometimes gather net money over train expenses in competition with water lines, and they should be allowed to do so, as their permanent way is expensive and fixed. It cannot be moved. The ship has its free right of way over all the seas, on which no taxes and no interest have to be paid; but the railroad is often doubly burdened by a tax not only upon its shares—which are only the evidence of ownership—but upon its real property, which is frequently assessed above its actual value.

In the high dry lands in the center of the continent a few people have sometimes confederated together and carved counties out of the desert where there was no necessity for their creation, and built court houses and school houses where they were not needed, simply because the establishment of these institutions gave them the power to tax the property of the new county to pay for the so-called improvements; the principal, almost the only, property on which taxes could be levied being the railroad by which the so-called county is traversed. And after all this comes the politician with his demand for the appointment of men who, though possessing no interest whatever in the property, or knowledge or experience in its management, shall practically control its business by fixing the rates of fares and freights. Surely the time has come to call a halt, and, in the words of the great jurist, for the conservative branch of the government to step in "between individual rights and public greed."

RAILROAD CONSOLIDATION.

By Gen. E. P. Alexander.

I am requested to write my views upon railroad consolidation, under circumstances precluding any but a very brief and hasty presentation. Yet it seems to me that even a very condensed presentation of some leading facts may serve in some degree to assist those willing to consider the railroad side of the subject. So with this much of apology in advance for what can be, at best, but a very deficient performance, I venture to set forth the line upon which I think an impartial and unprejudiced inquirer would approach the subject, and the conclusions to which he would be led.

In the first place, I think that such an inquirer would endeavor to form a clear conception of what a perfect system of transportation should be, and to note where and how our present system falls short of that ideal. He would then seek the reasons of these deficiencies, and taking them one by one, would inquire whether or not railroad consolidation would tend to increase or to diminish their sum. It is this line of inquiry which I propose to pursue.

It is unnecessary to dwell upon the great value of railroad transportation to the community. No other possible investment of a man's money can benefit his fellow citizens, near and remote, to the same degree that capital invested in a railroad does. Such investments should, therefore, be encouraged, and, if for no other reason, a community should willingly see its railroads prove profitable and secure investments.

But more especially is this true when it is remembered that railroad prosperity begins with its swifter, safer and more frequent trains, better cars and the employment of more men and disbursement of larger sums as wages, interest and dividends. It is a bad thing for a community when even the smallest merchant in it fails in his business, and many of his neighbors are sure to feel it in a greater or less degree. His landlord, his doctor, his butcher, his baker, his patrons, his creditors, and even his competitors in business, all come in for a share in his loss. How much more serious is the shrinkage of millions of dollars of invested capital, and the gradual depreciation in safe and efficient service of a great railroad

---

Reprinted by permission from the Railway Review of March 26, 1892.

upon which all our business interests and so much of our social pleasures depend?

And as the prosperity of large communities, of whole states even, may depend upon the ability of the railroads serving them to make their lines highways of freight and travel from distant sections, I am disposed to think that our impartial but intelligent inquirer may even put as the first requisite of an ideal railroad system that it shall be prosperous and self-sustaining, otherwise, whatever other excellences may be provided, the result might be like a recipe for hare soup without adequate provision for hare.

The next essential condition of an ideal transportation service is that its rates should be uniform. By uniform I mean the same to all persons similarly situated. There should be no rebates or secret allowances to secure the business of large shippers. Merchants should not have to go shopping and trading for rates, but should be able to feel confidently that all competitors stood upon an equal footing with the railroad as they do with the postoffice.

Another important condition of an ideal service, is that it should be as far-reaching as possible, and require dealing with the fewest officials to get rates to distant points, to trace for delays or damage, and to collect claims. Other things being equal that service is the best which reaches the farthest.

Last, but not least, I place the condition that rates should be reasonable. They should be high enough, but no higher, than to allow fair wages to employes, fair interest on the capital invested, and full maintenance of the road and equipment in the highest state of efficiency, safety and progress.

In this connection it should be noted that there are peculiar difficulties in the way of determining equitable railroad rates upon any particular article which are not generally understood. If it were possible to find out exactly each specific act of transportation costs it would be easy to fix a price which would refund the cost and a reasonable profit. Were that only possible there would be no railroad problems and no anti-railroad prejudice. But it is as utterly impossible to determine, for instance, what it costs a railroad to carry a barrel of flour a hundred miles, as to determine what it costs a doctor to prescribe for a headache, or a lawyer to give an opinion. In either case the actual outlay involved is practically nothing, but the ability to perform the act represents the entire capital of the railroad, or of the doctor, or of the lawyer. Hence, all three must graduate their charges for particular services by some other scale than by the actual cost of each service.

The only other equitable scale which has ever been devised, the world over, has been to proportion the charges to the value of the service rendered. A familiar illustration is found in the rates charged for postal service. The postoffice department pays the railroads for transportation by the pound, estimating all matter alike; but it charges the public, rates varying from one cent a pound to thirty-two cents a pound, depending upon the character of the matter transmitted. So railroads, the world over, have been compelled to classify all the products of the earth and of all manufactures and industries upon earth, and assign to each the proportion which it shall bear of railroad maintenance when it is transported by rail.

And here is where the trouble comes in. Every solitary one of these innumerable products (as numerous as the nouns in the English language), when it moves by rail is in competition both with other articles which may be used in its place, and with similar articles produced elsewhere, and the rate charged by the railroad is a material factor in the profits of the shipper. Naturally, interested parties will always think that their particular interests are made to bear an undue share of the expense and plausible arguments in justification of their complaints can always be constructed, by selecting some article of a lower classification, and showing that the actual service rendered by the railroad was the same in each case. That is held to prove that the railroad has "discriminated" against this article. Of course it has discriminated. It discriminates whenever it makes a rate. Like the postal service, it is obliged to discriminate, or it would have but a single rate for all articles, and the business of the country could not go on.

I do not mean for a moment to imply that the classifications now in general use are unimpeachable in the fairness of their discriminations. They are the gradual growth of experience and compromise, and changes are constantly taking place. But angels from Heaven could not make a classification which would satisfy everybody, and it would be almost a miracle if any two angels would fully agree upon any one complete classification. The trouble is, that there is no principle of equity to be appealed to in adjusting innumerable shades of differences, and this inherent difficulty, not generally appreciated, is the cause of much honestly meant, but unmerited, criticism of railroad management. It has, however, no direct bearing upon the immediate subject of present discussion, and what I have said about it is rather to eliminate it than to treat of it fully. For whether 10,000 miles of railroad are under a single management, or under 20 different ones; whether under government control, or under private individuals; rates will remain as they now are, based purely on discriminations, and as a whole they must be high enough to maintain the railroads and pay a reasonable interest on the investment. If rates fall short of that standard there must follow depreciation of the railroad's securities until their market value adjusts itself to the insufficient earnings.

From the foregoing we may now sum up the conditions most to be desired in the transportation service of the country as follows: 1st. The railroads should be self-sustaining. 2nd. Their service should be far-reaching. 3rd. Their rates should be uniform to all. 4th. Their rates should be reasonable.

We have now to consider whether the consolidation of our railroads into large systems will be promotive of these ends or otherwise. As to the first two conditions the argument is very short. It is beyond controversy that consolidation makes possible great economies in operation; far greater than is generally appreciated. But the result shows for itself in the low rates of freight at which the large systems of this country are successfully operated. It permits what is practically the doing away with middle men, and the middle men are usually very expensive men in every kind of business. The tendency of consolidation is therefore distinctly towards rendering railroads self-supporting.

Next, as to its effect in rendering far-reaching service, consolidation is the one essential and indispensable condition of such service. No road can fully represent its connections, or be held legally responsible for them, as it can for its own undertakings. Uniformity of rules, classifications, equipment, continuity of schedules, and innumerable minor refinements of safe and satisfactory service, follow and attend upon unity of management. There are fewer officials for the public to deal with, and these officials can fairly be held to a larger accountability, and have more power to accomplish the constant reforms and improvements which progress demands.

Next, we have to inquire into the tendency of consolidation to bring about uniformity or equality of rates to all shippers. This means, in other words, nothing but the abolishment of all secret arrangements by which concessions and rebates from the publicly quoted rates are given to favored parties. I think all will admit that the practice of giving such rebates is a grievous wrong— even the favored shippers who receive and enjoy them, and the ingenious officials who devise plans to pay them without detection. For the law already condemns them, and provides fine and imprisonment for both giver and receiver. But though the competitive business of the country is known to be full of them, and strenuous efforts have been made to make some examples of violators, I have never heard of a conviction and scarcely of a single prosecution. The offense is of a character too easy to conceal, and though it is really a robbery of the public and demoralizing to employes, it will never be eradicated while a strong temptation to commit it exists.

Now, of all the merits of consolidation, the chiefest one is this, that it tends to lessen and remove the temptation to secret rebating. Its effect in this direction is too obvious to require any argument. It insures a larger and more stable business independent of all risks and vicissitudes, permits a more economical transaction of it, and briefly diminishes the temptation to secure traffic by secret methods. No community would desire to see persons intrusted with important public functions brought to starvation, for pressing need often proves too great a temptation to private virtue. So it should not desire to see its transportation service in the hands of corporations upon the perpetual verge of bankruptcy, if it wishes to have a service uniform to all, and free from secret rebates.

There remains now to discuss but the fourth condition, that rates should be reasonable. The popular fear is that combination will result in extortion. But there are abundant facts to allay that fear which even the "way-faring man" may readily discern. In the first place, "consolidation," in the full sense of the word, cannot exist. It would imply a bringing under one management of the entire system of roads of the country, while the only consolidation possible at present, and what is now being discussed, is only a very partial consolidation. So I would say, in the first place, that there is no possible consolidation which will not necessarily leave out a great deal more than it takes in, and that the practical question is not as to what will be the results of an absolute and complete consolidation, but what is the tendency of partial consolidations in the present state of the development of our country.

Now, as to their tendency to result in extortionate rates, one very obvious fact is, that so far as it has yet gone in this country, and in foreign civilized countries, its tendency has been notoriously in the contrary direction. Ample statistics and illustrations could be cited did time and space permit; but Prof. Hadley, of Yale, one of the most accurate and eminent students of all railroad problems, and of its phases in all countries has summed up the facts in a single sentence, "consolidation of itself created through routes and long distance traffic." [Railroad Transportation, p. 13.] As long distance traffic is only possible under the lowest rates, the working tendency of consolidation has evidently not been toward extortion. I do not mean to say that it has ever, or anywhere. removed all complaints of discriminations, or of high rates upon some articles as compared with others. That would be a good deal to expect of the millennium itself. But I do not believe there exists an instance where a consolidation of railroads has resulted in extravagant profits, which is the only true test whether rates as a whole are exorbitant. Certainly the average results indicate that if there are exceptions to the rule that railroad investments in the south yield exceedingly poor returns, the exceptions are few and due to some peculiarly favorable circumstances. For the very prosperous year, 1890, the returns of the 17,077 miles of railroad in the South Atlantic states, including the two Virginias, the two Carolinas, Georgia and Florida, paid total dividends to stockholders of $3,360,000, an average of but $195 per mile, not two per cent upon ten thousand dollars per mile of stock. In 1886, in the same states, only nineteen per cent of the mileage paid any dividends at all upon stock, and only seventy-eight per cent paid interest upon their bonds.

But their remains one long rooted and most obstinate objection to railroad consolidation, which must be considered in the words in which it is usually expressed, although its only real meaning has already been discussed. It is said that railroad consolidation will "check competition." The essential meaning of that phrase is of course only that it will permit extortion. But before closing the argument upon it, it is well to consider for a moment the rather sentimental value which the public attaches to "competition." From the days in which there were many governmental monopolies, there has come down a prejudice against "monopoly" and a friendship for "competition" which are entirely to be commended and justified. But for all that, centuries ago it was discovered that there might possibly be too much even of a good thing, and that too much of some remedies, even of competition, might sometimes constitute another disease. From this conviction arose gradually innumerable forms of what was called "Protection," in the shape of tariffs, unions, brotherhoods, alliances and associations of every trade, profession and occupation on earth, until practically every living man today sees in his own business (which is the only one he understands fully) that, after competition has run to a reasonable extent, there must be some form of protection devised against competition gone mad. The correctness of this general belief is just now being notoriously emphasized by the calamitous effects of an over production of cotton.

A too abundant harvest has proven a national calamity. All other interests are suffering in sympathy with the cotton planters, and the latter are attempting to devise some scheme of "protection" by consolidation and co-operation. Even if there were no other arguments, the railroads could make a strong appeal upon analogy and equity for the same freedom of self-protection allowed their patrons, their employes and individuals generally. The railroad's welfare is no less worthy of consideration, for it is simply the welfare of many individuals combined to carry on works too large for the means of a single one. They furnish the means by which the weak may combine and compete with advantage against the strong, and no one who desires is denied the enjoyment of their privileges.

But apart from all this argument founded upon experience and upon reason, as to the danger of extortion resulting from consolidation, there remains one single statement of fact which is conclusive of the whole matter even without any argument The simple fact is, that extortion has been rendered impossible by laws lodging in state and interstate commissions the power of making all railroad rates. While these commissions exist extortion cannot exist, for it is provided that their sympathies and leanings shall not be toward the railroads.

Looking back now to the four conditions of an ideal railroad service which have been discussed as to the tendency of continued railroad consolidation to bring them about, it has appeared that, as to the first three, the tendency to produce self sustaining roads, far reaching service, and rates uniform to all is beyond question. As to the fourth condition, it does not appear that railroad consolidation, as far as it has yet been carried, has ever resulted in extortionate rates or extravagant profits; nor is it likely that such result could attend any partial consolidation which seems either probable or possible. But even were that the case there is always adequate protection for the public against extortion in the powers of state and interstate commissions.

It is, therefore, to the interests of the whole commercial and financial world that railroads should be assisted and encouraged to abandon the cut-throat policy which has heretofore prevailed among them, and by consolidation and co-operation endeavor to establish their securities as safe investments for rich and poor, and to keep pace with the general progress and improvement of the day in their methods and service.

It may be done quietly and gradually and without loss of any of the many millions of dollars invested in the securities of the properties involved, but even with a constant appreciation of them. But if not accomplished in this way it will finally come through sales at auction to highest bidders, a process which no legislation can check but which will take away from present owners many millions of dollars of values.

GOVERNMENT INTERFERENCE IN ENGLISH RAILWAY MANAGEMENT.

By W. M. Acworth.

"Of the many ways in which common-sense inferences about social affairs are flatly contradicted by events, one of the most curious is the way in which, the more things improve, the louder become the exclamations about their badness. . . . In proportion as the evil decreases the denunciation of it increases; and as fast as natural causes are shown to be powerful there grows up the belief that they are powerless."
—Mr. HERBERT SPENCER, in "A Plea for Liberty."

"The key to the solution of the railway problem lies in the thorough application of the principle of publicity to railway affairs. . . . The railway problem cannot be solved except in reliance on the principle of publicity. . . . There is danger lest the quietness with which the principle of publicity works should deprive it of the confidence it deserves."
—Prof. HENRY C. ADAMS, of the Michigan University and the Interstate Commerce Commission.

In these two quotations from distinguished authorities, the one English, the other American, the one dealing with affairs in general, the other referring to transportation questions in particular, there is to be found, I believe, the wisest guidance in the solution of the railway problem. The accuracy of this belief might be established by an appeal to the general history of all ages and all countries. For such a task, however, not columns but volumes would be required. I propose, therefore, to confine myself entirely to recent English railway history, being confident that even this limited field will supply illustrations and examples sufficient for our present purpose. Public attention in England has, in the last few years, been attracted by the following railway questions: freight rates, liability of the companies for accidents to their servants, hours of labor, public safety, cheap trains for the working classes, and punctuality.

The history of freight rates is in outline as follows: The special act of parliament incorporating a railway company—its charter as you would call it—has always fixed the maximum which might legally be charged. Further, as long ago as 1845 and 1854, the general law laid it down—in language that is reproduced almost

Reprinted by permission from The Independent of June 1, 1893.

verbatim by your act to regulate commerce—that rates must be reasonable, not giving to one customer undue preference or advantage over others, and that adequate facilities must be afforded for the interchange of traffic without delay, preference or obstruction; later acts have imposed on the companies the further obligations to publish their rates, and not to increase them without fourteen days' notice. Here then was a complete scheme of rate regulation, comprising first a fixed maximum, which the company took with its eyes open as condition precedent to leave to build its line; secondly, the obligation to hold the balance even between rival localities and trades, and lastly, publicity of rates in order that every one might be in a position to know if his legal rights were trenched upon. Of course, the machinery, being human in its origin and depending on human agency for its working, was very far from perfect. For one thing the maxima, fixed in the early days of railroading, were for the most part so high as to afford no practical check on the powers of the companies; for another, an appeal to the law courts, or to the railway commission, which, since 1873, has for most purposes of railway litigation taken their place, was both costly and troublesome; further, judgment sometimes went for the railway company, not on the abstract merits of the case, but merely because it was a more practiced and better-armed combatant than almost any conceivable trader or group of traders.

But, on the whole, the results were by no neans unsatisfactory. Rates were very rarely advanced, and by no means rarely reduced; on the whole the average tended steadily and not very slowly downward; while, on the other hand, the accommodation and service given in return for the rate tended steadily and by no means slowly upward. Rate wars, with their wild fluctuations, reducing all business for the time to little better than gambling, were unknown; the personal and secret discriminations which have discredited American railway management were unknown also. At the very time when America was ringing with the disclosures of the Hepburn committee, a committee of our House of Commons reported as the result of a searching investigation that, "on the whole of the evidence they acquit the railway companies of any grave dereliction of their duty to the public. It is remarkable that no witnesses have appeared to complain of preferences given to individuals by railway companies as acts of private favor or partiality." It was true that the English public had not the same legal power to control rates as is possessed by the state in most continental countries; but, on the other hand, rates could be varied to suit the varying exigencies of trade, while in France and Germany the necessary formalities occupy so much time that the reasons for a change have often arisen and disappeared again before the variation has received official sanction.

Such was the English system; such, alas! it is likely to remain no longer. But it is safe to say that those whose hands have destroyed it, did not know what they were really doing. The change came about in this way. In the course of fifty years many hundreds of separate lines had been chartered, each one with its own independent classification and schedule of maximum rates. The mass of different acts was so large, so confused, and sometimes so contradictory, that it was almost impossible to know what the powers of a company in a given case actually were. It was agreed on all hands that a codification of the powers of the different companies would be of public advantage. The companies were invited to undertake the work, and submitted draft codifications to Parliament as long ago as 1885. Naturally, where, for the sake of uniformity, it was necessary either to level up maxima or to level down, the companies preferred the former alternative. Equally naturally, their customers preferred the latter; and the companies' drafts disappeared in a storm of disapproval. Then the government took the matter in hand, and finally carried through Parliament in 1891 and 1892 a series of revisions which came into operation at the beginning of 1893.

Unfortunately, in the course of the intervening seven years the process had changed its character. It began by being a codification, it ended by becoming a reduction of maximum powers. It was originally intended to enable traders to know what charges the companies might legally make and for what services; it was turned aside into a means of enabling traders to economize in their expenses for transportation. Maxima were fixed by wholesale at points not only below the maxima on the faith of which the company expended its capital, but below the rates that were being at that moment actually charged. The reduction of revenue thereby caused to the companies might not seem very large, being estimated at some £300,000 on a gross income of £80,000,000. Put another way, however, and reckoned as falling wholly, as of course it must do, on the sum available for the ordinary shareholders, it meant an appreciable reduction of dividend. In any case, the sum was larger than the companies were prepared to surrender without a struggle. So, side by side with a series of rates compulsorily reduced, the first of January saw a second series of rates advanced by the companies at points where their statutory maxima had left them a margin for increase.

When the traders found that the results were not what they had expected they recommended an angry agitation all over the country. They began by declaring that the companies had been guilty of deliberate deception. This charge was easily enough disproved; but, far from consenting to learn by experience the disadvantages of State regulation, the traders are now going on to demand that the English government shall assume a control over railway rates more stringent than that ever exercised in Iowa or Wisconsin in the palmy days of the Granger legislation. A new

House of Commons' Committee is to meet and consider the question immediately. One proposal, which seems to meet with a certain amount of support, is that companies shall be at liberty to reduce rates at pleasure, but shall need the sanction of the Board of Trade before putting in force an increase. Another suggestion is that a new tribunal shall be appointed with power to fix reasonable rates in any individual case, on application. Such a tribunal is to be, we are told, "cheap and expeditious." How this desirable result is to be attained we are unfortunately not precisely informed. But that Parliament will move in the direction of further administrative interference is, I think, tolerably certain. Competent observers are, I also think, tolerably unanimous in believing that the further Parliament moves in this direction, the more serious will become the friction between the railways and their customers. This much at least is matter of history that, while denunciations of the arbitrary and extortionate conduct of the railway companies were increasing, the number of instances of such conduct was rapidly being diminished through the quiet but persistent action of publicity and public opinion, backed in rare instances by an appeal for justice to the courts of law, and that the situation has only become acute at the moment when the sharp sword of government interference has been used to cut asunder at one stroke a situation which might perhaps have taken a dozen or twenty years to disentangle itself. But it is time to turn to a different subject.

The Employers' Liability Act of 1880 for the first time made a master responsible to his servant for injuries caused by the negligence either of the master himself or of a fellow-servant. That the Act has done good in making masters more careful that injuries shall not occur is not denied. On the other hand it has not been without compensating disadvantages. It has encouraged a good deal of futile litigation, and the lawyers must have made out of it in fees a good deal more than the workmen have secured as compensation. In the railway service, however, its effect has been of almost unmixed benefit. For the passage of the Act stimulated most of the great companies to establish accident funds, which the men could, if they chose, join. Here are the details of the method in which such a fund works at the present moment on the Brighton Company's line: No man need join it unless he chooses, but out of 19,000 servants all but two were glad to do so when it was first started. If a man joins he pays in a sum of 6 or 9 or 12 cents per month and binds himself not to sue his employer under the powers of the Act. In return in case of accident he is entitled, according to the amount of his subscription, to 10s. or 15s. or £1 per week during disablement, while his representatives can claim £100 or £150 or £200, as the case may be, if the accident is fatal. Of course the men's contributions fall far short—they amount, I believe, to less than half—of the sum necessary to keep the fund solvent; but the company makes itself responsible for the balance. It will be noted, too, that the Insurance Fund pays compensation in all cases of accident however caused; while an action can only be brought with success in the rare instance (not one in fifty I was assured by the manager of the Brighton fund) in which negligence of employer or fellow-servant can be positively proved.

As far as railway companies are concerned—I say nothing one way or other about other trades as to which I have no special information—this compromise has worked most satisfactorily for the last dozen years. But contracting out of the Act has always been unpopular with the trade-union leaders, and this session the Government has introduced a bill to put an end to it. So far the humble requests of the railway servants to be let alone have met with but scant attention. Why 300,000 adult males, qualified to take part in the government of the country, are not to be considered qualified to decide for themselves whether they prefer the complete protection of an Accident Fund or the very incomplete protection of a right to extract money by a lawsuit out of the railway company in certain specific and comparatively rare instances, it is not very easy for one who is not a politician to understand.

A question similar in many respects to the last is that of railway servants' hours of labor. A committee of the House of Commons bearing this name sat and took evidence at great length during the sessions of 1891 and 1892, and a bill based upon their report was introduced this year by the board of trade. It has already passed through the House of Commons and been read a second time in the House of Lords, and within the next few days it is almost certain to receive the royal assent. The evidence before the committee went to show, what indeed everyone with any practical acquaintance with the subject knew already, that matters have vastly improved within the last few years; that, while on the lines of a few small and poor companies hours are still far too long, the great companies have, as a rule, set their house in order without waiting for the action of Parliament. Had the committee pushed its researches a little further back, it would, I believe, have found that in this matter the worst company of to-day does better than the best company of thirty years ago.

Indeed, there is considerable ground for believing that public opinion, combined with the pressure of the trade-unions, whose leaders are mostly inspired with longings for an ideal eight hours day, has driven the companies further than is desired by the mass of the railway servants themselves, only about ten per cent of whom are trade-unionists. Some color to this belief is given by a recent report of the inspecting officer of the board of trade in reference to an accident at Waldridge, in Northumberland last January:

" Taking the whole period for which I obtained returns" [writes Major Marindin], "namely from November 28th to February 4th, which is the busiest time of year, the average daily hours of duty were 14 hours and 41 minutes, and the average daily hours worked, deducting all stoppages, were 9 hours 5 minutes. . . . It is clear that the hours of work on these inclines during the busy season are exceedingly long, but the evidence on this head is remarkable. It seems that the company made offers to the men to reduce the hours by establishing two shifts; but the men were unanimous in asking that no change should be made, the company having acceded to their request that the regular working day should be 11 instead of 12 hours as heretofore. The men expressed themselves as being thoroughly contented with their lot, and it was most satisfactory to hear the terms in which they spoke of their employers. Under these circumstances, it would, in my opinion, be very undesirable to take any further action which might possibly have the effect of disturbing the harmony which evidently now exists upon this portion of the Northeastern Railway."

Parliament, however, is prepared to run this risk, tho' it is only right to say that attempts to fix a statutory working day for railway servants have been defeated by large majorities. The new bill provides that any person can complain to the Board of Trade that overwork is taking place on a railway; that the Board shall, thereupon, inquire, and if satisfied that there is a *prima facie* case, shall call upon the company to submit a schedule of the working time of its servants. This the Board may either approve or send back for amendment; it may further, if it thinks proper, draw up a schedule itself and require the company to adopt it. In case of non-compliance, it becomes the duty of the Board of Trade to prosecute the recalcitrant company before the Railway Commission, who can inflict a penalty of £100 a day for disobedience—so far as the bill relies on publicity for its motive power, it would seem unobjectionable. But a serious difficulty will probably be found in the fact that the Board of Trade will be driven by the pressure of London public opinion to interfere unnecessarily with the hours of labor in country districts. On lines in London eight hours may be a good day's work, while to a man whose trains come only six times in the day even sixteen hours of nominal service can hardly be called excessive. And yet the lay public are hardly likely to appreciate the difference at its real value.

Certainly in one very important matter the Board of Trade itself has failed to appreciate it. One of the most useful pieces of railway legislation ever placed upon the statute book was that which, some twenty years back, provided foi official investigation of all serious accidents The inspecting officers, experts of admitted capacity, could inquire, could report, could assign the blame and propose the remedy. There the powers ended; it was left to public opinion and the good sense of railway managers to do the rest. And they did it. The record of the English railways for safety grew better and better, till it might fairly be said that—considering the speed and the diversity of traffic—it was unequalled in the world. But, unfortunately, in the summer of 1889, there was a ghastly accident at Armagh, in Ireland, caused in the main by sheer personal stupidity. Not only were some eighty school children killed, but the result was to supply steam which enabled the legislative machine to turn out a new act, the Regulation of Railways Act, 1889. The Board of Trade obtained power to order, where previously it could only recommend, and, having got the power proceeded at once to use it. Broadly the Board did two things; it legislated mixed trains of freight and passengers out of existence, and it laid down a single uniform standard of safety appliances, the most elaborate and expensive known, as necessary to be used throughout the length and breadth of the country. If American readers will imagine the Atchison or the Denver and Rio Grande forbidden to carry passengers, except on exclusively passenger trains, and required to fit up the Hall or the Union Switch Company's automatic electric block over their entire system, they will be able to appreciate the situation in which Wales and Ireland and the Highlands of Scotland find themselves at this moment. The public is grumbling at the diminished service, while the railway companies are at their wit's end to raise capital for new appliances and revenue to meet the increased working expenses. As for building a new railway in these parts, no one but a millionaire philanthropist is likely to think of it. Doubtless, the Board of Trade, with its eye fixed on London and the crowded traffic of the great main lines, believes that it is acting rightly. The feeble voice of Caithness and Cardigan could hardly be expected to carry all the way to Westminster.

Another matter in which Parliament and Government departments have frequently interfered of late years has been that of workmen's trains. The history of the question is not without interest. About thirty years back several railway companies constructed new lines in London which swept away hundreds upon hundreds of houses occupied by the poorer classes. It was difficult to see where their occupants were to be re-housed. Parliament, therefore, laid upon each company an obligation to run a train morning and evening at nominal fares, so as to make it possible for the displaced workmen to seek new dwellings down the new line. Such was the origin of workmen's trains. But before long companies with large suburban areas still unbuilt on, the Great Eastern more particularly, found that workmen's trains were not without advantages even as a business speculation. The fares were low, but on the other hand the trains were full, and (in the morning at least) came at a time when they interfered with no other traffic. As long ago as 1883 an official report stated that the Great Eastern, being bound by law to run workmen's trains for a total distance of 25 miles, was in fact running 23 trains, with a mileage of 117¼ miles. In 1890 the number had increased to 49, and the distance run to 218¼ miles.

Meanwhile public opinion on the question has changed considerably. Railway companies were encouraged and exhorted to provide cheap trains, not merely for workmen whom they had displaced but for all persons who chose to avail themselves of them. In 1883 an Act remitted the larger part of the passenger tax in the case of all companies which could satisfy the Board of Trade that they were making adequate provision for workmen's accommodation. So far so good; but recently we have gone beyond mere encouragement and exhortation, and are coming to compulsion. The Great Eastern, which has found a commercial profit in giving exceptional facilities, is now regarded not merely as an example worthy of imitation, but as a standard to be compulsorily conformed to by other companies, which, from the fact that they do not encourage workmen's settlements, presumably fail to see any commercial advantage to themselves in so doing. Pressure is being applied to secure a reduction of the fares simultaneously with an extension of the time during which the cheap tickets are available from 7 to 8 A. M. Even 9 A. M. is now being put forward as reasonable. As a recent instance it may be mentioned that the Central London Railway, which obtained its act in 1891, is under an obligation, tho' its construction will not touch a single workman's house, to run not one train but three trains the whole length of the line (over six miles) for one penny.

The result of this legislative interference cannot be said so far to be very satisfactory. The Central London Company has had now for nearly two years the right to take possession of what is naturally the most valuable rapid transit route in the world. But so far it has not apparently seen its way to raise its capital and commence operations. Numerous other similar undertakings are likewise at a standstill. The traffic of London is increasing by leaps and bounds, and but little new accommodation is being provided to meet it. Before long we are likely to be brought face to face with the necessity of some new departure, perhaps in the direction of national or municipal subsidies to railway extensions. Commercial capital has been scared out of the business, not so much by what has actually happened as by a vague distrust of the form which the vicarious philanthropy of the legislature may ultimately assume. ' If the final result is to increase the rates and taxes on the workingman's house in order to subsidize the railway to carry him to and from his work for an unremunerative fare, it is difficult to see who besides the officials employed to control the elaborate financial adjustments will have gained by the transaction.

As an apt contrast to these various instances of positive legislation, it is worth while mentioning an attempt to have recourse to simple publicity which, so far, unfortunately, has missed the success which, at the outset, it seemed likely to attain. I refer to the matter of punctuality of train service. It is, I think, undeniable that on the whole, reckoning speed, frequency of trains, accommodation given, and fare charged, the English passenger service is, taking the country through, the best in the world. Punctuality, however, has never been our strong point. The congested state of our traffic always makes it difficult of attainment; dense fogs not infrequently make it impossible. Moreover, the ubiquity of competition naturally tempts the companies to promise a little more on paper than they are likely actually to realize in practice. Still there is no reason why the existing state of things should not be considerably improved. At least it is only fair that, where two companies promise to carry from A to B in the same time, the public should know that the one company keeps its promise, say, nine times out of ten, and the other perhaps only in one journey out of three.

Actuated by this idea a member of the House of Commons, in the session of 1889, moved for and obtained a return of the punctuality of trains arriving in London from the south; and in the year 1890 the inquiry was extended to all the metropolitan railways. The result of his action was all that could have been desired. Directors and managers found for the first time that details of train working were not beneath their notice; the merits or demerits of the different companies were freely canvassed in the newspapers; and a real improvement set in on the least punctual railways. Unfortunately the authorities at the board of trades had no sympathy with this line of action. Gentlemen accustomed to wield the cudgel of an act of Parliament, to give orders and see them obeyed, had naturally no belief in gentler methods, and looked upon the humbler office of purveyors of public information as beneath their dignity. The form of return had never been satisfactory. For the year 1891 it was made positively ridiculous. Moreover, the information was not published till too late to be of any interest. The return for the year 1891 came out in the late autumn of 1892. Naturally, the newspapers ignored this fragment of ancient history. So the board of trade declared that the public took no interest in the question, and discontinued the return. Better instance of the truth of Professor Adams' warning, that "there is danger lest the quietness with which the principle of publicity works should deprive it of the confidence it deserves," Professor Adams himself could hardly desire.

There is, however, no hope that the public will see the question from this point of view at the present moment. Two years back I wrote as follows (I must apologize for quoting myself, but I cannot better, and have no wish to alter, what I then said):

"Popular feeling is running strongly in the direction of substituting for the old English system of legal redress for proved injuries, of government inspection and publicity, a new system of direct state regulation, of constant and minute interference by a government department. The attempt to substitute the one system for the other, not as part of a well thought out and deliberately adopted course of policy, but by a series of haphazard and piecemeal decisions, can only lead to failure and disappointment."

That since this was written government interference with freight rates has resulted in failure and disappointment, is a matter of history. How much further we shall advance in the same direction, and how many more failures and disappointments we shall encounter in consequence, remains to be seen. Whether the English public will learn by experience before it is too late, or whether, having harassed private enterprise out of existence, they will awake one morning face to face with the necessity of taking over and working the railway system of the country themselves, the future alone can show.

London, England.

RAILWAY ASSOCIATIONS.
By Mr. Aldace F. Walker.

An important difference between the railway service of the United States and that of other countries is found in the fact that traffic by rail is here conducted by a great number of distinct corporations. These independent organizations are found in all the states and territories of the Union, maintaining lines of roads interlaced and interwoven through almost innumerable junction and crossing points, and actively competing with each other for the freight and passenger business of every section of the country. There are now in the United States over 150,000 miles of railroad owned by nearly fifteen hundred companies; this aggregate mileage is now operated by about six hundred and twenty-five separate corporations. The process of combination and amalgamation is a marked feature of the railway situation, but as yet it has proceeded only to the extent above indicated. At the present time there is practically no part of the country in which active competition does not exist between organically independent carriers. Even of so-called local points, situated upon the line of a single road, there are very few where traffic is not in some respects subject to competitive conditions, or where the transportation charges can be arbitrarily established by the carrier. Nor is railway competition confined to the various routes which may exist to and from the nearest market; but all markets are thrown open throughout the land; rates in a given direction are often regulated by those which exist in a precisely opposite direction; the price of each commodity added to the transportation charge determines the direction of the shipment or the source of supply. Moreover, the various water routes with which our country is favored have an almost incalculable influence upon the railway rates, the expense being very small when compared with the expense of constructing, maintaining and operating railway routes.

The contrast thus presented with the railway system of France, for example, where six great railway companies have a vast subdivision of the national domain assigned to each exclusively, is too marked to require comment. And in other European countries the competitive conditions which are found in the United States

---
Reprinted by permission from the Railway Review of January 4, 1890.

have been to a great extent eliminated through state ownership, by protective legislation, or by amalgamation of titles.

In our peculiar form of dual government, each state authorizes the construction of railroads within its boundary without control or supervision by the nation. Practically, no restrictions have been placed upon local railway building; and consolidations of ownership or of operative control are easily accomplished by the consent of state legislatures, coupled with concurrent action between adjoining states.

Answering the demands of the public for the freest possible interchange of products and commodities, an almost universal system of through traffic has come into existence; affording facilities which, while altogether unprecedented, no longer excite surprise. Each company might have contented itself with receiving passengers or freight, and delivering them at the end of its line to its connections; but this is by no means the case. On the contrary, the various companies have become accustomed to act together in establishing through rates of fare and through freight tariffs between most distant points, without regard to the hostile relations which necessarily exist among them in respect to · competitive traffic. Tickets can be universally purchased for remote destinations; freight is everywhere consigned to every other point. Customs have arisen in the provisions for through business and in the adjustment of traffic balances which have the force of law. The shipper does not pause to inquire concerning the route over which his goods are to be forwarded; he is informed of the established through rate, and he relies without anxiety upon the arrangements which the companies have established among themselves, concerning which he has little knowledge and less care.

The work of railway auditors and accountants has become enormous, involving the exact apportionment not only of each company's share in all receipts from through traffic, but also of losses and of liabilities for damages, as well as the distribution of car service charges and through line expenses. One of the great wants of the present time is a railway clearing house, or a series of clearing houses embracing territorial groups of roads, for the purpose of auditing their innumerable transactions upon a common basis, checking all charges with the established tariffs, and adjusting settlements between the various lines each with each other. It may be said in passing that such a railway clearing house was early organized in England, and was placed upon a legal foundation by act of parliament in the year 1850. Nearly every company in the United Kingdom now participates in its benefits. Its affairs are controlled by a committee, on which each line is represented; and its awards are made by law final and conclusive before the courts.

· When the act to regulate Commerce became effective on April 1, 1887, our railway system presented substantially the features outlined above, although many practical advances in conducting the details of universal intercommunication have since been adopted. It soon became manifest that every carrier, to some extent at least, was engaged in interstate commerce; and one consequence of this attempt at the national regulation of railways has been the perception by close observers that such regulation, to be successful, must be exclusive; in other words, that Federal control and state control conflict at innumerable points, so that their co-existence before many years will be found practically impossible.

The theory under which the Interstate Commerce law was framed, contemplated the maintenance of the independent existence of railway corporations as then constituted, subject to such organic changes as their owners might from time to time accomplish by contract among themselves in subordination to the laws of the several states under which they held their various charters, and all working together under a uniform national control. Although this was the first important occasion in which the Congress had undertaken to exercise the power intrusted to it by the Constitution, to regulate commerce among the several states, nevertheless the act was in most respects well considered and did not contemplate the creation of any obstacles or embarassments in the way of the free interchange of traffic. On the contrary, the maintenance of through routes and of through tariffs was provided for, and it was expressly made unlawful for any common carrier in any manner to prevent the continuous carriage of freights from the place of shipment to the place of destination. It became immediately obvious that many duties were incumbent upon carriers, some imposed and others recognized by the new law, which could be satisfactorily performed only through joint action among the roads.

There were in existence at that time many tariff organizations, commonly known as pools, which, in addition to the apportionment between competing lines of earnings derived from competitive traffic, performed many other important functions in making necessary arrangements of all kinds under which traffic might be systematically conducted. These organizations had been found indispensible for the proper and efficient transaction of railroad business; and when the pooling of freights was abandoned these existing organizations each became the nucleus of a reorganized association, exercising a certain supervision and control over tariffs and traffic arrangements. The form of their organization, and their purposes are not clearly understood by the public: in fact, their very existence has given rise in some sections to jealousy; they have been attacked from time to time before the Interstate Commerce Commission; state legislatures have attempted their suppression; and in Texas a judicial decision of the highest tribunal has held one of them to be organized in a form incompatible with the provisions of the constitution of the state.

At the present time the leading Railway Associations are the following: The Trunk Line Association, embracing the great railroads which operate between the Atlantic seaboard and the cities of Buffalo, Pittsburg and Wheeling; the Central Traffic Association, which includes most of the roads in the territory west of the Trunk Lines as far as Chicago and St. Louis; the Interstate Commerce Railway Association, with its affiliated organizations called the Western Freight Association, the Western States Passenger Association, and the Trans-Missouri Freight and Passenger Association, covering the region between Chicago and St. Louis on the one hand and the Rocky Mountains on the other; the Southern Railway and Steamship Association and the Southern Passenger Association, having their field in the southern states east of the Mississippi river; the Southern Interstate Association, working in the southwest beyond the Mississippi; and the Trans-Continental Association, embracing traffic to and from the Pacific coast. In addition to the foregoing there are a number of other associations, some of which have to do with the freight or passenger traffic of smaller sections of the country; some with selected articles of traffic; some are limited to particular subjects like classification, and the exchange of cars.

Their organization is very simple. The officer in charge is usually designated as commissioner, or chairman; and he is generally assisted by a secretary, an accountant or auditor, and a small staff of clerks who perform such services as are necessary in the preparation and publication of tariffs and the collection and distribution of statistics. They are purely voluntary, and are formed by agreement between the various lines which compose them, the details of which are expressed in articles of association subscribed by representatives of the several roads. These agreements are filed with the Interstate Commerce Commission, pursuant to the requirement of the act to regulate commerce, which provides for the filing of copies of all contracts, agreements or arrangements between common carriers in relation to traffic affected by the provisions of said act. Stated meetings are held from time to time, usually monthly, which are attended by a representative of each line, and which are usually presided over by the chairman or commissioner. Unanimous agreement is commonly required in order to effect a change in established rates, rules or regulations respecting traffic, subject, however, to a right or independent action which is reserved in case of failure to agree. In the event of disagreement between the lines arbitration is sometimes provided for. The duties of the chairman frequently embrace the investigation of cases where it is claimed that tariffs have not been maintained, or that the established rules and regulations which govern the handling of traffic have been departed from; the requirements of the association in such cases being in conformity with the provisions of the act to regulate commerce, which forbids the charging of a greater or less compensation for the transportation of passengers or property than is specified in the schedule of rates, fares and charges at the time in force, and which requires ten days' public notice of any advance in rates, together with three days' public notice of reductions.

The basis upon which these associations rest is simply good faith among the members. They are not corporations, and they exercise no corporate powers; yet they deal at times with questions of the utmost importance, and their influence is distinctly visible in every branch of the railway service. The subjects which they treat are not restricted to the territory which they respectively embrace, but the various associations are able, by negotiation with each other, to accomplish results in the management of long distance traffic that would otherwise be altogether impossible.

In order to correctly apprehend the relation which they bear to the governmental regulation of carriers, it is necessary first to understand precisely what is undertaken by the federal law under which all interstate commerce is now carried on. When this is properly appreciated it will be perceived that the work of the associations is directly in line with the administration of the law; in fact, that they owe their existence at the present time to the effort and desire of the carriers to transact their business in conformity with the statute; and that as a practical matter the act to regulate commerce would not be workable without the intervention of railway associations.

The object proposed by Congress, in enacting the Interstate Commerce law, may be perceived by ascertaining the then existing evils which that legislation proposed to remedy. The introduction of the bill was preceded by a long investigation, which re sulted in the formulation of an able report discussing broadly the general subject of the internal commerce of the country, its importance and the methods employed in carrying it on; and which embraced a concise and summary statement of conclusions entitled "The Causes of Complaint Against the Railroad System." The points covered by this indictment were eighteen in number, and there is scarcely one of them which is not comprehended within the significant word "discrimination." It was charged that local rates were unreasonably high as compared with through rates; that both were unreasonably high at non-competing points; that unjustifiable discriminations were constantly made between individuals; also between articles of freight and branches of business of a like character; also between localities; also by the use of secret special rates, rebates, drawbacks and concessions; also by secret cutting rates and fluctuations, demoralizing to legitimate business; also by the granting of free passes; by undue advantages afforded to business enterprises in which railway officials were interested; and otherwise as was set forth with particularity and detail.

Examined in the light of this report it is easy to perceive that the fundamental purpose of the Interstate Commerce law is the prevention of discrimination in every form. The first five sections of the statute declare the principles that are to regulate the internal commerce of the country, and the subsequent sections provide machinery for the enforcement of the rules thus first laid down. These rules are three in number: First, all railroad charges shall be reasonable and just; second, no unjust discrimination between persons by means of special rates, rebates, drawbacks, or other devices shall be permitted; third, no undue or unreasonable preference or advantage shall be given to any person, locality or description of traffic, in the establishment of tariffs.

These provisions comprise the foundation principles of the Interstate Commerce law; the famous fourth section being merely a declaration that the charge of a greater sum for a shorter than for a longer distance, shall constitute a preference or discrimination in favor of the more distant point, unless conditions and circumstances exist which make the service dissimilar; and the fifth, or anti-pooling section, was undoubtedly the result of a belief on the part of its authors that the pooling system, by stifling competition, tended to make rates unreasonably high.

The leading feature of the administrative portion of the law is found in the sixth section, which requires the establishment and publication by the carriers of tariffs showing rates, fares and charges for all interstate carriage of passengers and property, together with the classification of freight in force, and any rules or regulations which affect the rates. These tariffs are required to be filed with the Commission, and when established must be absolutely adhered to. The charge of a greater or less sum than the established rate is made a misdemeanor. This requirement that tariffs for all traffic shall be fixed in advance, made public and rigidly observed, is obviously designed to prevent discrimination. The task imposed upon the carriers by the passage of the law was an enormous one. It involved nothing less than the establishment of a full and complete system of schedules of rates, fares and charges, not only between the stations upon each road, but between all points in the United States under which through traffic might be handled by joint tariffs, which should be without preference, as between localities, and as between classes of traffic; which should be just and reasonable in every respect, and which should be made the measure by which all transportation charges should be governed, disregarding previous customs and usages, and suddenly bringing the entire interstate traffic of the country within the operation of a procrustean rule. Sixty days were allowed for this task before the law became operative. The work is by no means finished yet. The various details necessary to be covered in the establishment of tariffs, classifications, rates, rules and regulations controlling transportation of persons and property are almost innumerable. Tariffs and traffic regulations must necessarily be alike upon the lines of carriers engaged in joint operations, or holding competitive relations with each other. Harmonious action between carriers was an absolute necessity in order to enable them to take the first step in obedience to the administrative sections of the Interstate Commerce law. This cause compelled the continuance, for the purpose above described, of such associations as had previously been in existence, and the development of a system for the conduct of traffic, in which the existing associations play an important part. The Interstate Commerce Commission, in its first annual report, recognized this feature of the situation in carefully chosen words, as follows:

"VOLUNTARY ASSOCIATION OF RAILROAD MANAGERS.

"Nearly every railroad in its origin has been independent of all others, and in the early history of such roads they were commonly provided for as local conveniences, with no provision of the great highways of trade and communication which they have since become. It was in many cases thought to be important that a road should be kept as distinct in its business from all others as possible, and at their termini in some instances they are not allowed to have the same freight or passenger stations with other roads, lest the local draymen and hackmen should be deprived of a profitable employment.

"When the great possibilities of railroad service came to be better understood these primitive notions of local benefits gave way before a more enlightened public sentiment, and the fact was recognized that the public interest would be best subserved by making the connection between the roads as close as possible, in order that the commerce between different sections and localities might go on steadily and uninterruptedly. The railroad companies perceived also that their interest lay in the same direction. * * *

." To make railroads of the greatest possible service to the country, contract relations would be essential, because there would need to be joint tariffs, joint running arrangements, an interchange of cars and a giving of credit to a large extent, some of which were obviously beyond the reach of compulsory legislation, and even if they were not, could be best settled and all the incidents and qualifications fixed by the voluntary action of the parties in control of the roads respectively.

"Agreement upon these and kindred matters became, therefore, a settled policy; short, independent lines of road seemed to lose their identity and to become parts of great trunk lines, and associations were formed which embraced all the managers of roads in a state or section of the country. To these associations were remitted many questions of common interest, including such as are above referred to. Classification was also confided to such associations, it being evident that differences in classification were serious obstacles to a harmonious and satisfactory interchange of traffic. But what perhaps more than anything else influenced the formation of such associations and the conferring upon them of large authority, was the liability, which was constantly imminent, that destructive wars of rates would spring up between competing roads to the serious injury of the parties and the general disturbance of business.

"Accordingly, one of the chief functions of such associations has been the fixing of rates and the devising of means whereby their several members can be compelled or induced to observe the rates when fixed. And in devising these means the chief difficulty was encountered. Agreements upon rates were voluntary arrangements which could be departed from at pleasure, and if they had behind them no sanction, they were not likely to stand in the way of a war of rates when the provocation to one seemed sufficient. Accordingly, the scheme of pooling freights or the earnings from traffic was devised and put in force through the agency of these associations, as a means whereby steadiness in rates might be maintained. The scheme was one which was made use of in other countries and had been found of service to the roads.

"The pooling system was looked upon with distrust by the public, mainly because it seemed to be a scheme whereby competition between the roads could be obviated and rates for railroad service put up or kept up to unreasonable figures. But if railroad managers supposed that by this scheme they were to stop competition among themselves, the result has not answered their expectations. Competition has still gone on; each road striving to obtain as large a share of the business as possible, and no agreement among them could altogether prevent a yielding to the pressure of shippers for lower rates. * * *

"The pooling of freights and of railroad earnings, so far as the commission has knowledge or information on the subject, came to an end when the act took effect. But as pooling was only one of several purposes had in view in forming railroad associations, the leading associations have not been dissolved, but have been continued in existence for other objects. Among these objects are the making of regulations for uninterrupted and harmonious railroad communication and exchange of traffic within the territory embraced by their workings. Some regulations, in addition to those made by the law, are almost, if not altogether, indispensable. Thus, while the seventh section of the act forbids the carriers preventing shipments from being continuous by the device of changing time schedules, carriage in different cars, etc., it has not undertaken to provide for the making of such time schedules as would facilitate the continuous shipment, or to prescribe rules for the loading and movement of cars for that purpose. However desirable this might have been, if it were practicable to make rules which, while general in their nature, should be sufficiently definite of enforcement as laws, it was doubtless perceived by Congress that these and many other matters of detail, though they might be of high importance, could not be wisely and effectively dealt with by general legislation, but that such legislation must chiefly be restricted to provisions for regulation and to prevent abuse.

"Moreover, these matters of detail, to a considerable extent, involve the element of contract, and also of credit, when one company becomes the agent for another in the sale of tickets and the collection of freight moneys; and they then require the assenting minds of parties, and the number of parties whose minds are to be brought into accord being commonly very considerable, an association of officers or agents is made the means of bringing about the desired unity of action, and is also made a common arbiter, to prevent frequent and serious disturbances.

"Classification also, as has been said, is not by the act taken out of the hands of the carriers, though a certain power of supervision is vested in the commission; and classification is not only best made by joint action, but if it were not so made and the methods of the roads thereby brought into harmony, it would probably become indispensable, however undesirable it might otherwise be, for the law to undertake to provide for it. Moreover, when classification is made and put into effect it becomes necessary to make provisions for inspecting or some sort of supervision of its application, in order to prevent its being employed as a device for giving preferences as between shippers. A fraudulent classification, through connivance of the agent in making out deceptive shipping bills, has often been resorted to for this purpose; and as the fraud affects the competing carriers as well as the shippers who are discriminated against by means of the cheat, the carriers and the public alike are interested in such a supervision of the work of all the roads as will be likely to detect the fraud. Self-interest on the part of the carriers will impel to this supervision, and it is most generally done through some common agency. If it shall be fairly done as between the carriers themselves, it will tend to the protection of the public; and the benefits will be on the same line with those the act undertakes to establish or provide for."

JOINT TRAFFIC.

It will be observed that the traffic which lies within the scope of association control may be considered under two distinct relations, as joint traffic and as competitive traffic. Joint traffic is defined in the act to regulate commerce as "where passengers and freight pass over continuous lines or routes operated by more than one common carrier, and the several common carriers operating such lines or routes establish joint tariffs of rates or fares or charges for such continuous lines or routes." The general nature of the work of the associations in respect to joint traffic has been already indicated. Through their agency arrangements of all kinds are consummated under which joint service is made possible, and constant improvements in its extent and facilities are brought about. The principle subjects of negotiation and concerted action are the following: rates, classification of freight, apportionment of earnings, and inspection. Other points relating to through traffic, such as time table arrangements, exchange of cars and settlement of traffic balances are usually adjusted by individual connecting lines.

Lines where traffic originates are expected to establish and publish through rates to points of ultimate destination, but such rates must necessarily be made by agreement between the various lines composing such through routes, and the necessary agreements would be too infinite in number to be practically possible without the assistance of associations. The present extremely complicated system is the result of long years of negotiation and contest. The effect of rates which exist in one section of the country upon those made between very distant points, can be appreciated only by careful study. Certain principles in the relation of rates to each other and in the use of established differences, sometimes called differentials, have been worked out, usually by some arbitration or agreement, founded upon just reasons and presenting a medium between the claims of competing points. These adjustments are found in every section of the country and are made upon the broadest principles. While one community and another, upon a narrow view of its geographical situation, has from time to time made complaint of an alleged unfair adjustment of its rates, instances have been very few in which the lines have been unable to demonstrate that the tariffs, in fact, were just and reasonable, upon the requirements of the whole situation involved. Through rates are almost invariably somewhat less than the sum of the local rates, and are necessarily established by concerted action in view of the relation of rates at one point to those at others. The mileage rate of the shortest line is taken as the maximum. No line, however circuitous, can expect to participate in the traffic if its rates are higher; and cases are found where the effort is made to attract travel to longer routes by the employment of a lower rate than is charged by direct routes between the same points.

Much has been said in relation to the importance of a uniform classification of freight throughout the land. A common classification even in a single state requires concerted action. Every article of merchandise must be taken up and considered with relation to the various considerations embraced in the establishment of its just and reasonable classification; in addition to this the development of the traffic of every line must be kept in mind, and the classification of each commodity must be sufficiently low to permit of its free movement. Prior to the passage of the act to regulate commerce thirty-seven different classifications were in use in the territory of the Central Traffic Association. The great bulk of interstate traffic throughout the United States is now handled under four classifications. The progress which has been made in this direction would have been impossible but for the fact of the existence of railway associations, in which the subject has been efficiently handled. At the present time a conference of representatives of all the associations is in existence, meeting from time to time and engaged in the work of still further simplifying and harmonizing the present differences, with a view, if possible, to ultimately establish a single uniform classification of freight.

The subject of the apportionment of receipts from joint traffic between the various lines which unite to form through routes is one of the utmost importance to the carriers, but in which the general public has little interest. Shippers are concerned solely with the question of the rate which they are required to pay as an aggregate through rate from the initial point to the point of destination. The division thereof between the various roads which unite in performing the service is of no consequence to the public, although of great consequence to the carriers. These divisions have been and are a constant subject of negotiation and modification. In determining the share of a through rate which any given link will receive, a great variety of elements are taken into account. A common basis where the lines participating in the division are relatively equal is that of mileage, under which the through rate is prorated according to the length of the various roads. This basis, however, is by no means universal. Weak lines, or roads where the traffic is light and expenses are high, are accustomed to claim and are usually conceded an additional allowance in the division of the earnings upon through traffic. Sometimes this concession takes the form of an arbitrary allowance for an expensive bridge, or for a mountainous haul; sometimes an arbitrary mileage is assigned, one and a half, twice or even thrice the actual mileage of the line in question; sometimes an arbitrary division of the total through rate is awarded, under which a short branch line, or feeder, may receive one third or even one half of the total income; sometimes the adjustment is made upon the relative local rates charged in different sections of the country, so that roads where traffic is thin and low rates are impossible, divide with other lines having a heavy tonnage and low freight charges upon the basis of the sums received by each respectively for their local traffic. These matters are necessarily the subject of frequent negotiation, and are often adjusted between large sections of the country east and west, or north and south, by concerted action through the associations which represent the lines in the various sections involved in the question. It often occurs that lines are willing, for the sake of increasing their own traffic, to concede to their connections a larger share in the earnings of joint business than would naturally accrue to them. Lines having more than one outlet are sometimes able to sell their traffic to the highest bidder. Some standard is usually adjusted for a considerable extent of territory, designed to effect an equitable distribution of the results of joint traffic between the lines of which various through routes are composed. Were it not for the existence of associations where understandings already reached are maintained, and necessary changes are effected from time to time, confusion would at once arise and chaos would speedily folllow.

The advantages to shippers and passengers arising from the through billing of freight, and through tickets under the coupon system, need not be enlarged upon..

The importance of the inspection of freight is found in the fact that, without it, advantages would be continually obtained by shippers as against each other. It becomes necessary, therefore, to establish bureaus not controlled by individual roads, which would be under the constant inducement of permitting preferences in order to obtain traffic, but organized under associations of carriers where interest requires that the rules of shipment be universally and equally applied to all. This inspection service includes the examination of freight at various points for the purpose of ascertaining that it is properly classified; that the established rates are duly applied, and that the weight is accurately given. The law is very stringent in its requisition that all rates, rules and regulations shall be strictly observed, and even imposes a penalty upon shippers who misdescribe their freight for the purpose of obtaining lower rates. Notwithstanding these provisions of the statute, the monthly reports of the various inspection bureaus now in operation, and which should be largely increased, show hundreds of cases of discrimination and fraud which are corrected by the carriers through their agency.

COMPETITIVE TRAFFIC.

Coming now to the field of competitive traffic, a branch of the subject is reached in respect to which great sensitiveness exists in the apprehension of the public. There can be no doubt, however, that this feeling largely arises from a failure to clearly understand certain principles which lie at its foundation, or at least from the fact that the subject is usually viewed from one side only. The desirability of the preservation of competition will not be denied, but it should not be forgotten that in transportation there may be too much competition, as well as too little; for example, competition between railroads and water lines, which proceeds to the extent of driving the latter out of existence as channels of commerce, can hardly be claimed to be for the best interest of the public at large; and the same thing may be true of competition between competing railroad routes.

In other words, competition as a fact cannot be preserved unless the necessary agencies for competition are maintained. To turn loose upon the same field of operations several wealthy corporations, with the requirement that they must forever compete and that under no circumstances shall concerted action be allowed, would presently result in the extinction of one or more of them. This has been so often practically demonstrated in cases where competition between rival roads has driven the weaker to the wall and resulted in its absorption by lease or other form of combination, and the extinction of the competition originally proposed, that its statement has become a truism.

Again, adequate railway service requires the maintenance of the road and its equipment in the most perfect and efficient form, together with the constant provision of employes of the highest skill obtainable. Good public service cannot be rendered unless the rates are adequate to its support, and adequate also to insure the continuance in the field of the necessary capital. Whenever carriers fail to harmonize their conflicting interests by the adoption of corresponding tariffs a war of rates ensues, and in every rate war the public as well as the carriers must suffer. It is a common idea that competition means lower rates and nothing more. On the contrary, competition may exist, and does exist, where rates are well maintained. The very fact that different routes are open, of itself presents the essential element of competition. The facilities and advantages of competing routes are the subject of selection by shippers and passengers while rates may be alike on all. It cannot be denied that the public generally is more interested in safe and efficient railway service than in extremely low railway rates. Rates may easily be so low as to render such service impossible. The public is best served by rates which are reasonable, uniform and firmly maintained. This is precisely what the Act to regulate commerce demands. English tribunals have affirmed healthy competition to be that in which various transportation routes are kept open which are "practically independent of one another, fairly alternative, and reasonably calculated to keep one another in check."

Looking at the question of competitive rates as affected by the requirements of the act to regulate commerce, it will easily be seen that some degree of concurrent action between the competitors is indispensable. Although in denouncing discrimination the act in terms applies to individual carriers, a moment's reflection will show that discrimination in rates between competing carriers is equally prejudicial to the public interest. Suppose, for example, that there were only two lines of road between New York City and Chicago, and that the charges upon one were twenty per cent lower than upon the other. So far as volume of traffic is concerned, the immediate result would be to turn all business to which a choice of the two routes was open, upon the road giving the lowest rate, but so far as the manufacturing public is concerned, every establishment situated upon the line of the other road would at once be placed at a disadvantage impossible to overcome. Nor is this confined to rates alone. If, for example, one trunk line from the eastern seaboard to the west, transports sugar at its net weight, deducting the weight of the barrels, while the regulations in force upon the other lines demand that the gross weight shall be employed in applying the same tariff rate, the refineries upon the latter roads are placed at a disadvantage sufficient to exclude them from the territory reached by the other line; or if one line returns without expense, tank cars furnished by shippers of oil, while another line exacts a charge for the return of such cars, the refineries located upon the latter line are discriminated against to an extent which would soon close their works. Hundreds of instances like the foregoing might be readily enumerated, in which the failure to apply similar rules and regulations, as well as similar tariffs, by competing lines of road would result almost immediately in the destruction of important industries. It is absolutely essential that discrimination be prevented by the formulation of rules, regulations and tariffs between competing lines, which shall work out exact justice to the patrons of all. This is one of the results accomplished through the agency of railroad associations. It may be said that by preserving absolute independence of action the desire to secure competitive traffic would compel the line which wished to maintain a higher rate to reduce its charge to the basis fixed by its rival; but this would not necessarily follow, and if it did follow the result would be a series of reductions, causing great disturbance to business, and ultimately resulting in the elimination of one or the other of the competitive agencies.

Again, enlarging the field of vision, and taking the case of carriers from different competing points to the same markets, or from different markets to the same field of distribution, discrimination necessarily produces a similar result to that above described. One point or the other is excluded, and the public is wronged. The only remedy possible is the establishment of a corresponding or a relatively equivalent rate to or from the different points in question which will prevent unjust discrimination, preference or advantage, and serve the whole public equally.

And once more, consider a complicated network of roads which operates through a wide sweep of territory in which the products are all competitive and all markets are common; the law leaves them to fix their rates each for itself; without co-operation the transportation charges would immediately become grossly discriminative, and in the end almost certainly would become inadequate to sustain the service, while inflicting great wrong upon innumerable communities.

Association among competitive carriers for the adjustment of their rates and their traffic regulations, is required by sound public policy. It makes possible the handling of traffic which is competitive as between individuals and between localities, without preference and without discrimination. It is required upon similar considerations to those under which towns, cities, states and the nation itself are organized for concerted action in matters of common interest, and for the prevention of anarchy. It establishes rates co-ordinated with the value of the service, which are necessarily adjusted to the expenses of the shortest routes. It assists to preserve all existing lines in competitive existence. It affords an organized support to the enforcement of the regulative statutes. Association is the servant of the law. Without it there can be no adjustment of tariffs made which will conform to the administrative provisions of the act. The law implies associate action as a necessary prerequisite to obedience.

One of the objects of association among competitive carriers, therefore, is the establishment of a forum, or meeting place, where rates, rules or regulations governing the transportation of all commodities can be arranged by concurrent action, and where all the elements attending the fixing of rates by one or more of the lines may be given full force in reaching the resultant. In this correlation of forces, the most direct and economical route dominates the rest. If the ruling rate thus fixed is not a reasonable one, the act to regulate commerce provides control.

An inspection of the actual work taken up by the associations at their meetings will show that the raising of rates is not, by any means, their important function. Undoubtedly one of their leading principles is the maintenance of rates upon a durable and permanent basis. Proposed changes in tariffs are discussed in association meetings, and are acted upon with care. Considerations based upon the exigencies of business and the stimulation of traffic are those most frequently urged, while the necessity for the maintenance of revenue counterbalances, to some extent, the pressure that is constantly brought to bear for reductions here, there and everywhere. The scale of rates throughout the United States, as is well known, has been constantly shrinking through a long term of years. At times a general scheme of advancing rates may be devised and agreed upon, for the purpose of putting an end to a rate war or of taking advantage of an outside condition like that which arises upon the annual closing of lake navigation; but such advances as are accomplished are usually trivial, arising from the lining up of rates previously reduced to meet some special emergency, or from the removal of some factor of disturbance. The general tendency is always in the direction of lower rates. In respect to this matter the association system is conservative. It tends to check unnecessary reductions, but it is inadequate to stem the tide in its universal ebb. It is estimated that the rate changes considered at association meetings constitute almost one-half of the business presented; and that about ninety per cent of such proposed rate changes are propositions for reduction, which are so accomplished as to prevent the preferences and discriminations that would ensue if each line were to make reductions for itself.

At the present time the usual rate question is in respect to relative rates. It is claimed that the rate at some point is too high when compared with the rate at some other point, or that the rate on a given commodity is too high in comparison with the rate upon some analogous article, or upon the same article from other sources of supply. A complaint that rates are excessive in themselves, or as compared with the value of the service, is very seldom seriously made.

CO-OPERATIVE MANAGEMENT.

Certain distinctions that exist between the business of transportation and other branches of industry, in respect to the practical effect of associated management, cannot properly be overlooked. There is no governmental regulation of the price of lead, or sugar, or oil. Manufacturing and mining combinations, presumably intended to restrict production and increase profits, are regarded with suspicion by reason of the fact that no control exists upon the prices to be charged. The regulation of the tariffs of common carriers, on the contrary, has become an established feature of our legislation and jurisprudence. The danger apprehended in the one case is altogether absent in the other.

Another marked difference between railroads and other business enterprises lies in the fact that if the latter find their work unprofitable, it is open to them at any time to close their doors. The loss involved is, of course, serious; and a struggle for continued existence is often maintained until bankruptcy ensues; but the result of a lockout or a failure is confined to the owners and the operatives of the particular plant involved; the public are supplied from other sources. In the case of a railroad under similar circumstances the operations of the road can seldom stop. The road must stay in existence, and the courts assume its operation when bankruptcy has destroyed the value of the original investment. New capital is brought in through receivers' certificates, and the wheels continue to turn. If the discontinuance of a line is determined upon, the public as well as the owners and operatives suffer. Some competitor or some larger system has usually found it for its interest to assume the operation of bankrupt roads; but several instances of abandonment have actually occurred, and others are in sight; cases even exist where state officials are seeking by legal process to compel the maintenance of worthless branches, for the benefit of the local communities through which they run.

Again, the tendency to lower rates in railroad service under the stress of unregulated competition has a violence of which citizens engaged in other branches of business are wholly ignorant. It resembles the rush of the cataract. The education of the freight agent has been in the direction of maintaining tonnage at almost any cost. The net results are shown in the accounts of the operating department, which is separately organized. One effect of the law has been to extend the scope of all reductions by making general what was formerly restricted, localized and often secret. Where, in the days before the law, a single rate was cut, the freight agent must now reduce a tariff; and while he points with pride to the increasing tonnage of the line, the loss of net revenue may be excused as a result of the operation of the statute.

It has become a common criticism upon the present form of congressional regulation of railway traffic, that while it prevents discrimination and protects the public, it altogether fails to protect the carriers. It presents no method of restraint upon impecunious, extravagant, speculative or unreasonably aggressive railway management; it leaves the doors of competition open to the most circuitous routes; it puts the strong lines at the mercy of the weak, and makes it possible for a road that should never have been built to fix rates which all other competing roads must perforce accept.

And this, in truth, is an obvious defect. The Congress has assumed the task of making provision against rates which are unreasonably high, and rates which are not relatively equal, without providing for the prevention of rates unreasonably low, or for the protection of investments which now form an immense proportion of the country's wealth, represented by securities which are not found alone in the vaults of capitalists, but which in many cases, constitute the only source of income for the comparatively poor and the otherwise hopelessly dependent. The scheme of governmental regulation will not be rounded and complete until this omission is supplied.

State ownership, or direct national control of the railway system of the country, is at times suggested as a remedy; but this may be at once dismissed as chimerical. No greater injury could befall our republican institutions than the establishment of a branch of the public service which would throw open to the field of politics the railway service of the land.

Legislative regulation in the direction of the prevention of rates unnecessarily low is not impossible, although it has not been seriously considered. If it were simply to take the form of a provision that rates once established should not be reduced, except at stated periods or after prolonged announcement, it would materially improve the existing situation in some respects. Such restrictions, however, might at times operate unjustly, and occasionally would divert traffic for a time into unreasonable channels. So long as carriers are independent, and some of them irresponsible, occasions will arise where prompt action may be necessary.

The theory of the law up to the present time has been that railway owners, having the rate-making power in their own hands, are competent to protect their revenues. If the premises were correct the conclusion would follow; but the theory is applied to a situation where independent action by six hundred different carriers is preserved; and it is not true, as a practical matter, that any one of them can control its own rates. On the contrary, the rates of every line are, to a greater or less degree, at the mercy of its rivals. There is but one way in which the prosperity, or even the prolonged existence, of independent railway corporations can be maintained under existing legislation; namely, through co-operation among railways themselves in preserving their tariffs from destruction.

This co-operation may take two forms; associate action, subject to the regulation of the law, or consolidation of titles and control.

Railway consolidations, or "trusts," as they are often unthinkingly termed, are among the popular bugbears of the day. Some of the distinctions which differentiate them from the "trusts" that have been formed in other directions, have been alluded to above; and it is safe to say that no consolidations or combinations among railroads are imminent at the present time which are likely to operate otherwise than favorably to public interests. But the public mind is aroused upon the general subject, and, while usually just, it is not ready to distinguish. It is undeniable that the present time is not a favorable one for the unification of competing roads in common ownership, or even in joint control. The American system has been established upon a contrary basis, involving the maintenance of competitive conditions. As a last resort, and in default of any other solution of the question, actual immense consolidations may eventually arise. At the present time their necessity has not been demonstrated to the public eye, and their formation would arouse antagonism in many quarters. As has been well said, however, unless railway managers can associate, railway owners must combine.

When revolutions of this character occur, the movement is usually sudden and unexpected. The association experiment, which is now in progress of trial, is unmistakably in the nature of a breakwater against the so-called railway "trust." If this fact can be clearly recognized, and the usefulness of railway associations sustained, while their power is strengthened, the existing system, for a time, at least, can be preserved. In order to secure this result it is necessary that the public should understand the nature of their work and their value, and that their results should receive some governmental sanction. Central bureaus, with power to establish and adjust reasonable rates through large sections of territory where traffic is competitive, are indispensably required. This is going far beyond the work of the present associations, but the matter can be arranged by the roads among themselves, through the employment of a reasonable amount of good sense and as much good faith as usually pertains to ordinary business transactions, provided that their tariffs continued to be recognized as *prima facie* just, though subject to proper revision and control, and their arbitrations are supported by authority for the enforcement of awards. In controversies between man and man an award of arbitrators may be made the basis of a suit at law, and a judgment is rendered in order to compel the payment of money so found due. A money judgment, however, is not appropriate to awards between competing carriers. They relate to the establishment of rates, the adjustment of divisions, and the preparation of rules and regulations for the conduct of traffic. They deal with the future, not the past, and mandatory process is required for their execution. It is believed that an amendment to the sixteenth section of the act to regulate commerce might very properly provide that the courts of the United States, sitting in equity, should entertain jurisdiction of awards rendered in arbitrations between carriers, or between associations of carriers, respecting interstate commerce, and should have power to enforce them by any appropriate process, subject to the rules which govern the consideration of awards for the payment of money in courts of law.

This idea is not novel; in 1885 the Railway Commissioners of the state of Kansas used the following significant language:

"Since the violent fluctuations of rates, consequent on rate wars between rival lines, result, usually, in discriminative benefits to a few at the ultimate expense of the public, means should be taken to at least moderate this disturbing element to the business interests of the country. As a means to this end, we venture to suggest that contracts or agreements between rival companies to carry on interstate traffic upon given rates, providing those rates are reasonable and just, should be invested with a legal status and be enforceable with appropriate sanctions."

In the same year a somewhat similar thought was thus stated by Hon. T. M. Cooley:

"The question then presents itself whether the final solution for the 'railroad problem' is not likely to be found in treating the railroad interest as constituting in a certain sense a section by itself of the political community, and then combining in its management the state, representing the popular will and general interests, with some definite, recognized authority on the part of those immediately concerned; much as state and local authority are now combined for the government of municipalities."

The wisdom of these pregnant utterances has been demonstrated by the result of the experiment which has been conducted for nearly three years upon narrower lines. The statesman who can effect the required co-ordination of governmental regulation with associated railway management, will prolong for many years the American system of universally competitive railway service.

Without some such provision the statute is incomplete. The only other natural solution of existing difficulties appears to be through actual consolidations of ownership, by which all traffic in great sections of the country can be brought under the control of a single mind.

www.ingramcontent.com/pod-product-compliance
Lightning Source LLC
Chambersburg PA
CBHW032051230426
43672CB00009B/1556